RELIGION IN CONTEXT

Recent Studies in Lonergan

Timothy P. Fallon, S.J.
Philip Boo Riley

COLLEGE THEOLOGY SOCIETY
RESOURCES IN RELIGION · 4

UNIVERSITY
PRESS OF
AMERICA

Lanham · New York · London

Library of Congress Cataloging-in-Publication Data

Religion in context : recent studies in Lonergan / edited by Timothy P. Fallon,
Philip Boo Riley.
p. cm—(Resources in religion ; 4)
"Co-published by arrangement with the College Theology Society"—T.p. verso.
Includes bibliographical references and index.
1. Lonergan, Bernard J.F. 2. Theology, Doctrinal—20th century. 3. Catholic
Church—Doctrines—History—20th century. 4. Philosophy, Modern—20th
century.
I. Fallon, Timothy P., 1922–   . II. Riley, Philip Boo, 1951–   .
III. College Theology Society. IV. Series.
BX4705.L7133R45   1988   230'.2.0924—dc 19   88–21772 CIP
ISBN 0–8191–7137–9 (alk. paper)
ISBN 0–8191–7138–7 (pbk. : alk. paper)

Contents

Series Editor's Preface

The College Theology Society co-publishes CTS Resources in Religion with University Press of America. This series includes anthologies, translations and textbooks which provide important resources for effective scholarship and teaching. The College Theology Society is a professional association of college and university professors numbering over 800 members in all fifty states, Canada and Europe. The Resource Series reflects the interests in both scholarship and pedagogy of the Society's membership while at the same time providing significant publications on religious issues.

The Research and Publications Committee of the CTS has sole editorial responsibility for the selection, design and production of CTS Resources in Religion, CTS Studies in Religion and CTS Reprints in Religion. Further information regarding these series can be obtained from the Editors. The sales and distribution of the volumes in these three series are the responsibility of University Press of America.

My special thanks to John McCarthy, Loyola University of Chicago, who has helped to see this volume through to its completion. He assumes the position of Chair and Editor of Research and Publications beginning December 1987.

Managing Editor
Leonard Biallas
Quincy, Il 62301

Chair, Publications Committee
Robert Masson
Milwaukee, WI 53233

Foreword

The present age has been described as a time of crisis, transition, fragmentation, turmoil, decline, expansion, progress, pluralism, and confusion. These various epithets offered many times in recent years, point to a profound cultural change reverberating throughout our world. Far from being an established or timeless institution immune to this phenomenon, religious traditions have themselves been profoundly affected by these changes. Indeed, this cultural change has become the context in which religion—its insights and institutions, traditions and values—today must be understood, assessed, and lived out.

This re-assessment of religion was a primary motivation behind the life-work of theologian and philosopher Bernard Lonergan, S.J. It is not surprising to find the following definition in his major work, *Method in Theology*: "A theology mediates between a cultural matrix and the significance and role of a religion in that matrix."[1] Far from a static, completed system, the theology Lonergan had in mind is dynamic and multifaceted, engaging not only the traditional loci of scripture and tradition, but new advances in historical studies, human and social sciences, and philosophy as well. The mediation Lonergan intended is in accord with the maxim from Leo XIII cited in the epilogue of *Insight*: *vetera novis augere et perficere*, to enlarge and enrich the old with the new.[2] Theology conceived along these lines engages in a *transposition* of what is noble and enduringly valid from our religious heritage to meet the challenges of our present cultural context. In the process, both the religious traditions and the culture are altered. Lonergan's contribution to a theology envisioned as mediation lies not so much in

---

[1] *Method in Theology* (New York: Herder and Herder, 1972), xi.

[2] *Insight: A Study of Human Understanding* (New York: Philosophical Library, 1958), 747.

an exemplary specialized work or discipline as it does in the province of method. It is Lonergan's achievement to have articulated a radical method that cuts across and unites all facets of human inquiry. With self–knowledge, consciousness of oneself as an intellectual, moral, and religious subject, as his starting point, Lonergan argued that positions in philosophy, theology, and the human sciences are rooted in the subject's conscious and intentional operations and can therefore be governed, criticized and verified through a method that adverts to this foundational fact. Using the term "transcendental method"—or "generalized empirical method" as he later came to call it—Lonergan presented not a system deductively yielding solutions to problems but a framework in which problems can be creatively engaged, understood, and resolved by intelligent and responsible subjects. It is for this reason that Frederick Crowe, S.J., has characterized Lonergan's life–work as a *"organum novissimum*," a new organon beyond the original organon of Aristotelian logic and the *Novum Organon* of Francis Bacon's experimental science.[3] In this fashion Lonergan's achievement is to have invited and enabled others to engage in ongoing and creative collaboration in shaping and healing our present culture.

The essays presented in this volume were written in the spirit of such collaboration by a group aware of and engaging in the radical transformation Lonergan has called for. They are drawn from a 1984 international symposium held in honor of Lonergan at Santa Clara University. Methodical collaboration was conceived as the guiding principle of the symposium, and to that end no formal papers were read during the main sessions. Rather, the meetings were given over to panel presentations, responses, and small scale discussions through which individuals could engage one another's ideas more directly. The papers presented here, as in the companion volume *Religion and Culture*,[4] were all written after the symposium took place with the idea that the interchange the symposium made possible would inform the authors' thinking and writing. The source of the unity of these papers on the current context of religion, then, is twofold: Lonergan's methodological perspective, in terms of which all authors work out their positions; and the sympo-

---

[3] *The Lonergan Enterprise* (Cambridge, Mass.: Cowley Publications, 1980), Ch. I.

[4] *Religion and Culture: Essays in Honor of Bernard Lonergan, S.J.*, eds. Timothy P. Fallon, S.J., and Philip Boo Riley, (Albany: State University of New York Press, 1986).

sium collaboration out of which their various efforts grew. It remains to provide a brief overview of each contribution.

The first two essays articulate the type of cultural transformation called for by Lonergan's program. Frederick Lawrence argues that Lonergan's life work is best seen as a "political theology." After drawing on Metz to present the emergence of the political approach to theology, Lawrence traces and relates the moral and practical aspects of Lonergan's work on economics to his concern with the critical role of education in cultural progress. It is this emphasis on transformation that unites into a political mode Lonergan's appeals to insight, self-appropriation, collaboration, foundations rooted in interiority, functional specialization, etc. Far from being ends in themselves, these nctions constitute Lonergan's eminently practical contribution to the healing transformation of contemporary culture. The next essay, by Hugo Meynell, takes Lonergan's perspective into the social sciences. Meynell argues that both Marxist and Weberian value–free sciences are based on faulty epistemologies. That Lonergan's critical account of knowing and doing can offer an alternative basis is sketched through a critique of Peter Winch's understanding of social science and a work by the Marxist anthropologist Roland Barthes, *Mythologies*. Meynell's analysis strives to make clear why Lonergan's position on normative judgment and truth can be transformative by liberating social science and social criticism from the biases and relativism with which they are presently afflicted.

The next three essays are more programmatic, offering presentations of the scope and intention of Lonergan's transformative work in today's cultural context from the perspectives of systematic theology, philosophy, and economics. Robert Doran, S.J., begins with the definition of theology noted above and argues, like Lawrence, that such a theology must be a theology of praxis, oriented to the transformation of culture and history. Doran proposes to locate such a transforming theology in a theory of History based on two sets of categories derived from Lonergan: a threefold dialectic of subject, culture, and community and the scale of values sketched in *Method in Theology*. Decline stems from various combinations of breakdown in the dialectics and distortions of the integral scale of values. Its reversal and the promotion of cultural healing on a global scale is a task to which today's theology must contribute. Philip McShane likewise works out the implications of Lonergan's program for a transformative theology, this time working out the implication of Lonergan's conception of the science of economics. In a characteristically wide ranging, playful and personal way, McShane documents and works out the significance of Lonergan's difficult development of *Method in Theology's* functional specialties. He then argues that functional specialization seen not simply as a group of eight theological tasks but as a personal and cultural challenge alone provides the theological sciences with the means to address the actual context of theology today. Thomas McPartland argues that Lonergan's critical, and therefore truly transformed, epistemology allows one to advance the intrinsically historical character of philosophy without succumbing to the specter of historical relativism. The key is to shift philosophy's foundations from the traditional ones of logic and metaphysics to cognitive performance, to one's response to the invariant norms resident in the subject's pure desire to know. McPartland then investigates the conditions for a community to promote fidelity to it. Engaged with the normative achievement of the past, such a philosophic community would come to take on a therapeutic function in today's culture. For philosophy's contribution to the reversal of cultural decline consists in a call to conversion, to awakening and enacting fidelity to the transcendent dynamism of the pure desire to know.

The next three essays focus on specific theological issues. Nancy Ring takes up the theme of transformation with respect to theological language and symbol. Following Lonergan's notion of the constitutive dimension of meaning and value in human living, Ring sketches the role of language as a carrier and generator of meaning. She argues that transformation of persons and communities is best achieved by re-fashioning the images foundational to the language and symbols through which they live their lives. In this vein, she calls on theologians to advert to the role of images and imagination, and to see their task as methodical control of the way language and symbols shape and transform the way Christians live out their faith today. Vernon Gregson is concerned with the problem of evil and the subjective dimensions of the doctrine of soteriology. Using Ricoeur's analysis of the West's symbolization of the experience of evil as a basis, Gregson argues for the profound transformation involved in reversing the tendency in the tradition (and in human psyches) to interpret the cross juridically and objectively, in a retributive fashion according to the *lex talionis*. As an alternative, he suggests Lonergan's and Sebastian Moore's more vital and psychological reflections on the "symbolic dynamic" of the crucifixion. On this model, argues Gregson, the mystery of Jesus' death on the cross is presented in such a way that the redemptive power of God's love, the transformation of evil into good, can be appropriated as a primary and vital element in Christian living. Eugene Webb turns to another Christian doctrine, the Trinity, and examines the 4th and 5th century trinitarian development on the basis of Lonergan's intentionality analysis. Offering both historical and philosophical analysis, Webb grounds in conscious operations and explains the distinct meanings intended by such key terms to the development as *ousia, prosopon, physis*, and *hypostasis*. His study shows the fruitfulness of intentionality analysis for the understanding of a distant and complex moment in the Christian tradition, so much so that it may be a key to recovering and preserving the affirmation of the central mystery of Christian faith, the Incarnation, achieved at Chalcedon.

The final two essays of the volume compare Lonergan to other major figures who have significantly contributed to the cultural transformation we owe, in large measure, to modern philosophy. John C. Robertson compares Lonergan's and Whitehead's use of the "subjectivist principle" as a basis for critical metaphysics. Robertson challenges Schubert Ogden's earlier contention that, following Whitehead's criticism of Western philosophy, Lonergan's metaphysics is based on an intellectualist and therefore abstract and diminished account of experience. He does so by adverting to Lonergan's distinction between the worlds of meaning and of immediacy and the objects proper to each, arguing that Lonergan's full subject is no less dynamic and concrete than Whitehead's. With this issue clarified, it is easier to see the complementarity relationship between these two advocates of a critical theistic metaphysics. Vincent Potter, S.J. turns our attention to the American philosopher, Charles S. Peirce. Potter argues that for both Lonergan and Peirce knowledge is primarily discursive, this following from Lonergan's emphasis on judgment and Peirce's on inference as constitutive of knowing. From this it follows that there are no first principles in "the traditional sense," i.e., self-evidently true concepts immediately grasped by intuition. In their own ways, then, Lonergan and Peirce are seen, through the transformation they helped achieve, to critically ground human cognition in cognitive performance. Further study of such complementarity, suggests Potter, would greatly contribute to Lonergan's call for Catholic thought to shift from classicist to historically-minded foundations.

This short account of the origins and content of this volume would be incomplete without acknowledgement of the assistance we have received from friends and colleagues. Among the many who helped plan the 1984 Lonergan Symposium we single out for special mention Frederick Crowe, S.J., David Oyler, Paul Marcoux, Michael Rende, Terry Tekippe, Elizabeth and Mark Morelli, and Frederick and Sue Lawrence. We want to acknowledge in particular the colleagues who creatively and tirelessly organized the symposium panels: Joseph Flanagan, S.J., Michael O'Callaghan, Sean McEvenue, and William Mathews, S.J. Special thanks go to the committee of volunteers at Santa Clara who helped master the myriad practical details associated with getting over one hundred scholars to the right place at the right time: Dennis Rosselli, Louise Dillon, Arthur and Lorraine Bennett, Kevin St. George, Daniel Rivers, Maurus Straumanis, and Megan Mulvihill. Without the support of Santa Clara University's departments of Philosophy and Religious Studies, and their respective secretaries, Sheila Speciale and Ethel Johnston, neither the symposium nor this publication would have proceeded as smoothly as they did. Robert Masson, of the CTS Publications Committee, is to be thanked for overseeing the production of this volume, as is Leonard J. Biallas for his painstaking efforts as copy editor. Especially we would like to thank David J. Buerger of Santa Clara University's Personal Computer Center for his long and patient help in teaching us how to typeset this book on a personal computer. Finally, we gratefully acknowledge the financial support provided by the following: at Santa Clara University, the Jesuit Community, the Bannan Foundation, and William Rewak, S.J. through the Santa Clara University President's Fund; the Method Institute founded by the Jesuits of Upper Canada and the Lonergan Trust Fund; the Loyola Jesuits (Montreal) University Fund; James McGuire and Guy Guiffre; and the National Endowment for the Humanities. Without such assistance and encouragement, the symposium and publication would not have been possible.

It remains to dedicate this volume. We and our colleagues were saddened to learn last year of the death of Michael O'Callaghan, a distinguished and long-time contributor to Lonergan Studies. His study of Lonergan, *Unity in Theology: Lonergan's Framework for Theology in its New Context*, his work on contemporary theological discussion, his co-editorship of the Lonergan Studies Newsletter, and other endeavors have made him a friend and collaborator to many. His ever patient,

Foreword

helpful, and gentlemanly presence will be sorely missed. This volume
is dedicated to Michael's memory, whose life and work provides us all
with an inspiring model for our own lives of dedicated scholarship.

TPF   PBR
Santa Clara University
September, 1987

Chapter 1

Lonergan As Political Theologian

Frederick G. Lawrence

1.1   The Emergence of Political Theology

In today's parlance, political theology is one in a series of attempts since the 1960's on the part of Roman Catholic and Protestant theologians to come to grips with the foundations for Christianity in the light of the contemporary crisis of culture. After World War I theology had reached a type of equilibrium, with the Protestants constellated around the three giants: Karl Barth, Rudolph Bultmann, Paul Tillich; and the Catholics still operating under the auspices of the Scholasticism called forth by Pope Leo XIII's mandate for a renewal of Thomism in 1879. At the close of the Second Vatican Council (1962–1965), those prevailing liberal and neo-orthodox solutions to the mediation between Christianity and modern cultures had suddenly become irretrievably passé, valiant and estimable as they had been.

What contributed to this shift? A significant factor proved to be the recognition that none of the dominant theologies had really come to terms with the crisis of modern culture in a way that was sufficiently profound or adequately differentiated. These deficiencies were registered within the mainly academic context of European and North

1

American theology through the increasing influence of the 19th century masters of suspicion: Karl Marx and Friedrich Nietzsche.

Nietzsche's critique of modernity had sounded the enervating effects upon life in the West of the invasion of cultures and the various forms of reflection upon culture by historical consciousness in terms of nihilism and the death of God. He had limned the outcome of the liberal-democratic and socialist solutions to the political problem in his unforgettable image of the Last Man:

> 'We have discovered happiness,' say the Last Men and blink.
>
> ...A little poison now and then: that produces pleasant dreams. And a lot of poison at last, for a pleasant death.
>
> ...'Formerly all the world was mad,' say the most acute of them and blink.
>
> They are clever and know everything that has ever happened; so there is no end to their mockery. They still quarrel, but they soon make up–otherwise indigestion would result.
>
> They have their little pleasure for the day and their little pleasure for the night: but they respect health.
>
> 'We have discovered happiness,' say the Last Men and blink.[1]

So from *Zarathustra*.

This radical crisis of meaning and value was the issue in such diverse schools as the "God-is-dead" theologies of Thomas Altizer, Gabriel Vahanian and Paul van Buren; in the universal historical theology of Wolfhart Pannenberg; in the post-Bultmannian hermeneutical theologies of Gerhard Ebeling, Ernst Fuchs, Heinrich Ott; and the post-Heideggerian theology of Karl Rahner–all Christian theologies whose stars rose in the mid-sixties. Philosopher Hans-Georg Gadamer, whose *Truth and Method* became required reading for theologians in the sixties and seventies, resumed Heidegger's meditation upon the crisis indicated by Nietzsche and formulated the issue as follows: since all normative traditions have been rendered radically questionable, hermeneutics (the auxiliary science of skilled interpretation) has become a universal issue.

---

[1] Friedrich Nietzsche, *Thus Spoke Zarathustra*, R. Hollingsdale, trans. (Harmondsworth, England: Penguin Books, 1972), Prologue, n. 5 (46-47).

That universal and comprehensive challenge of hermeneutics to theology has usually been met in two ways.

The first way is to trim academic theology down to conventional scholarly dimensions, after which the theological task is sub-contracted out to a set of sub-disciplines that divide up the data on Christian religion for ever more minute critical study. In the second effort to meet the challenge of hermeneutics, theology is swallowed up by a transcendental-metaphysical (as in Rahner) or by an out-and-out ontological reflection (as in Process Theology). These responses to the universal hermeneutic issue—fragmenting, on the one hand, and totalizing on the other—bear the earmarks of that sort of interpretation which Marx, in his famous eleventh Thesis on Feuerbach said needed to be supplanted by practice. It became a real question whether theology was anything more than either a species of intellectual history or an academically domesticated speculation without any practical bearing or importance.[2]

During the sixties and seventies, this question became ever more inescapable. At the same time a common awareness was starting to emerge of the spiritual impoverishment spawned by what were cynically labeled "state-controlled monopolies"in the East and "monopoly-controlled states"in the West. And in the Third World, mounting dissatisfaction in the face of the dependency engendered by colonialist and imperialist policies of advanced industrial societies (called national security states) was spreading at the popular, grass-roots level. In brief, the stage was set for prevailing trends in theology to shift from the different kinds of hermeneutical solutions to the problem of mediating Christianity with contemporary cultures to the approaches that styled themselves political or liberation theologies.[3]

By 1970 it was already manifest that there were two distinct originating points for political theology: from within an academic context in advanced industrial societies, and from what had come to be called base communities in Third World countries. It is clear that both styles of theology are seeking to come to terms with the universal hermeneutic problem as portrayed by Nietzsche, Heidegger, Gadamer, and Ricoeur. But it is no less evident that the heading under which they mean to

---

[2] F. Lawrence, "Method and Theology as Hermeneutical," *Creativity and Method: Essays in Honor of B. Lonergan, S.J.*, M. Lamb, ed. (Milwaukee: Marquette University Press, 1981), 79-104.

[3] Matthew Lamb, *Solidarity with Victims* (New York: Crossroad, 1982).

engage that issue is Marx's imperative of changing rather than merely interpreting history.

Where does the work of Bernard Lonergan stand in this development? In particular, what can Lonergan's methodological proposals, given their decidedly transcendental character, yield by way of a historical and transformative theology? A useful point of departure for this query is found in Johann Baptist Metz's formulation of political theology as a praxis-oriented correction of what he saw as the shortcomings of Rahner's idealist-transcendental view of theology.

According to Metz, Rahner's epistemological and metaphysical mediation of the transcendental, universal, and absolute horizon yields a lack of clarity with regard to both categorial revelation and to historical time. How does it really do justice to the specificity, contingency, and the concreteness of Christian meaning and value? In Rahner, doesn't the transcendental become "noumenalized" in the Kantian sense, i.e., (1) interiorized within the "already-in-there-now"; (2) existentialized in terms of an account of attitudes whose concrete historical mediation is so vague, and for which so little is really at stake, that that mediation seems ultimately not to matter; (3) privatized in the sense of being mystical, as in a vacuum from the social and political; and (4) ahistorical to the extent that it eliminates the need for existential history as the condition for individual and social identity?[4]

Metz's alternative would be post-idealist and so just the opposite. His central category of memory is a recognition of existential history as the knowledge of the past that makes social continuity and identity possible. Metz's emphasis on narrative is opposed to history as a dimension of museum culture in which past life is observed as an object in the sense that it has no meaning whatsoever for our lives. It is selectively and symbolically engaging; it doesn't pretend to be exhaustive. His alternative is ethical; it is not beyond good and evil, and it praises as well as blames. As Christian, Metz's program is not a history of the winners but a history of the losers, a history of suffering. It is apologetic insofar as in his narrative approach the theodicy question is central. It is prophetic in so far as it points out a direction for the future in terms of one's ethical, apologetic, and symbolic stance. And it is existential in so far as individually and collectively we cannot function without

---

[4] See J.B. Metz, *Faith and Society and History: Toward a Practical Fundamental Theology* (New York: Crossroad, 1980).

such a memory—it is constitutive of ourselves.[5]

Metz's position emerges from encounter on a number of fronts. He has been unable to reconcile himself with the virtual silence of German theologians about Auschwitz; he has been influenced deeply by many years of intermittent encounter in person and conversation with Marxist philosopher Ernst Bloch; he has tried to take seriously the Frankfurt School's Marxist insights into the entwinement of knowledge and human interests; and he has absorbed Walter Benjamin's serious criticism of emancipatory critique in terms of a salvaging critique. Metz undertook to retrieve in a memorative and symbolic way the theodicy question centered on the problem of moral evil as symbolized by Auschwitz. Existential and narrative history as a story of suffering is confronted with the saving story and dangerous memory of Jesus who suffered and died and was raised again.[6]

The outcome of this confrontation is that two aspects of negativity absolutely critical to Christian and Jewish religion are once again made central: first, the radical difference between God as mystery and everything else; and second, the objective absurdity of the mystery of iniquity, sin. The second negativity Metz deals with in the light of the narrative resources provided by the incognito Jesus of Nazareth, called a fool by Herod and a rebel by Pilate. In contrast to Moltmann who transposes the issues of unreconciled evil into the Godhead via Luther's theology of the cross, Metz replaces Aquinas' notorious agnosticism with regard to God by his own agnosticism centered on Jesus. This constitutes a move towards understanding the content of redemption as a law of the cross, symbolically mediated by the dangerous memory of the passion, death, and resurrection of Jesus.

The point of a program like Metz's is communicative: the concrete reorientation of practice. This communicative practice takes two principal forms. The first is response to and encouragement and support of what is going forward in Third World basic Christian communities. This form has as its chief premise the recognition of the shift from a culturally monocentric Christianity, a post-Tridentine, Romanized control

---

[5] J. B. Metz, "Glaube als gefährliche Erinnerung," *Theologische Meditationen: Hilfe zum Glauben*, H. Küng), ed. (Einsiedeln: Benziger, 1971), 22-38; and "The Future *ex Memoria Passionis*," in *Hope and the Future of Man*, E. Cousins, ed. (Philadelphia: Westminster Press, 1972) 117-131.

[6] F. Lawrence, "Transcendence as Interruption: Theology in a Political Mode," in *Transcendence and the Sacred*, A. Olson and L. Rouner, eds. (University of Notre Dame Press, 1981), 208-225.

of meaning deployed by a sort of monolithic, bureaucratic structure—
what Lonergan often spoke of as "the Church with its lid on" for over
four centuries—to a culturally polycentric Church, as emergent, so to
speak, from the grassroots upwards rather than from Rome downwards.

The second form of this practice (exemplified by Metz's *laudatio*
for Ernesto Cardenal[7]) is solidarity with emancipatory political movements. This does not mean siding with leftist politics. For example,
in his Boston College lectures, Metz has emphasized how he pleaded
with his acquaintances among the Sandinistas to try for a third way,
reducible neither to U.S.-style liberal capitalism nor to Russian- or
Cuban-style socialism.

So what does Metz's political theology do? It starts from biographically rooted resistance to evil, has recourse to dangerous Christian
memories, and tries concretely to mediate an anthropological revolution informed by those memories in relation to a plurality of cultural
contexts. It tries to illuminate concrete judgments concerning specific
policies and plans in relation to the technological, the economic, and
the political goods of order.

What is the place of Bernard Lonergan in such a development? I
would argue he stands squarely in the middle of it. For can't Metz's concrete engagement with political and social orders be seen as one version
of what is meant by the very first sentence of *Method in Theology*: "A
theology mediates between a cultural matrix and the significance and
role of a religion in that matrix?"[8] In what follows I will develop this
point by extending it into a twofold claim about Lonergan's life-work:
first, from the beginning right until the end of his career, Lonergan was
ever a political theologian in Metz's sense; second, Lonergan not only
enacted political theology throughout his life, but he thematized the
dynamics of ascent required for doing political theology at the level of
our times.

1.2   Lonergan and Political Theology

There are three dimensions of Lonergan's life-long pursuit of political theology to be examined; namely, his reflections on economics, on

    [7] J.B. Metz, *The Emergent Church: The Future of Christianity in a Postbour-
geois World* (New York: Crossroad, 1981).
    [8] Bernard Lonergan, S.J., *Method in Theology* (New York: Herder and Herder,
1972) xi.

education, and on culture.

1.2.1 Economics

What are we to make then, of Lonergan's blatant and overwhelming preoccupation with economics in relation to morality and democracy? This is a preoccupation that emerges from a number of influences dating back to the 1930's: his encounter with Louis Watt's attempt to come to terms with the economic teachings of Leo XIII, his provocation by *Quadragesimo Anno*, his return to Canada in a depression, with Major Douglas's ideas about Social Credit being propagated in Canada. These elicited from Lonergan what he later called "a long, hard, uphill climb" towards an understanding of the good of order precisely in its economic dimension, an understanding that would "reveal how moral precepts have both a basis in economic process and so an effective application to it."[9]

Lonergan noted that the moral requirement for a family wage was good in itself, but altogether vague in relation to economic reality. What happens when the businesses that strive to pay such a wage go out of business and the ones that don't bother with such a demand succeed? In other words, a moral imperative is vague whenever it is not grounded in the concrete intelligibility of the subject matter to which it is to be applied. Moreover, what if the imperative assumed a pre-exchange, traditional, agrarian economy rather than a modern, industrial, exchange economy? And what if it failed to distinguish (within complex sets of distinguishable goods of order) the good of order as familial from the good of order as economic? Just as economic criteria may be out of place in the conduct of familial morality, so also familial criteria may not be directly appropriate in the properly economic sphere.

To approach the issue at stake here from another angle: What is the relationship of the economic order to the political order, an order which is distinct from it and is supposed to dispose of it? What if modern social and political theories of both left and right tend to install economics as the basic social science, in the sense that economic

---

[9] Bernard Lonergan, S.J., "Healing and Creating in History," *Bernard Lonergan: Three Lectures*, E. O'Connor, ed. (Thomas More Institute, Montreal, 1975), 59, 65. (Reprinted in *A Third Collection: Papers by Bernard J.F. Lonergan, S.J.*, F.E. Crowe, S.J., ed. (New York: Paulist Press, 1985), 100-109).

exigencies tend to control politics rather than the other way round?
By the same token, what happens when the properly economic sphere
gets mixed up with the political (in the ignoble sense), and so both
economics and politics have their specific intelligibilities obscured and
both become detached from morality?

Thus was Lonergan absorbed by the critical need to understand the
nature of a modern exchange economy, both for the good of the ecology
disposed of by the economy, as well as for the good of the ecologies (such
as political cultures) which are supposed to dispose of the economy. In
his spare time for about fourteen years, Lonergan gave himself to this
task. The result was a roughly 130 page analysis of the production of
goods and the circulation of money, as well as scattered reflections on
finance and credit.

In his early work on economics, Lonergan was striving—with what
success probably none of us will live to know—to make a contribution
to our culture by working out fundamental ideas on the production
of goods and the circulation of money—ideas such as his notion of
"pure surplus income."[10]   One of his more ironic comments in this
early manuscript reflects his view on just this point: "Now it is true,"
he writes, "that our culture cannot be accused of mistaken ideas on
pure surplus income as it has been defined in the essay. For on that
precise topic it has no ideas whatever." ([1944], 97)

It is important to understand that Lonergan's concern for economics
was just part of a broader practical and political caring. A statement from a 1943 review of André Maurois' biography shows this. "A
Catholic weekly," he wrote,

> ...must, because Catholic, pay tribute to any humanism in our
> inhuman day. The count of those who know letters and so un-
> derstand men dwindles perpetually. Foreign affairs are bungled
> by pressure-groups with a shadow of insight into the culture and
> history and minds of other nations. Domestic affairs gain mo-
> mentum as they approach the technician's utopia, when a suc-
> cession of security plans will have made citizens into guinea-pigs
> for the grandscale experiments of commissars, under the labora-
> tory conditions guaranteed by a secret police. As Maurois found

---

[10]References to Lonergan's economic manuscripts will give page numbers and
dates of the MS in the text. The manuscripts are available in North America at
the Lonergan Research Centers at Regis College (Toronto), Boston College, Santa
Clara University and Lonergan College at Concordia University (Montreal).

in France, the humanist with his love of reconciliation, of order, of spreading understanding, has little leverage in such a world.[11]

In 1941 Lonergan wrote in favor of Canada's Antigonish Movement, saying, "The essence of the cooperative movement is to teach free enterprise to those who in a regime of free enterprise have not got the initiative to look out for themselves." And he went on, "Why does the proletariat today include almost everyone? Why is the control of industry in the hands of fewer and fewer? Radically, it is our own fault. We leave our affairs to others because we are too indolent and too stupid to get to work and run them ourselves. The results are palpably ruinous. A system of free enterprise cannot survive if only a few practice free enterprise."[12] I hasten to add that we must not be too quick to read our own notions into what Lonergan meant by free enterprise. For he has stated explicitly:

> Very definitely I should say that the issue of free enterprise is proximately scientific but ultimately existential. It is proximately scientific inasmuch as one has to refuse to mean by free enterprise what has been going on in the West for the past 200 years. One has to mean what is revealed as possible by a functional analysis in macroeconomics. But the issue is ultimately existential, for one has to choose between praxis and technique. Planning is a technique by which a few people take upon themselves the office of deciding what vast numbers of other people are to do, whether they are to do it, and what will happen to them if they don't. That is what planning means. And it is not particularly intelligent because it uses old ideas that everybody understands or knows are good; it is not a source of initiative. Free enterprise is a set-up in which individuals are free to figure out what can be done, whether they will do it; and if they so decide they take upon themselves the risk of doing it .... The issue between planning and free enterprise is existential in two manners. It arises in as much as it is doubtful whether the people are totally corrupt. If people are totally corrupt then planning is inevitable. They can't help themselves. In the manner that they are not, you have some hope. But it is also existential inasmuch as one's decision on the issue tells something about the kind of

---

[11]Bernard Lonergan, S.J., "Review: *I Remember, I Remember*, by Andre Maurois," *The Canadian Register*, Quebec Edition, February 20, 1943, 8.

[12]Bernard Lonergan, S.J., "Review: *Masters of Their Own Destiny* by M.M. Coady," *Montreal Beacon*, May 2, 1941, 3.

person one is. Our age is an age of technique; our behaviorists, positivists, newsmen, politicians know and think a great deal of technique and very little of praxis, and one can catch the virus. But deciding one way or the other is existential.[13]

1.2.2   Education

It is clear that for the great majority of people to be capable of knowing "what is revealed as possible by functional analysis in economics," the analysis not only has to be done and applied, but communicated as well. And this is a vast educational undertaking. So we come to the second dimension of Lonergan's enterprise as political theology, the educational. Early on, Lonergan had written that the alternative to democracy's being "a noble experiment that failed" and to "the doom of quiet death by uninspired regimentation under an intellectually uninspired bureaucracy" is "to train and equip the masses to achieve economic independence."[14] In a typescript associated with his economic analysis, Lonergan had written,

> ...the liberal dream of an automatic economy has, like all dreams, at long last been broken. The necessity of rational control has ceased to be a question, and the one issue is the locus of that control. Is it to be absolutist, from above downwards? Is it to be democratic from below upwards? Plainly, it can be democratic only in the measure in which economic science succeeds in uttering not counsels to rulers but precepts to mankind, not specific remedies and plans to increase the power of bureaucracies, but universal laws which men themselves administrate in the personal conduct of their lives .... [T]o deny the possibility of a new science and new precepts is, I am convinced, to deny the possibility of the survival of democracy.[15]

The point is that, as Lonergan conceived the issue, the educational role of economic science is not the replacement of practical wisdom by

---

[13] Comments in a Dialog session at the Lonergan Workshop, Boston College, June, 1977. (Transcripts are available at the Lonergan Centers noted in n. 10 above). Such is the orientation of Lonergan's reflections on economics.

[14] Bernard Lonergan, S.J., "Review: *Masters of Their Own Destiny* by M.M. Coady," *Montreal Beacon*, May 2, 1941, 3.

[15] Cited by Philip McShane, "Features of Generalized Empirical Method and the Actual Context of Economics," in *Creativity and Method*, M. Lamb, ed. (Milwaukee: Marquette University Press, 1980), 557-558.

technique, but the development of a practical wisdom that can respond with integrity to the exigencies of the economic cycles in their basic and surplus expansions. Such practical judgments and decisions, of course, will immediately affect the standard of our living. And, as Lonergan expressed the issue so well, in his first economics manuscript:

> Now to change one's standard of living in any notable fashion is to live in a different fashion. It presupposes a grasp of new ideas. If the ideas are to be above the level of currently successful advertising, serious education must be undertaken. Finally, coming to grasp what serious education really is, and nonetheless, coming to accept that challenge constitute the greatest challenge to the modern economy. ([1944], 65)

Serious reflection on practical and political life, from Plato and Aristotle until Rousseau and Locke in the 17th and 18th centuries, right down to Lenin, Mao and Dewey in our own century, has always expressly and integrally entailed reflection on education. The reason for this, of course, is that education is the reproduction of our culture. It inculcates the terminal values by which a society lives, passes on skills and disciplines proper to the roles and tasks at work in any institutional set-up, and hands down the rationales for the diverse goods of order operative in any society. So it is that the context for radical educational practice and reflection on that practice involves, in turn, radical reflection on culture and cultures. This task, a concern of Lonergan since the earliest stages of his career, constitutes a third dimension of his political theology.

1.2.3 Culture

Radical reflection on culture is already implicit and even often explicit in the short quotations I have already cited above. By way of illustrating this overall concern with culture I turn now to Lonergan's great hermeneutic encounter and conversation with the thought of Thomas Aquinas, recorded in his breathtaking works, *Grace and Freedom* and *Verbum: Word and Idea in Aquinas.*[16] The chief and direct aim of his

---

[16] Bernard Lonergan, S.J., *Grace and Freedom: Operative Grace in the Thought of St. Thomas Aquinas*, J. Patout Burns, ed., (London : Darton, Longman & Todd,

work with Aquinas in the late 30s and 40s was, as he put it, "reaching up to the mind of Aquinas."[17] But the underlying interest that had long since preoccupied him was not so much the possible use of Thomas as a source-book for fertile theological speculation as so many have done (and which he did too). It was found, rather, in some hunches he already had about method or methodology, in the unique sense in which he would use that term, viz., primarily as a practical as opposed to a technical category.

For Lonergan reflection on culture has to do not just with thematizing the meanings and values embodied in a way of life, but with what Lonergan later called "the control of meaning,"[18] where by "control" is not meant something authoritarian or logical or technical but rather attunement with the deepest exigencies of human liberty. It is in this context that Lonergan's work on Aquinas can be appreciated. For *Grace and Freedom* was not only a magnificent retrieval of the extraordinary development by Aquinas of explanatory theory upon a large cluster of theological issues that were always to remain central to Lonergan's thought. It was not merely a re-appreciation of what Lonergan would later call the systematic exigence in doing theology. It was also the outcome of his own development of a powerful foundational a priori that specifies empirically verifiable invariants within the evolution and development of meaning towards theoretical apprehension.

It is no wonder, then, that understanding was not only the theme of *Verbum*, but developing understanding was the performative method at work there too. As Lonergan put it:

> Only by the slow repetitious, circular work of going over and over the data, by catching here a little insight and there another, by following through false leads and cumulative changes in one's initial suppositions and perspectives and concepts, can one hope to attain such a development of one's own understanding as to hope to understand what

1971) and *Verbum : Word and Idea in Aquinas*, David Burrell, ed., (Notre Dame : University of Notre Dame Press, 1967).

[17] Bernard Lonergan, S.J., *Insight: A Study in Human Understanding* (New York: The Philosophical Library, 1957), 748.

[18] Bernard Lonergan, S.J., "Dimensions of Meaning," *Collection: Papers by Bernard Lonergan, S.J.*, F.E. Crowe, ed. (London: Darton, Longman & Todd, 1967), 252-267.

Aquinas understood and meant.[19]

My point here, of course, is the change undergone by Lonergan, as well as how he came to that change. To cite the final page of *Insight*:

> After spending years reaching up to the mind of Aquinas, I came to a twofold conclusion. On the one hand, that reaching had changed me profoundly. On the other hand, that change was the essential benefit. For not only did it make me capable of grasping what, in the light of my conclusions, the *vetera* [the old things in Aquinas, what Aquinas himself meant] really were, but it also opened up the challenging vistas on what the *nova* [the new, what Aquinas never really thought of himself] could be.[20]

As we know, Lonergan claimed to give a "Thomist" and intellectualist reading of Aquinas in contrast to a "Thomistic" and conceptualist one. But Lonergan was never really interested in Thomism. Yes, we do have to acknowledge that for many years he described his efforts in terms of a transposition of Aquinas' position to meet the issues of our day. Yet beyond this, what Lonergan owes to Aquinas is not *vetera* to be transposed, but the realization that theology embraces far more than an explanatory theorization of what believers already know by faith. In his encounter with Aquinas, Lonergan met up with a view of theology as "a principle for the moulding and transformation of culture"[21] which is exactly what I take to be the point of political theology.

Aquinas provided Lonergan with a proximate model of the political theologian as diagnosing and proposing a remedy for the derailments of a culture. Aquinas gave him a living example of uncovering and formulating the issues in a culture which a creative evocation of any *vetera* would have to meet. That is why Lonergan could eventually write the following in face of his own and our situation.

> Modernity lacks roots. Its values lack balance and depth. Much of its science is destructive of man. Catholics in the

---

[19] *Verbum*, 216.

[20] *Insight*, 748 [parenthetical additions mine].

[21] Bernard Lonergan, S.J., "Theology in Its New Context,"in *Second Collection: Papers by Bernard J.F.Lonergan, S.J.*, eds. W. Ryan and B. Tyrrell (London: Darton, Longman & Todd, 1974), 62.

> 20th Century are faced with a problem similar to that met
> by Aquinas in the 13th Century. Then Greek and Arabic
> culture was pouring into Western Europe and, if it was not
> to destroy Christendom, it had to be known, assimilated,
> transformed. Today modern culture, in many ways more
> stupendous than any that ever existed, is surging round us.
> It too has to be known, assimilated, transformed.[22]

Notice that in this quotation what is at stake in Lonergan's relationship
to Aquinas is not just a task of understanding his past meanings and
re-expressing that meaning in a way that is comprehensible in the contemporary context. For Lonergan, the Leonine program of increasing
and perfecting *vetera* with the *nova* encompassed a far vaster challenge,
viz., that of knowing, assimilating and transforming the contemporary
cultural context.

Insight, that 748-paged "essay in aid of a personal appropriation of
one's rational self-consciousness," is a truly awe-inspiring documenta-
tion of just part of Lonergan's assimilating and transforming modern
culture. It is clear that the time he spent coming to grips with what
Aquinas meant by understanding helped Lonergan immensely in his
job, inasmuch as he discovered that the key to uncovering the intelligibility at the basis of all science and all action is what he came
to call *generalized empirical method*: an expansion of awareness that
attends to the data of consciousness even as we advert intelligently,
reasonably, and responsibly to any data we happen to be inquiring
about or interested in. In other words, other philosophers may have
attended explicitly to the data of consciousness before, but none of
them focused upon the act of understanding or insight in quite the
same way Lonergan has done. This focus enabled him to make the
striking claim in *Insight*, "Thoroughly understand what it is to understand, and not only will you understand the broad lines of all there is
to be understood but also you will possess a fixed base, an invariant
pattern, opening upon all further developments of understanding."[23]
Insight into insight—something Lonergan never could have discovered
and articulated in quite the same way he did without subjecting himself
to that long and hard tutelage under Aquinas—would become a key to
providing modernity with the roots, the balance, the depth it lacks by

---

[22]Bernard Lonergan, S. J., "Belief: Today's Issue," *Second Collection*, 99.
[23]*Insight*, xxviii.

helping to transform both its human and its natural sciences as well as its common sense.

Insight—understanding at the levels of intelligence, of reasonableness, and of affectivity and responsibility—is the heart of meaning and value; it is the core of the self-meaning by which we mutually mediate and constitute each other; and it is the key to the control of cultural meaning. So, too, is insight central not merely for theology as faith seeking systematic understanding but for theology as "somehow mediating God's meaning into the whole of human affairs."[24] Because, as Lonergan wrote, "theology is called upon to influence the cultural context, to translate the Word of God and so project it into new mentalities and new situations."[25] Universal concepts or even theories can never be practice; but insight is practice itself, besides being the component in practice overall without which that practice would not be properly human.

Moreover, insight, even as it goes beyond what is intrinsically conditioned by space and time, is not only into but actually *in* images, especially in direct acts of understanding and in affective insights on the level of consciousness as responsible. Hence, insight is crucial to the dimensions of the imaginal, the symbolic, the mythic, the metaphorical, endowing these with their torque and their twist as they communicate between ourselves as organisms and ourselves as intelligent, reasonable, responsible, and in love.

Insight into insight: it is an empirically verifiable grasp of psychological fact. Lonergan's discovery that both Aquinas and Aristotle—neither of whom were bothered by the critical or epistemological question as to how we know that we know—had insight into insight as the grounding for the theories they expressed in terms of metaphysical causes delivered him from two temptations: the primacy of metaphysics (the questions about the first causes of being) and modernity's vaunted primacy of epistemology (the post-Cartesian question about knowledge) along with its correlative assumption of the primacy of the subject/object split. Lonergan's question about what we are doing when we are knowing—what he names the cognitional-theoretic question—is a practical question about practice as human, i.e., as intelligent, reasonable, responsible, loving. That is *the* method question. Such things as epistemology and metaphysics or any kind of theory are

---

[24] Bernard Lonergan, S.J., "Theology in its New Context," *Second Collection*, 62.
[25] "Theology in its New Context," 62.

therefore secondary.

Now to ask and answer the question of what I am doing whenever I think I am knowing in any area of my living brings us right back to the threshold of practical and political philosophy and theology. Because adequately facing that question also involves asking and answering the practical and political question regarding the right or most choiceworthy way to live, the issue that forms the matrix of all authentic philosophy and theology. This is why Lonergan stated expressly, in the introduction to *Insight*, that "more than all else, the aim of the book is to issue an invitation to a personal, decisive act." This is why he calls the book's program "both concrete and practical."[26] This is why he can specify the project of appropriation in his essay as involving not just problems of learning and of identification but of orientation as well.[27] And, because genuineness is the operator of human intellectual development, the appropriation of one's rational self-consciousness makes extraordinary practical demands upon the whole person.[28] As Lonergan expressed the matter (in a language still tainted by a residual faculty psychology): "cognitional appropriation of truth is solidary with volitional and sensitive appropriation."[29] The "You must change your life!" of Rilke's great poem is very much to the point here.

Lonergan's next great work, *Method in Theology*, turned out to be a summary and elegantly rounded off result of over two more decades of painstaking thought, accomplished while he was teaching his famous Christology and Trinity courses at the Gregorian. I was one of those fortunate enough to have attended one or another of Lonergan's method seminars and to have gotten hold of notes from others, as well as from courses during those years on such topics as existentialism, mathematical logic and philosophy of education, so *Method*'s maddeningly dense, allusive, and elliptical style only makes me appreciate all the more keenly just how much of a summary it is.

In *Method in Theology* the massive project of *Insight* suddenly gets us up into a context of interiority and culture that, stunningly enough, is even broader and more profound than what had been envisaged by that former work. The sea change involved here may perhaps be telegraphed to you by the following contrast. *Insight* provided "five-

---

[26] *Insight*, xix, xvii.
[27] *Insight*, 558-562.
[28] *Insight*, xix, xvii.
[29] *Insight*, 558.

finger exercises" required for the job of appropriating one's consciousness, i.e. of learning, identifying, reorientating. But it presupposed
that its readers possess what Lonergan called "a sufficiently cultured
consciousness."[30] But *Method* goes on to explicate the social, cultural,
and existential conditions for the *emergence* of that "sufficiently cultured consciousness." It does so in terms of its treatment of the structure of the human good; of feelings and the normative scale of values; of
beliefs; of intersubjective, artistic, symbolic, linguistic, and incarnate
meaning; of the stages of meaning and the differentiations of consciousness; and above all, of those vertical exercises of liberty and radical
changes in orientation achieved through religious and moral conversion
which occur in the context of human and otherworldly falling in love.
In other words, *Method* sketches out the philosophy and theology of
action that specifies the actual and concrete context for the practice of
Insight.

It remains, though, that our appropriation of this philosophy and
theology of action is still only propaedeutic. Such a procedure would
only be fulfilling the conditions needed to appropriate Lonergan's bold
transposition in *Method* of Aquinas' practice of theology as *lectio* (ex-
egesis), *quaestio* and *disputatio* (speculative theology), and *praedicatio*
(preaching), into a functionally specialized framework for creative collaboration in molding and transforming culture, which is to say, for
political theology at the level of today's culture.

When I speak of appropriating the functional specialties as a framework for creative collaboration, I do not mean primarily becoming fa-
miliarized with a pattern that simply organizes a division of labor for
a team of scholars and practitioners. No, I intend rather further differentiation of one's interiority as an interpreter and agent in the world.
Just as a person skilled in mathematics can look at an equation and
tell whether or not it is a quadratic equation, so one who has appropriated the formally dynamic structures of one's conscious intentionality
can read the world in terms of elements, functions, realms and stages
of meaning as by a certain kind of X-ray-like vision. So too a person
can appropriate oneself as morally converted, and then "read" his or
her concrete situation in the light of the eighteen-fold structure of the
human good, along with the range of radical variations that it would
undergo in accord with diversely held terminal values as vital or social

---

[30] *Insight,* xxviii.

or cultural or personal or religious.[31] And so, furthermore, can one appropriate the structures immanent and operative in human reflection on humankind's self-constitution by meaning and value; and one can sort out the empirically accessible outcomes of human progress and decline through the X-ray-like vision wrought by functionally specialized reading and interacting.

1.3   Political Theology and Education

Although without benefit of a community dedicated to building up within themselves this kind of capacity for making sense of humankind's making sense of itself, Lonergan managed both to perform and thematize these conditions and operations to be realized within our interiority. This effort was political theology in so far as it is essential to taking a practical and political stance towards the future in the light of the past. Lonergan's heuristics for political theology contrast rather sharply with the style manifest thus far in the political theology of Metz. And this disarming person, Metz, admits quite honestly that his paradigm, as he calls it, is quite open to Lonergan's perspective. The rhetoric of Metz's reaction against the sorts of inauthentic styles of professionalization and specialization in the academy, with its instrumentalist *divide et impera* rationale, can tend to sound like a plea for dedifferentiation as rooted in self-transcendent openness, and as both based upon and orientated towards communication. Again, Metz's truly prophetic contention that in Catholic and Christian theology generally banality is more to be feared than naiveté, can tend to suggest that both historical critical research and argumentative or properly systematic theology are relatively insignificant; but Lonergan's heuristics for political theology both makes room for these and reintegrates and re-orients them as parts within a larger whole whose finality is communicative and transformative practice. Therefore, an obvious and direct aim of Lonergan's effort as a political theologian is the transformation of the procedures and institutions of theological education.

But it is the measure of Lonergan's significance as a political theologian, however, that his efforts and reflections were never really narrowly theological in the sense of a parochial concentration upon the institutions and conventions of Christian theology. To be sure, until he was

---

[31]See *Method*, 47-52.

seventy-eight Lonergan "did what he could" (as, with Damon Runyon, he loved to say) to shift the probabilities for the emergence and survival of theology as a principle for shaping and transforming culture. He spent a lifetime teaching and studying and writing; and he maintained a virtually symbiotic relationship with the Thomas More Institute for Adult Education in Montreal. But, I want to argue, precisely because he was a political theologian in the deepest sense, education had always really been Lonergan's line, as it had been for his beloved Newman. Just as Lonergan had inherited Aquinas' large vision of theology as "a principle for molding and transforming culture," so too did he argue that, "[a] completely genuine development of the thought of St. Thomas will command in all the universities of the modern world the same admiration and respect that St. Thomas himself commanded in the medieval University of Paris."[32] Consequently, I believe it can be consistently argued that there is made available in the concrete and practical programs of *Insight* and *Method* a framework for healing the fragmented and alienated modern multiversity and a strategy for creative collaboration within the university.

In universities today education for specialized professionals (technocrats or bureaucrats) has all but supplanted genuinely liberal education; and education for careers has practically displaced education for citizenship. Anyone who knows what goes on in universities today cannot but agree that they have become seminaries for what Max Weber called "specialists without spirit or vision and voluptuaries without heart."[33] If there is a possibility for a revival of liberal and liberating education that is not simply anachronistically oblivious of the claims of authentic and needed specialization, I believe that it resides in the virtualities of Lonergan's method. For just as *Insight* and *Method* specify the conditions for theology as a principle for shaping and transforming culture, so, too, can they be used heuristically for determining the implementation of the core of liberal and liberating education for citizenship.

At the university level of liberal or of specialized (i.e., professional and even theological) education, what would happen if we clearly started to envisage two sides of the problem in the following way? On the one

---

[32] *Verbum*, 220.

[33] Max Weber, *The Protestant Ethic and the Spirit of Capitalism*, Talcott Parsons, trans. (New York: Charles Scribner & Sons, 1958), 182: "Fachmenschen ohne Geist und Lustmenschen ohne Herz".

hand, what if we inquired about core liberal education in terms of generating the conditions needed in order to be able to read, as they are
intended to be read, *Insight* and *Method in Theology*? What would
need to be done for both students and teachers to attain this sufficiently cultured consciousness? On the other hand, there is the task
sketched out by those books, viz., self-appropriation: all the learning,
identifying and reorienting of ourselves (as students and as teachers)
that are required for (individually and communally) achieving such a
differentiated interiority as would be prepared to exercise a healing and
creative practice within contemporary culture. Surely, there can be a
spiralling interplay between these two educational tasks of acquiring a
sufficiently cultured consciousness and of appropriating it.

In trying to imagine what such a process might entail we can be
helped by the example of Aristotle's project of practical and political philosophy and theology as articulated in his *Ethics* and *Politics*.
We note that, here too, pedagogy and philosophical and theological
reflection are integrally combined. Aristotle's procedure is a matter
of ascent: one starts from the chaos of ends towards which people are
likely to be orientated, one moves through the performative and habit-
ual grasp that virtuous people have of what is just and what is noble,
and one climbs gradually up to a philosophical, theological apprehension of the highest or the most choiceworthy way of life. This pedagogy
should be reminiscent not just of Plato's ascent from the cave but of
the pedagogy of *Insight*: from the polymorphic consciousness of the
bewildered, disorientated subject to the appropriation of one's rational
self-consciousness.

But all those added conditions not directly or adequately envisaged
by *Insight* will have to be explicitly dealt with too. For *Insight*'s attain-
ment of intellectual self-transcendence is only possible on the basis of a
moral conversion from pre-moral ends or satisfactions to true value and
the truly good; and genuinely moral conversion is only possible on the
basis of the religious conversion caused by the gift of God's love. So the
process of ascent in education will involve not merely the restoration
of the centrality of the practical and political question concerning the
right way to live. It will also require first, an individual and communal
process of purification and enlightenment; and, second, the fostering of
the breakthrough experiences that are conditions for real purification
and enlightenment, viz., moral and religious conversion.

I am convinced that what is true of undergraduate education must *mutatis mutandis* be true also of theological education and of every other sort of professional and specialized education. If they are not rooted in education as the sort of ascent we can spell out in terms of the normative structures uncovered in *Insight* and *Method*, then they are simply reproducing the causes of the contemporary crisis of culture rather than developing creative and healing solutions to it. My sense is that the vision of such a transformation of education with all its ramifications for the arts and sciences and for politics is the main stem of Lonergan's achievement as a political theologian, and that his properly theological works together with his yet to be published work on economics are its most precious flowerings.

Chapter 2

Values in Social Science: Foundations and Applications

Hugo Meynell

Ezekiel Bulver, a fictional savant of the nineteenth century, is someone who I believe is insufficiently known to social scientists. The turning point in his life came when he heard his father trying to prove to his mother that the square on the hypotenuse of a right-angled triangle is equal in area to the sum of the squares on the other two sides. His mother won the argument by declaring, "You only say that because you're a man." The young Bulver realized that he need never again attend to the tiresome question of whether the arguments presented to him were sound or unsound; if he wanted to dismiss them, he had only to direct attention to the psychological history or socio-economic circumstances of those who advanced them.[1]

To repudiate Bulverism is not to maintain that a person's history and socio-economic circumstances are never worth citing in explanation

---

[1] Bulver was invented by C.S. Lewis. See his *Undeceptions*, ed. Walter Hooper (London: Bles, 1970), 223-228. Christians have sometimes played the same trick when they have been too ready to attribute disagreements with them to "sin."

of her beliefs. But if such citing is by way of refutation, it must first be shown why the arguments underlying the beliefs are of themselves unsound. It must also be made clear why the arguments of the person conducting the refutation are not determined by factors of the same kind, and hence equally unsound. If some socio-economic or psychological determinants (say, membership of the proletariat) tend to help one in making true judgments, while others (say, membership of the bourgeoisie) tend to have the opposite effect, then it must be shown why this is so. A generalised Bulverism would, of course, invalidate all beliefs whatever as equally due to factors other than intelligent and reasonable assessment of relevant evidence. It seems to me that the contradictory of such a generalised Bulverism, and of all other sets of propositions which entail that no one can ever intelligently, reasonably, or responsibly assent to them, is the beginning of wisdom in social science. To draw out its implications is to show how social sciences and social criticism could be put on a comprehensively critical base—as I shall try to bring out in the course of this essay. Bulver's most conspicuous followers, of course, are the Freudians and the Marxists, so far as they fall into the trap of accounting for their opponents' positions exclusively in terms of class ideology or infant sexuality, while tacitly excluding themselves, as of course they must, from the scope of the explanations which they see fit to apply to other human beings. How rare is the man, as Lonergan remarks, who admits that he himself never says what he says or writes what he writes because he has good reason for doing so; or that he never makes a responsible decision, least of all in submitting to the learned public books and articles which imply that no human being ever makes a responsible decision.[2]

The place of a society's own self-understanding, in the explanation given of its acts and institutions by the social scientist, has been something of a crux in sociology and anthropology. Peter Winch cites R.G. Collingwood to the effect that some accounts of "primitive" societies offered by anthropologists seem to mask "a half-conscious conspiracy to bring into ridicule and contempt civilizations different from our own."[3] In accordance with this corrupt motive, the anthropologist will assume that he himself has the categories appropriate for understanding the

---

[2] See B. Lonergan, *Method in Theology* (London: Darton, Longman and Todd, 1972), 16-17.

[3] Peter Winch, *The Idea of a Social Science* (London: Routledge and Kegan Paul, 1958), 103.

actions and institutions characteristic of the society which he is studying, while the members of that society are themselves unable to do
so, since their own conceptions are mere "ideology" or whatever. As
against this, Winch insists that the anthropologist, if he is to understand an action or an institution even within the most "primitive" of
societies, must understand it in the same terms as the members of that
society themselves. Suppose that an observer, O, is offering as explanation, for N's having voted in a certain way, that N is trying to preserve
industrial peace. "Then it should be noted that the force of O's explanation rests on the fact that the concepts which appear in it must
be grasped not merely by O and his hearers, but also by N himself."[4]
To understand why someone who is a member of another society does
something, one would infer, so far from treating his own explanation as
so much ideology, is both to understand and to adopt that explanation.

In appreciation and criticism of Winch, Alasdair MacIntyre remarks
that many social commentators, non-Marxist as well as Marxist, make
a distinction between those motives which agents appeal to which in
fact determine their actions, and those which do not; this is a necessary condition of there being such a phenomenon as "ideology" or
"false consciousness."[5] Such a distinction, together with those influ-
ential conceptions which depend on it, seems not to make any sense
on Winch's view. Furthermore, MacIntyre points out, Winch appears
to agree with the authorities whom he opposes in presupposing that to
investigate a society in terms intelligible to its members, and to investigate it in terms not so intelligible, are mutually exclusive alternatives.[6]
Also, Winch's account makes certain types of social change unintelligible, that is, those which involve the transition from one system of
beliefs to another and the consequent raising of questions of the kind
that Winch rejects.[7] It may be concluded that what Winch would conceive as the *whole* of social science is in fact its proper *starting-point*.[8]
"What I take to be Winch's mistaken thesis" writes MacIntyre, "is that
we cannot go beyond a society's own self-description.... What I take to
be his true thesis" he continues, is "that we must not do this except and

---

[4] Winch, 46.
[5] A. MacIntyre, "The Idea of a Social Science," in *Rationality*, ed. Bryan Wilson
(Oxford: Blackwell, 1970), 118.
[6] A. MacIntyre, 121.
[7] A. MacIntyre, 129.
[8] A. MacIntyre, 123.

until we have grasped the criteria embodied in that self-description."[9]

Bernard Lonergan wrote very little on the basic problems of social science; yet his thinking is highly relevant to them. The foundations of a social science, on his account, amount to the contradictory of a generalised Bulverism; that every sane human being in every society acts *to some extent* in a rational manner. What is definitive of social science is that what is being investigated, as well as the investigator, is to a certain extent rational, and has to be understood as such. A being is rational to the extent that it attends to experience; that it envisages a range of hypotheses; and that it judges as probably or certainly so the hypotheses which best fit the evidence. To understand an alien society is to see *how far* its beliefs, actions and institutions evince such rationality (so far Winch is right); and *how far* (here MacIntyre would be correct against Winch) they are due to its limitation due to desire, fear, religious sanctions, lack of a tradition of unrestricted inquiry, and so on. Such an account would agree with Winch that to understand a society in its own terms is a *necessary* condition of the kind of understanding aimed at by the social scientists; with MacIntyre that it is all the same not a *sufficient* condition.

What role in social science, if any, should be taken by Max Weber's principle that the conclusions of such a science must be "value-free"?[10] Lonergan's answer to this question, I suggest, is implied by his distinction between the third and the fourth of his "functional specialties," History and Dialectic.[11] It is one thing to determine what persons of other epochs, or of other societies and cultures in our own epoch, were up to; it is another thing to take up an attitude of praise or of censure towards this. It is a gross but, unfortunately, very common intellectual vice to confound the two activities; to allow your value-judgments about Hitler, Jesus, Ayn Rand, Lenin or Luther to distort your inquiry, which ought to be conducted strictly by intelligent and reasonable investigation of the available evidence, as to what these individuals said or did or meant by their sayings and doings. So far, Lonergan is entirely in the spirit of Weber. However, Weber thought that the value-judgment which one might arrive at *after* conducting one's investigation could not

---

[9] A. MacIntyre, 130.

[10] I have recently been much enlightened on this topic through reading an M.A. thesis by Shabbir Akhtar, "A Defense of Value-Free Social Inquiry" (University of Calgary, 1983).

[11] See *Method*, Chapters 5, 8, 9, and 10.

itself be based on rational principles, but must depend in the last resort on something arbitrary which he called "faith." In this a wide range of twentieth-century thinkers, from positivists to existentialists, have in effect followed him. But on Lonergan's principles, the making of such a value-judgment is every bit as reasonable, or at least can be so, as the establishment of what was going on; one is merely making a distinct use or application of reason. We can, after all, establish that the human agents we are studying were more or less reasonable and responsible in what they did, and commend or condemn them accordingly. They will have been responsible so far as they acted on their reasonable judgment of what was the best thing to do, rather than according to the biases due to their individual circumstances or membership of their group or class.

On Lonergan's account, then, we can objectively establish how it is with persons or cultures, without either neglecting their own point of view, or capitulating to it; and we can objectively evaluate them. The *frisson* with which we are inclined spontaneously to react to the notion of "objective evaluation" is due partly to our (proper and Weberian) instinct, which distrusts confusion between establishing what the facts were on the one hand, and taking up an approving or disapproving attitude to them on the other; and partly to a (improper and superstitious but also perhaps Weberian[12]) prejudice that we cannot be objective about what we cannot take a look at. That, of course, if one follows through its implications, is just as destructive of objective physics, and objective knowledge of other minds, as it is of objective values. That philosophers *are* following through these implications accounts for the rising tide of relativism, in my view appallingly dangerous for the future of culture, which seems to be inundating analytical philosophy from the later Wittgenstein through Thomas Kuhn to Richard Rorty.[13]

---

[12]I am, regrettably, not enough of a Weber scholar to know how far this attribution is just in detail. But a disciple of Lonergan might well ask what Weber's espousal of the ideal of value-freedom amounted to, apart from a sharp distinction between the sociological equivalents of "History" and "Dialectic." If it amounted to more than this, he might go on to ask whether the denial of an element of evaluation in the conclusions of social science as such was perhaps based on the prejudice that what cannot be looked at is not a proper object of science; a prejudice which of course rules out electrons and neutrinos from the province of science just as effectively as it rules out good and evil. For a conveniently brief account of Weber's thought, see Julien Freund, *The Sociology of Max Weber* (Harmondsworth: Penguin Books, 1972).

[13]I have tried to argue this in "Doubts About Wittgenstein's Influence", *Philos-*

Can the human sciences articulate norms? It seems to follow from
what I have said that, on the basis of Lonergan's theory of knowledge,
they can certainly do so. A good society is one which is characterized
by, and promotes, intelligent, reasonable and responsible action; a bad
society is one which is not and does not. What are the means by which
such a society may best be promoted? They are, the treatment of the
self-deceptions and *scotoses* by which people justify the avoidance of
intelligent, reasonable and responsible action, like the treatment at the
hands of Napoleon Solo of the agents of *Thrush*. It is the business of
every intellectual to criticise his social environment in the light of the
ideal of objective good, and to encourage others to do so.[14]

Corrupt societies foster and are fostered by corrupt language; and it
is consequently one important function of intellectual criticism to keep
up a running battle against this. George Orwell wrote of an article by
a well-known scientist of strong political opinions:

> A thing that is especially noticeable is the English, ...at
> once pompous and slovenly, in which it is written. It is not
> pedantic to draw attention to this, because the connection
> between totalitarian habits of thought and the corruption
> of language is an important subject which has not been suf-
> ficiently studied. Like all writers of his school, Professor X
> has a strong tendency to drop into Latin when anything
> unpleasant has to be said ... To say 'Party loyalty means
> doing dirt on your conscience' would be too crude; to say
> '(Virtues) based on excessive concern with individual rec-
> titude need reorienting in the direction of social responsi-
> bility' comes to much the same thing, but far less courage
> is required for saying it. The long, vague words express
> the intended meaning and at the same time blur the moral
> squalor of what is being done.[15]

What strikes me about the *aporia* as to the practical applications
of social science is something rather like the emperor's lack of clothes
in the fairy story—so obvious that it is nearly always overlooked. *You*

---

ophy, 57 (1982), 251-259.

[14] See Lonergan's remarks on the role of "cosmopolis" in *Insight: A Study of
Human Understanding* (London: Longmans, Green and Co., 1957), 238-42, 633,
690.

[15] In the journal *Polemic*; quoted by the London *Observer*, September 9, 1968.

cannot at once honestly and usefully criticize a society or any of its institutions without some underlying conception of what is objectively better and objectively worse, and why it is so. The manner in which contemporary analytical philosophy swings between positivism and relativism, both of which in effect either forget about this fact or abandon the problem which it constitutes as insoluble, gives little ground for encouragement. And the ideal of "value-freedom" in social science, unless adopted with the qualifications which I have already mentioned, leads straight to the same impasse; one can be "objective" only about what is the case ("facts"), not about how good or bad it is, let alone what ought to be done about it ("values").

Marxism might well be hoped to provide some kind of solution to this difficulty, but I think such a hope would be illusory. If Marxists have effectively exposed the corruptions and obfuscations of others, it is not implausible to maintain that they themselves have been similarly at fault; and that not so much *in spite of* as *because of* their characteristic doctrines. The fatal ambiguity in Marxist theories of value may be brought out by the following question. Ought a person—would it be right and good for her—to commit herself to the bringing-about of a socialist revolution in a capitalist country, or not? According to what seems the standard Marxist view, ethics is simply a consequence of class position; such a commitment will be "good" from the proletarian point of view, "bad" from the bourgeois point of view, and that is that. And yet the whole intellectual and practical effort of Marxists from the time of Marx himself has been based on the assumption that the revolution, and the classless society which will be its ultimate issue, is really *worth* striving for, that post-revolutionary society will be *better* than pre-revolutionary society. The enormous moral force of a work like *Capital* is entirely dissipated, if this is not assumed; for example, if the reader keeps saying to himself, "Well, this is a fine expression of the proletarian point of view; but of course there is a bourgeois one which is equally valid in its own terms." The issue is masked for Marxists by their conviction that the revolution and the classless society are in any case inevitable in the long run; so that the question of whether an action or a policy is "good" or "right" can be evaded in favour of the question whether it is "progressive," or helpful in bringing about the society of the future.

The way of thinking exemplified in *Insight* corroborates many of the basic theses of Marxism, though it is entirely without the fatal axiological ambiguity just described. According to it, by the attentive,intelligent and reasonable use of our minds we may progressively come to know not just what is true-for-those-of-our-economic-and-social-position, or good-for-them, but what is actually true and actually good. Cognitive and moral self-transcendence, in other words, whereby, from within one's particular material and social milieu, one comes to know what is true and good prior to and independently of one's material and social milieu, is really possible; in contrast to the prima facie implications of historical materialism, where the "true" and the "good" reduce to the practical and to what promotes the revolution here and now.[16] On the other hand, it may be agreed whole-heartedly with the Marxists that one's economic and class position is apt to influence enormously the data to which one will attend, the theoretical and practical possibilities which one will be able or willing to envisage, and the judgments and decisions which will occur to one, or which one will be capable of regarding as a serious option.

It is a main application of Lonergan's philosophy that, with regard to any claim in metaphysics or ethics or the human sciences, one should try to detect how far it is expressive of the basic position, how far of the basic counterposition. In accordance with the basic position, the real is what is to be known by the threefold cognitional process of attentiveness to experience, intelligent inquiry, and reasonable reflection. According to the basic counterposition, the real is what confronts the pre-critical extroverted consciousness common to human beings and animals. The basic counterposition as reflected in Marxism seems to amount roughly to this, where values are concerned. Good and bad are not objects for simple extroversion, and so not real in the last analysis. What *are* real are groups and classes of human beings acting within an environment developed to some stage or other by technology; their morality, their law, and their religion are all means of stabilizing the position of privileged groups and classes in relation to others. There is no point, consequently, in asking whether the revolution is "good" to engage in, whether the classless society is the "right" state of affairs for which to aim. These will be striven for by the proletariat and resisted by the bourgeoisie, each of whom will use terms like "good" and "right" accordingly. The basic position expressed in Marxism is this. What is

---

[16] Cf. the second of Marx's *Theses on Feuerbach.* I have developed this criticism of Marxism at greater length in *Freud, Marx and Morals* (London: The Macmillan Co., 1981), Ch. 4.

good is that human beings should co-operate and enjoy life to the full. Material and social circumstances which frustrate this, by giving the few a satisfying human life at the expense of the many, should be done away with; as should the "ideologies" which give specious justification to these evils.

But Marxism does at least supply the illusion of a comprehensive critique of contemporary society; its influence on many minds is surely due to the apparent lack of alternatives. This is illustrated by Roland Barthes' *Mythologies*,[17] which brings out with consummate wit and brilliance how a particular artifact or social institution may act on persons in such a way as to prevent them attending to certain significant data, and to stop them from asking certain important questions. This ought to issue in a general account of truth as that which one tends to reach by an unrestricted questioning of the widest possible range of data, as in effect on Lonergan's account; and of the good as an aspect of this. But in fact, due to lack of an adequate epistemology, it does not. The result is that Barthes is far more convincing and effective when he describes his "myths" in detail, than when he tries to give a theoretical account of what "myth" is and of what is wrong with it. Marxist dogmas and terminology crowd in at that point, *faute de mieux*.

What annoys Barthes fundamentally in what he calls "myth" is the "naturalness" with which common sense and the media dress up a reality which is in fact determined by history—in other words, making that seem inevitable which could and perhaps ought to be other than it is. He wants to track down the "ideological abuse" which is hidden "on the decorative display of what-goes-without-saying."[18] A critic complains that he does not "understand" a rather subversive writer, who shows the complacent self-deceptions of our society for what they are; the critic's audience in relief turns away from the author as not worth worrying about.[19] Another way of getting rid of inconvenient intellectuals is "telling them to run along and get on with the emotions and the ineffable."[20] To make mild fun of some social institutions may be officially encouraged, as it tends to make people oblivious of the

---

[17] Roland Barthes, *Mythologies*, translated by A. Lavers. (New York: Hill and Wang, 1981.)

[18] Barthes, 11.

[19] Barthes, 34.

[20] Barthes, 35.

real social wrongs which they contain, and the still greater enormities of which they prevent the acknowledgement and removal. "A little 'confessed' evil saves one from acknowledging a lot of hidden evil."[21] The moving sight of a priest who does charitable work for the poor, especially when he seems perfectly dressed up for the part, may be "the alibi which a sizeable part of the nation uses...to substitute with impunity the signs of charity for the reality of justice."[22] A popular women's magazine has an article about women who are both writers and mothers. What is the underlying message? It "says to women: you are worth just as much as men; and to men: your women will never be anything but women." In every feature of the magazine, according to Barthes, there is a kind of double action, to "lock the gynaceum", and "then and only then release women inside."[23]

A child's toys get him quickly inured to a world of soldiers, postmen and Vespas. "Toys here reveal the list of all the things the adult does not find unusual: war, bureaucracy, ugliness ...etc."[24] And confronted with the elaborate and ready-made objects which so many modern toys are, as opposed to, say, the old-fashioned wooden building-blocks, the child finds himself as an owner and a user rather than as a creator.[25] Wine is a delightful substance enough, especially in France; but it is less delightful there when one remembers that much of it is due (this example is, of course, no longer up-to-date) to "big settlers in Algeria who impose on the Muslims, on the very land of which they have been dispossessed, a crop of which they have no need, while they lack even bread."[26] Portrayals of remote countries or cultures, in pictures or in films, tend to resort to a picturesque exoticism which lulls one into failing to ask serious and perhaps disturbing questions about how they came to be as they are.[27] A picture on the front of a magazine of a young negro saluting the French flag may impose on you the conviction that France is a great empire, all of whose sons, of whatever race or color, serve her with wholehearted devotion; and silence within you unworthy suspicions about colonial exploitation.[28]

---

[21]Barthes, 42.
[22]Barthes, 49.
[23]Barthes, 51.
[24]Barthes, 53.
[25]Barthes, 53-4.
[26]Barthes, 61.
[27]Barthes, 96.
[28]Barthes, 116. Barthes' notion of "myth" as used if not as explained by him,

What, for Barthes, is the essence of "myth"? What seems to emerge
from his discussion of examples is that myth is something deplorable;
that it consists in putting over assumptions which are not clearly con-
ceptualized, but which falsify or conceal how things are; and where
the falsification and concealment tend to benefit the more fortunate
classes of society and ipso facto to preserve the status quo. This is
what Barthes' examples and his immediate discussion of them *bring
out*; but his lack of an adequate epistemology prevents him from saying
clearly what he is about. He complains that we can hardly avoid drift-
ing from one myth to another, and that in our alienated state within
bourgeois society we cannot achieve more than an unstable grasp of
reality.[29] But there is an awe-inspiring crudity, which is again related
to certain strands in Marxism (pragmatism, the worship of the working
man), about his conception of what it is to grasp reality directly, to
speak immediately about things. The real is the "already-out-there-
now" with a vengeance, known basically in physical interaction, and
by no means through anything so recondite as reasonable judgment
based on intelligent inquiry into the evidence of sensation. No wonder that the student of myths, the "mythologist," is at several moves
from reality. In the case, say, of a car or an airplane, "the mechanic,
the engineer, even the user, 'speak the object,' but the mythologist is
condemned to metalanguage."[30] Even as a revolutionary he is only
vicarious—presumably because he is not directly subverting the institutions which put about the myths. The critic of myth in bourgeois
society, for Barthes, must operate exclusively in the mode of sarcasm;[31]
about positive and real good, enmeshed as he is in today's evils, he cannot speak. "The mythologist is not even in a Moses-like situation; he
cannot see the promised land. For him, tomorrow's positivity is entirely hidden by today's negativity. All the values of his undertaking
appear to him as acts of destruction."[32] But this need not be so. If one

---

seems instructively close to that in *Insight*; where myth consists of emotion-laden
images connected with the known unknown which involves a distortion of reality.
See *Insight*, 543-47.

[29] Barthes, *Mythologies*, 159.
[30] Barthes, 158.
[31] Barthes, 157.
[32] Barthes, 157. Barthes writes: "Wine is objectively good, and *at the same time*,
the goodness of wine is a myth: here is the *aporia*. The mythologist gets out of
this as best he can."(158) But all he needs to get out of his *aporia* is an adequate
epistemology; a general account of the mental operations involved in knowing what

takes seriously the possibility of moral self-transcendence, one will be able clearly to envisage and confidently to state how the present social situation might be objectively improved. But historical materialism, which tends to bind human judgment too closely to practice within the immediate situation, is not consistent with such self-transcendence. It is for this reason that I believe that Lonergan's work shows how social science and social criticism could be put on a comprehensively critical base more satisfactory than that provided by Marxism, or any other philosophy at present fashionable.

---

is true and knowing and doing what is good, and of the manner in which "myth" frustrates this. The goodness of wine may form part of a complex of beliefs and assumptions which tends to distract people from the existence of remediable suffering and injustice; but people may also believe that wine is good when they fearlessly attend to evidence, even in the teeth of disapproval of the powers that be (whether bourgeois or socialist), and unrestrictedly ask questions. Barthes' suggestion that "myth" in his sense is somehow less characteristic of the political left than of the right (148) strikes me as a lamentable piece of special pleading, again due to the influence rather of Marxist dogmatics than of comprehensively critical principle.

Chapter 3

The Analogy of Dialectic and The Systematics of History

Robert M. Doran

In this paper I will present in summary fashion some insights reached along the way toward writing the first installment on a systematic theology.[1] I began with the assumptions, first, that, if a theology mediates between a cultural matrix and the significance and role of a religion within that matrix,[2] then the first task in constructing a contemporary systematic theology would involve working out basic terms and relations for understanding the cultural matrix being addressed; and second, that these terms and relations would be found by reflecting on Bernard Lonergan's understanding of the structure of society, especially in the seventh chapter of *Insight*.

The first assumption was significantly expanded, however, as the work proceeded, and the expansion was largely due to following through

---

[1] Robert M. Doran, *The Analogy of Dialectic : Categories for a Systematic Theology* (manuscript in process).

[2] Bernard Lonergan, *Method in Theology* (New York; Herder and Herder, 1972), xi.

on the second assumption. For what Lonergan offers is not simply guidance for the sizing up of a given situation. His reflections on society and its immanent dialectic of community contain a key to the heuristic anticipation of an understanding of the intelligible core of historical process itself. After several years of work, I have come to see that the principal general categories of a systematic theology can be derived from reflecting on Lonergan's contributions to an understanding of history. The significance of this insight for the construction of a systematic theology lies in the fact that Christian doctrines can thus be understood in the context of a general-categorial understanding of history. Systematic theology becomes throughout a theological theory of history, as the realities named by the special categories are mediated with the realities articulated in the general categories of a theory of history.[3] Systematics thus becomes praxis, in that it articulates the meaning constitutive of Christian fellowship, witness, and service as the latter exercise a catalytic agency in evoking an alternative situation more closely approximating the kingdom of God in this world.

My first assumption, then, while broadened far beyond its original scope and range, retains an element of truth. The understanding of theology as mediating between a cultural matrix and the significance and role of a religion within that matrix does imply that the theologian addresses one situation only to evoke another one. A mediating theology has not only a disclosive but also a transformative function with respect to its situation. In the perspective provided by Lonergan's understanding of the entire theological enterprise as constituted by eight distinct but related functional specialties, where the first four specialties mediate in indirect discourse from the past into the present, and the second four in direct discourse from the present into the future, the burden of the transformative function falls upon the second phase. What remains true from my first assumption is that a theologian working in the second phase—in foundations, doctrines, systematics, and communications—has to understand, and articulate his or her understanding of, the situation which is being addressed and of the alternative situation which one would evoke. But the widening of the scope and range of this assumption involved for me the grasp of what I would call the heuristic structure of *any* situation, the a priori element involved in the theological understanding of history itself. I

---

[3] On general and special categories, see *Method in Theology*, 281-93.

will attempt to set forth here the basic elements of this understanding.

3.1   The Analogy of Dialectic

The principal categories that I would offer to express an understanding of the structure of history are *the analogy of dialectic* and *the integral scale of values*. These will become the principal general categories of a systematic theology that would understand the meaning of Christian doctrines in the light of an understanding of history. The realities named in the principal Christian doctrines—in David Tracy's summation "God, Christ, grace; creation-redemption-eschatology; church-world; nature-grace, grace-sin; revelation; faith, hope, love; word-sacrament; cross-resurrection-incarnation"[4]—are to be understood in this systematic theology within the overall context of the dialectics of the subject, culture, and community, as these dialectical processes are related to one another by the structure of the scale of values.

The dialectic of the subject and the dialectic of community are discussed by Lonergan in the chapters on common sense in *Insight*.[5] The dialectic of culture is my own contribution. The scale of values is set forth by Lonergan in *Method in Theology*,[6] and my own efforts have been to understand three of the levels of value—social, cultural, personal—as constituted, respectively, by the three dialectics of community, culture, and the subject, and to specify the relations which prevail among the various levels of value both from below and from above. What would these relations be in a line of pure progress in history? How does the breakdown of these relations enable us to achieve some understanding of the dynamics of decline? These are questions to which I would suggest a response. The category of the analogy of dialectic expresses my understanding of the dialectics of the subject, culture, and community. And I try to relate these to one another by specifying their respective functions within the integral scale of values.

---

[4] David Tracy, *The Analogical Imagination: Christian Theology and the Culture of Pluralism* (New York: Crossroad, 1981), 373. Lonergan offers an interrelation, grounded in method, of five sets of the special categories in *Method in Theology*, 290-1.

[5] Bernard Lonergan, *Insight: A Study of Human Understanding* (paperback ed., San Francisco: Harper and Row,1978), 187-206, 211-18.

[6] Lonergan, *Method in Theology*, 31-2.

Each of the three dialectics is internally constituted as "a concrete unfolding of linked but opposed principles of change."[7] The principles constitutive of the dialectic of the subject are neural demands for psychic integration and conscious representation, on the one hand, and the censorship over these demands exercised by dramatically patterned intelligence and imagination, on the other hand.[8] The principles constitutive of the dialectic of community are spontaneous intersubjectivity and the practical intelligence that institutes the technological, economic, and political structures of society.[9] The principles constitutive of the dialectic of culture are cosmological and anthropological constitutive meaning, which are two diverse but interrelated sets of insights regarding the direction that can be found or missed in the movement of life.[10] The dialectics are analogous, first, in that each is an embodiment of the creative tension of limitation and transcendence constituting an unfolding of linked but opposed principles of change;[11] second, in that each is a dialectic of contraries, not of contradictories; and third, in that in each case the integrity of the dialectic is a function of a third principle of higher synthesis beyond the principles internally constitutive of the respective dialectic.

A dialectic of contraries, as opposed to a dialectic of contradictories, is a particular realization of the single but complex notion of dialectic in which the constitutive principles are to work harmoniously in the unfolding of the changes that emerge from their interaction. The processes of individual, social, and cultural change proceed along a line of pure progress to the extent that they are marked by the integral unfolding of the changes emergent from both of the constitutive principles of the relevant dialectic.[12] A dialectic of contraries is a mat-

---

[7]Lonergan, *Insight*, 217.

[8]Lonergan, *Insight*, 189-91. On the ultimate primacy of the dramatic pattern of experience, see my paper, "Dramatic Artistry in the Third Stage of Meaning," in *Lonergan Workshop*, Vol. 2, ed. Frederick Lawrence (Chico, CA: Scholars Press, 1981), 147-99.

[9]Lonergan, *Insight*, 211-18.

[10]On cosmological and anthropological constitutive meaning, see Eric Voegelin, *Order and History*, Vol. 1, *Israel and Revelation* (Baton Rouge, LA: Louisiana State University Press, 1956), 56. On the experience of life as a movement with a direction to be found or missed, see Voegelin: "The Gospel and Culture," in *Jesus and Man's Hope*, eds. D.C. Miller and D. Y. Hadidian (Pittsburgh: Pittsburgh Theological Seminary, 1971), 59-101.

[11]Lonergan, *Insight*, 472-9.

[12]"...Dialectic is a pure form with general implications; it is applicable to any

ter, not of either/or, but of both/and: both neural demand functions and the constructive censorship—in Jungian terms, both the unconscious and the ego; both spontaneous intersubjectivity and practical common sense; both cosmological and anthropological meaning and truth. The respective dialectics of the subject, community, and culture are integral dialectics to the extent that the processes of change that they constitute are a function of the harmonious interaction of both of the opposed principles of change internally constitutive of the dialectic. Each dialectic becomes distorted when the changes are a function of the dominance of one principle over the other, that is to say, when the dialectic of contraries is treated as if it were a dialectic of contradictories—either neural demands or the (now repressive) censorship, either spontaneous intersubjectivity or practical (and now exclusively instrumentalized) intelligence, either cosmological or anthropological (become mechanomorphic) constitutive meaning. In a distorted dialectic, each internally constitutive principle is displaced from its normative function in the concrete unfolding of linked but opposed principles, and the displacements affect the entire process of change emergent in the skewed dialectic.

A dialectic of contradictories does function, however, with respect to a third principle of higher synthesis responsible for the integrity of the respective dialectics. The integral dialectic of neural demand functions and the censorship is a function of the charity that Lonergan calls universal willingness.[13] The integral dialectic of spontaneous intersubjectivity and practical common sense is a function of genuine cultural values. And genuine cultural values, themselves constituted by the integration of cosmological and anthropological meaning and truth, are a function of a soteriological differentiation of consciousness. A dialectic of contradictories operates with respect to these principles of higher

---

concrete unfolding of linked but opposed principles that are modified cumulatively by the unfolding; it can envisage at once the conscious and the non-conscious either in a single subject or in an aggregate and succession of subjects; it is adjustable to any course of events, from an ideal line of pure progress resulting from the harmonious working of the opposed principles, to any degree of conflict, aberration, break-down, and disintegration ..." *Insight*, 244.

[13] Lonergan, *Insight*, 624. Some Jungians do not differentiate contraries from contradictories. The ego and the unconscious are contraries to be synthesized in a higher unity; good and evil are contradictories, the only resolution of which is a choice of one or the other. See Robert M. Doran, "Jungian Psychology and Christian Spirituality," *Review for Religious* 38, 4 (1979), 497-510; 5 (1979), 742-52; 6 (1979), 857-66.

synthesis: either universal willingness or some blend of the biases; either authentic or inauthentic culture; either soteriological meaning and truth or bondage to a one-sided vision of reality that either overly immanentizes the ultimate measure of integrity (the cosmological horizon) or renders this measure so inaccessible to the questing mind and heart (the anthropological horizon) that it is eventually rejected altogether (the death of God and the end of history proclaimed by contemporary post-structuralists).

3.2   The Dialectic of Community

"Society" is a generic term embracing five elements: technological institutions, the economic system, the political order, primordial intersubjectivity, and culture. Culture has two dimensions: the everyday level of meanings and values informing a given way of life, and the reflexive or superstructural level of scientific, philosophic, scholarly, and theological objectifications.

I said above that there is a dialectic of community internally constituted by the linked but opposed principles of spontaneous intersubjectivity and practical intelligence. Spontaneous intersubjectivity is one of the five elements constitutive of a society. Practical intelligence is the source of three of the other elements: technology, the economic system, and the political order. The dialectic of community is the concrete unfolding of the changes that result from the tension of spontaneous intersubjectivity with the dimensions of society emergent from commonsense practicality. The integrity of the dialectic, and so of the society that it informs "rests on the concrete unity of opposed principles; the dominance of either principle results in a distortion, and the distortion both weakens the dominance and strengthens the opposed principle to restore an equilibrium."[14]

The integrity or distortion of the dialectic of community is a function, proximately, of the everyday level of culture, and remotely of the reflexive scientific, scholarly, philosophical, and theological dimension of culture. ".... [I]f men are to meet the challenge set by major decline and its longer cycle, it will be through their culture that they do so."[15] Spontaneous intersubjectivity, technology, economic relations,

---

[14]Lonergan, *Insight*, 233.
[15]*Insight*, 236.

politics, and the everyday level of culture constitute the infrastructure of a society; the reflexive level constitutes a society's superstructure. Culture, in both its everyday infrastructural and its reflexive superstructural dimensions, is the condition of the possibility of the integrity of the dialectic of spontaneous intersubjectivity and the technological-economic-political structures created by practical intelligence for the sake of social order.

In *Insight* Lonergan speaks of a dimension of consciousness that he calls cosmopolis, which informs an intellectual collaboration that assumes responsibility for the integrity of the dialectic of community by attending to the cultural values operative at both the infrastructural and superstructural levels of culture. The integrity of the dialectic of community is a function of neither of the principles internally constitutive of the dialectic, but of culture. Culture is to see to the harmonious cooperation, the creative tension, of intersubjectivity and practicality, through which the community becomes, if you want, a work of art. Authentic cultural values constitute a higher synthesis of the internally constitutive poles of the dialectic of community, a synthesis upon which the integrity of the dialectic depends. Conversely, the breakdown of the dialectic is due to a culture that either has been "forced into an ivory tower of ineffectualness by the social surd" or has "capitulate[d] to its absurdity" by becoming practical.[16] Cosmopolis assumes the responsibility of preventing either of these defaults of transpractical intelligence in the constitution of the meanings and values informing a given way of life.

The analysis to this point is transcendental. It is grounded in the concrete unity-in-tension that is human consciousness itself, the unity-in-duality of sensitive spontaneity and ordering intelligence.[17] Any situation is constituted in part by a particular condition, more or less integral or distorted, of the dialectic of community. But a theology that would mediate between a cultural matrix and the significance and role of Christian faith within that matrix must specify more concretely the factors that constitute the particular dialectic that the theology would address. I understand the significant dialectic of community

---

[16] *Insight*, 237. On cosmopolis, 238-42.

[17] Cosmopolis "stands on a basic analysis of the compound-in-tension that is man." *Insight*, 241. On the transcendental grounding of the dialectics of contraries in the unity-in-duality of consciousness, see Robert M. Doran, "Duality and Dialectic," a paper delivered at the 1986 Lonergan Workshop at Boston College.

today to be global. Almost every regional cultural matrix today must
be understood in terms of planetary structural realities at the levels of
technology, economics, and politics. These realities have been created
in large part by the exploits of competing and escalating imperialistic
systems. I use the term imperialism in accord with a modification of
Joseph Schumpeter's definition: "the objectless disposition on the part
of a state to unlimited forcible expansion." [18]

The modification is to the effect that such a disposition can constitute either a state or an economic macrosystem controlling even states.
At its base imperialism is constituted by a neglect of the limitation poles
in the three dialectics of community, culture, and the subject: a neglect
of spontaneous intersubjectivity, of cosmological constitutive meaning,
and of aesthetic participation in the movement of life. The distortion of
imperialistic praxis represents a skewing of the threefold dialectic in the
direction of transcendence: of practical intelligence become exclusively
instrumental reason, of anthropological meaning become mechanomorphic nihilism, of censorship become repressive of the major portion of
the materials through which persons can make a work of art out of
their lives. And in each case the distortion weakens the dominant principle and calls forth the reversal of the derailed dialectic by evoking
the contribution of the neglected element. But the suppressed element,
when awakened, can be just as tyrannical as was its suppressor. From
the suppressed intersubjectivity, there can result mob violence; from
neglected cosmological meaning a demonic entrapment on the great
mandala that would measure on purely intracosmic standards whatever human integrity it still acknowledges; from the repressed psyche,
a psychotic breakdown.

The task is one of reversing the distortion of the dialectic of community due to the ascendancy of the practical intelligence that institutes
technological, economic, and political structures, over the contrary but
essential exigencies of intersubjective spontaneity; this task is the responsibility of the cosmopolitan intellectual collaboration that, by as-
suming responsibility for the integrity of culture, is, in Hannah Arendt's
words, to "develop a new guarantee which can be found only in a new
political principle, a new law on earth, whose validity this time must
comprehend the whole of humanity while its power must remain strictly

---

[18] Joseph Schumpeter, *Imperialism/Social Classes: Two Essays*, trans. Heinz
Norden (New York: New American Library, 1951), 6.

limited, rooted in and controlled by newly defined territorial entities."[19]
The combined facts, that, first, technological institutions, an economic
system, and a political order are constitutive elements of society, and,
second, that these realities are to be understood ultimately in global
terms, lead to the conclusion that the dialectic of community is today
a global tension. Because culture is the condition of the possibility of
the integrity of the dialectic of community, cosmopolitan intellectual
collaboration is confronted with a demand for the generation of world-
cultural values capable of synthesizing the internally constitutive poles
of a global dialectic of community.[20]

The perversions of the dialectic of community constituted by the objectless disposition to forcible expansion that is imperialism are rooted
in the aberration of intelligence that Critical Theory calls the exclusive
instrumentalization of reason, and Lonergan the general bias of common sense. Practicality or instrumental intelligence in originating and
developing capital and technology, the economy and the state, can be
properly subordinate to the constitution of the human world as a work
of art only by being brought into and maintained in a state of taut balance or poised equilibrium with spontaneous intersubjectivity. And this
is possible only by the subjection to the higher, non-instrumentalized
specialization of intelligence that constitutes and indeed generates authentic cultural values. For this it needs to be invested with the detachment that is needed to honor long-range, ultimate, and theoretical
questions. The dramatic artistry of subjects in community requires that
detachment if it is to preserve intact the delicate and nuanced unfolding
of the dialectic of intersubjectivity and practicality in the constitution
of the social order. The function of culture is to render intellectual
comprehension of and existential engagement in social reality critical,
dialectical, and normative: critical, because any social situation is a
compound of the intelligible and the unintelligible, the good and the
evil, and one must be able to judge the difference; dialectical, because
our intellectual and existential participation in society must advance
the intelligible and good dimensions of the situation and reverse the
unintelligible and evil dimensions (the dialectic of contradictories), and
because the intelligible and good are a function of the integral dialectic

---

[19] Hannah Arendt, *The Origins of Totalitarianism* (New York: Harcourt, Brace,
and Jovanovich, 1973), ix.

[20] On world-cultural humanity, see Lewis Mumford, *The Transformations of Man*
(New York: Harper and Row, 1956), 137-68.

of intersubjectivity and practicality (a dialectic of contraries) and the unintelligible and evil are a function of the distortion of this dialectic; normative, in that neither of the principles internally constitutive of the dialectic is the immanent form of the intelligibility and goodness of the situation. That intelligibility and goodness must be rooted in the higher synthesis of cultural meanings and values embracing both poles of the dialectic in a concrete unity-in-tension.

One of the major principles of the transcendental analysis of historical process—a principle that will become clearer when we discuss the scale of values—is that only cultural values commensurate with the proportions of the social dialectic can assure the integrity of the dialectic itself. This means that if the social dialectic itself is of global proportions, the culture that would sustain it in its integrity must be in some sense a world culture. The integral dialectic of community today calls for schemes of recurrence in the social infrastructure that are both global and alternative to the schemes that emerge from the competing and escalating imperialisms. These alternative schemes depend upon a set of cultural values that are both different from those informing the imperialistic systems and capable of uniting in crosscultural community and collaboration the members of the various regionally circumscribed cultural traditions of humankind. Cosmopolis today must see to the generation of those cultural values, at both levels of culture. The possibility and necessity of the vast interdisciplinary effort required to meet this task constitute the intellectual context of a contemporary Christian systematic theology. Such a theology must be part of that wider interdisciplinary collaboration, employing categories used in other fields as well, but also providing its own special categories. I propose the general systematic rubric of the analogy of dialectic, as a framework in which theology can assume these responsibilities.

3.3   The Integral Scale of Values

The position just stated regarding the relation between the dialectic of community at the level of the social order and the need for cultural values commensurate with the demands of the common good implies a particular stance on the scale of values in general which we must articulate before moving on to other instances of dialectic. The pertinence of the dialectics of culture and the subject for an understanding of history will emerge in the course of our discussion of the integral scale of values and especially of the relations among the various levels of the scale.

Lonergan presents the following account of the scale of values:

> ...we may distinguish vital, social, cultural, personal, and religious values in an ascending order. Vital values, such as health and strength, grace and vigor, normally are preferred to avoiding the work, privations, pains involved in acquiring, maintaining, restoring them. Social values, such as the good of order which conditions the vital values of the whole community, have to be preferred to the vital values of individual members of the community. Cultural values do not exist without the underpinning of vital and social values, but nonetheless they rank higher. Not on bread alone doth man live. Over and above mere living and operating, men have to find a meaning and value in their living and operating. It is the function of culture to discover, express, validate, criticize, correct, develop, improve such meaning and value. Personal value is the person in his self-transcendence, as loving and being loved, as originator of values in himself and in his milieu, as an inspiration and invitation to others to do likewise. Religious values, finally, are at the heart of the meaning and value of man's living and man's world.[21]

I would offer the following understanding of the scale of values.

First, technology, economic relations, and the legal and political stratum of society, in dialectical relation with intersubjective spontaneity, with the dialectic constituted as a function of the everyday level of culture, compose the *infrastructure* of a healthy society.

Second, the *superstructure* of such a society lies in the reflexive, objectifying dimension of culture.

Third, the infrastructure is thus constituted by the vital, social, and everyday cultural levels of value, and the superstructure by reflexively articulated cultural values.

Fourth, beyond these levels of value constitutive of the infrastructure and superstructure of society lie the levels of personal and religious value.

Fifth, the relations among the levels of value may be understood in part as follows: the higher levels condition the schemes of recurrence of

---

[21]Lonergan, *Method in Theology*, 31-2.

the more basic levels, while problems in the effective recurrence of the more basic levels offer an occasion for, and establish the proportions to be met by, the questions that prompt the needed developments at the higher levels. Thus religious values condition the possibility of personal integrity. Personal integrity conditions the possibility of genuine cultural values. At the reflexive level of culture such integrity would inform the cosmopolitan intellectual collaboration of which we spoke above, one function of which is to keep alive in the infrastructure a concern for the integrity of cultural values. Cultural integrity conditions the possibility of a just social order, where justice is a function of the integral dialectic of community. And a just social order conditions the possibility of the equitable distribution of vital goods in such a way as to assure liberation not only from hunger and misery but also from servitude and personal degradation, from hopelessness and meaninglessness. Conversely, problems in the effective recurrence of vital goods for the whole community can be met only by a reversal of distortions in the dialectic of community at the level of social values. A new dynamic equilibrium between intersubjective interaction and technological, economic, and political changes demands a transformation at the everyday level of culture. The latter transformation frequently calls for and depends upon reflexive scholarly and theoretical developments at the superstructural level of culture. And new cultural values at both levels call for changes at the level of personal integrity. The latter, finally, depends for its sustenance and consistency on the religious development of the person.

There are, then, two basic and mutual sets of relations among the levels of value: a movement from above downwards determines the integral functioning of the scale; a movement from below upwards demands the creativity that will result in new developments, further differentiations, at the higher levels.

Sixth, the integrity of the superstructure thus conditions that of the infrastructure.

Seventh, the breakdown of infrastructural integrity consequently calls for developments at the superstructural level of culture.

And eighth, the personal integrity of the individual and the authenticity of his or her religious life, while they lie beyond both infrastructure and superstructure, are essential to the integral unfolding of historical process.

A society, then, is composed of an infrastructure and a superstructure. But the condition of any given society depends on what in fact constitutes these two dimensions of that society. The society is healthy to the extent that its infrastructure is constituted by the dialectical tension of intersubjective interaction with the technological, economic, and political institutions emergent from practical intelligence. The cultural values operative at the everyday level determine the integrity of this basic social dialectic.[22] But the breakdown of everyday cultural values can at times be reversed only by prolonged and difficult collaborative scholarly and theoretical labor at the superstructural level, labor that aims at either the restoration of cultural values that have been eclipsed, or, as in periods of epochal change such as our own, the generation of a new and more inclusive set of cultural values. The cultural values in general of a healthy society are constituted by the operative assumptions consequent upon the pursuit of the beautiful in story and song, ritual and dance, art and literature; the pursuit of the intelligible in science, scholarship, and common sense; the pursuit of the true in philosophy and theology; and the pursuit of the good in all questions regarding the normative relations among the elements constitutive of the human world. The values constituting cultural integrity are the transcendental values of the beautiful, the intelligible, the true, and the good. The operative assumptions that they engender to govern a particular way of life would permit the subordination of practicality in the origination and development of capital and technology, the economy and the state, to the construction of the human world, of human relations, and of human subjects as works of art; they would see that practicality is maintained in a taut balance with the exigencies of intersubjective communication and interaction, and so would guard against the exclusive instrumentalization of intelligence and reason responsible for the current distortions of the dialectic of community.

Personal and religious values are to be understood in relation to the values internally constitutive of the social infrastructure and the cultural superstructure. While they lie beyond these, they are not for that reason to be regarded as constituting a realm of privacy irrelevant to cultural and social process. While the values that constitute

---

[22] Note that the basic social dialectic is between practicality and intersubjectivity, not (as Marxists maintain) within practicality (the dialectic of forces and relations of production). For an approximation to our position, see Jürgen Habermas, "Labor and Interaction: Remarks on Hegel's Jena *Philosophy of Mind*," in Habermas, *Theory and Practice*, trans. John Viertel (Boston: Beacon Press, 1973), 142-69.

cultural integrity condition the possibility of an integral dialectic of community at the level of social values, these cultural values in turn can be promoted only by persons of moral and intellectual integrity. And the person as a self-transcendent originator of values in self and world does not exist, is in fact an impossibility, without the gift of God's grace. Higher levels of value thus condition the possibility of the recurrent realization of more basic levels: no personal integrity without divine grace, no genuine cultural values without personal integrity, no good social order without cultural integrity, and no vital values for the whole community without a good social order. The movement from above downwards among the levels of value is thus the movement of conditioning. The movement from below, on the other hand, is in part one of differentiation and creativity. Problems in the effective realization of more basic levels are solved by new developments at higher levels, developments which must be commensurate with the problems they are meant to solve. Thus a breakdown of the schemes of recurrence supplying vital values to the whole community calls for a higher integration of the dialectic of community, whether through new technological developments, new economic relations, new forms of political organization, through the adaptation of the sensitive spontaneity of intersubjective groups, or through some combination of these various elements of the dialectic. The conversion of the dialectic of community from distortion to integrity calls for either the restoration of cultural values that have suffered eclipse or the differentiation of new, more inclusive, and more refined cultural values. Cultural values are authentic to the extent that they meet the proportions of the problems generated by the distorted dialectic of community. Whether eclipsed cultural values are to be restored or, as in periods of axial cultural changes, new cultural values are to be generated, a conversion of persons to a new level of integrity in their constitution of the world, of human relations, and of themselves as works of dramatic art is required. And because the sustained integrity of self-transcendent persons is impossible without the gift of the divinely originated solution to the problem of evil, the whole process is in effect a supplication for an ever more refined and purified relationship with God.

What is required of the relations among technology, the economy, and politics if these practical arrangements, while a product of instrumentalized intelligence, are to be a function of the integral praxis that would constitute the human world as a work of art, and so if they would emerge in creative tension with the intersubjective base of community? The primary requirement is that legal and political institutions be an element not of the superstructure but of the infrastructure of society. Genuine cultural values keep the political in its place in the infrastructure, where it is to mediate between culture in its everyday dimension and the economic and technological institutions of a society, with a view to placing and maintaining these in dialectical relation with intersubjective interaction. Thus while the mediation from the superstructural to the infrastructural level of culture is one function of cosmopolis, the mediation from the infrastructural level of culture to the economy, to capital formation, and to the intersubjective community is the responsibility of the authentic political specialization of common sense.

On the other hand, when the integral scale of values is neglected, as in the societies spawned by the competing and escalating imperialisms, legal and political institutions slip out of the infra- structure and constitute the lowest level of a mendacious superstructural edifice erected for the sake of preserving a distorted dialectic between practicality and the intersubjective community. Law and politics then become a function of economic relations rather than the guarantee of the dialectic between these relations and intersubjective groups. Slipping out of the infrastructure, they become a mendacious but quite public determinant of the meanings and values informing the way of life of segments of the community. They usurp the prerogatives of culture. Genuine culture retreats into the margins of society. The effective culture is merely the creation and instrument of distorted practicality. When the political specialization, defaulting on its legitimate and necessary infrastructural function, invades the domain of culture, genuine culture surrenders its function of autonomously determining the meanings and values that, through political integrity, would otherwise inform the economy and the institutions of technology as dialectical counterparts of intersubjective interaction. As culture retreats, morality and religion follow suit, and become merely private concerns. The entire structure of the scale of values is upset by the derailment of the political: a derailment that is rooted in the loss of the tension of practicality and intersubjectivity which it is the responsibility of culture to inform and of politics to implement and maintain.[23] The authentic political specialization of

---

[23] My analysis differs from the Marxist position on at least four counts: first, the more dominant role assigned to the dialectical functioning of intersubjective spontaneity in the infrastructure; second, the consequent subordination of practicality

common sense is to meet the recurrent problem of effective agreement
through rational persuasion guided by genuine cultural values. But
under the dominance of the distortions generated by bias it becomes
in a recurrent fashion the inauthentic instrument of the process that
produces the social surd. The subordination of the genuine function of
politics to the distorted dialectic of community can be prevented only
by an everyday culture that has not become instrumentally practical.

I follow Lonergan in maintaining that an authentic everyday culture
depends on the development of a dimension of consciousness that recognizes and implements the immanent norms of intelligence and indeed
of the entire scale of values. This cosmopolitan mentality operative at
the superstructural level is to generate and support, first, a culture in
which "[d]elight and suffering, laughter and tears, joy and sorrow, aspi-
ration and frustration, achievement and failure, wit and humor, stand
not within practicality but above it;"[24] second, a philosophy that appropriates a normative order of inquiry; and third, a human science
that is not only empirical but also critical, dialectical, and normative,
because grounded in that philosophic appropriation.

Culture, philosophy, and human science, then, are reflexes of a distorted infrastructure only when they have surrendered to the exclusive
instrumentalization of intelligence and reason responsible for the distortion. The genuine relation of superstructure and infrastructure is quite
the reverse of that which Marx discovered in capitalism and which, ironically, his followers promoted in state socialism. Theology is to evoke
a superstructure that, through the philosophy, the human science, and
the culture it sponsors, would have a profound impact on the everyday
cultural, the political, the economic, and the technological dimensions
of the infrastructure.

3.4   The Dialectic of the Subject

The cultural superstructure can influence the social infrastructure and
direct it toward integrity only if it takes its stand on the immanent
duality of consciousness that gives rise in the first place to the dialectic

---

to the dramatic constitution of the world as a work of art; third, the recognition
of cultural integrity's responsibility for the infrastructural dialectic; and fourth, the
inclusion of the legal and political in the infrastructure of society.

[24] Lonergan, *Insight*, 236,

of community. At the level of the dialectic of community, this duality manifests itself in the tension of spontaneous intersubjectivity and practical intelligence. But its more radical manifestation is to be found in a dialectic constitutive of the subjects composing a society. The integrity of the dialectic of the subject at the level of personal value is the condition of the possibility of the cultural values that would guarantee an integral dialectic of community at the level of social values.

The dialectic of the dramatic and existential subject is a tension between neural demand functions and that preconscious collaboration of imagination and intelligence that Freud called the censorship and that Lonergan helps us understand within a more inclusive horizon than that available to Freud. The dialectic of the subject constitutes a second instance of the analogy of dialectic.

The integral dialectic of the subject is a condition of the possibility of the cosmopolitan collaboration that assumes the integrity of culture as its responsibility; for it is the immanent intelligibility of personal value as the ground of cultural values. The dialectic of the subject figures in the scale of values in such a way that, while personal integrity grounds the authentic function of culture in a movement from above downwards *among the levels of value*, distortions in the realm of personal value are statistically almost inevitable if personal development is solely a matter of a movement from below upwards *in human consciousness*; and these distortions are to be understood precisely in terms of a breakdown of the integral dialectic of the subject, due to some blend of the several biases that distort the concrete unfolding of the linked but opposed principles of neural demand functions and the censorship. A higher integration in the subject that functions from above downwards in human consciousness is required if persons of integrity are to be available to promote the cultural values that can sustain the integral dialectic of community in the social order. That higher integration is affected by the gift of charity, as the latter imparts an antecedent and in the limit universal willingness. This willingness constitutes the immanent intelligibility of religious values.

The dialectic of subjective development functions within the dialectic of community. The dialectic of community sets the conditions that stimulate our vital spontaneities and mold the orientation of our intelligence as the latter negotiates, with the help of imagination, the spontaneities stimulated by the social situation. These spontaneities, as neural demand functions, constitute one pole of the dialectic of the subject. The other pole consists of the dramatic intelligence in collaboration with imagination that, as censor, negotiates the neural demands. A creative tension of neural demands and the censorship analogous to that which we have already seen between intersubjective spontaneity and practical intelligence is required for the integrity of the dialectic of the subject. The dialectic is distorted in the direction of limitation when neural demands overwhelm intelligent, reasonable, and responsible powers of negotiation; it is distorted in the direction of transcendence when these powers of negotiation become repressive of the very factors they are meant to attend to. In either case a reversal of the distortion is invited through an appeal to the claims of the neglected factor.

The ground of our capacity to shape the elements stimulated by the dialectic of community into a work of dramatic art, through the constructive rather than repressive functioning of the censorship, lies in the sensitive psyche's relative aesthetic liberation from both neural process below and instrumentalization from above. Then intelligence can artistically subordinate neural process to psychic determinations. The censorship is the collaboration of the psyche, through imagination, with intelligence in the effecting of this subordination. It is constructive if oriented to insight and responsible decision, and repressive if directed against these. In my own interpretation of this matter, the orientation of the censorship against insight can be rooted in either of its constitutive elements: in intelligence itself, as in general bias, or in the psychic component, as in the other forms of bias, each of which impairs the psyche's aesthetic liberation from the neural undertow and so its ability to collaborate with intelligence in admitting images into consciousness for insight. As we move from individual through group to dramatic bias, the problem becomes progressively more a problem of psychic development; dramatic bias is the least available to conscious control and free self-correction.

Just as the integrity of the dialectic of community is grounded, not in either of its internally constitutive principles taken singly but in the higher synthesis provided by authentic cultural values, so the dialectic of the subject is grounded not in neural demands nor in the censorship, but in the higher synthesis of an antecedent universal willingness that must be offered and accepted as a gift, as grace, as a feature of personal development not achievable on the basis of one's own immanent resources. If the movement from below in conscious development is not met by a movement from above, development will almost inevitably fall victim to some blend of the biases. The movement from above is the gift, the grace, of an antecedent and in the limit universal willingness, of the detachment of divinely bestowed charity. Without this grace, a functioning relation of conditioning from above downwards among the levels of value is impossible; for the highest level of value would lie in the personal, and bias would prevent an integral development precisely at that level. Personal integrity is not self-grounding. Only a living relationship of partnership and love with the absolute limit of the process of going beyond renders possible sustained development. That relationship is the communication of a willingness that conforms, not to inadequately developed human intelligence, but to God's understanding of the world order which God has chosen and created and which God sustains in being through the whole course of its emergent process.

3.5   The Dialectic of Culture

Cultural values mediate between personal values and social values. If the latter two levels of value are constituted by an integral dialectic of limitation and transcendence, we may suspect that the same is true of authentic cultural values. But our discussion of the issue of cultural values and of a dialectic of culture is more convincing, if it proceeds not from some a priori base of transcendental analysis, however valid, but from a concrete consideration of the crisis of cultural values in a situation where the dialectic of community is globally distorted by the competing and escalating agents of imperialistic ambition. Our attention can shift at this point, then, to the relations that obtain *from below upwards* among the levels of value. The social-infrastructural dialectic of community today is a matter of global proportions, due to the socioeconomic relations and political realities that constitute a globally interdependent commonwealth. These relations and realities demand the generation of cultural values that are more complex in structure and inclusive of more historically transmitted materials than would be the cultural values that might function as ordering factors for less extensive and more regionally circumscribed technoeconomic and political relationships. The meanings and values, the culture, adequate to the proportions of a globally interdependent technological, economic, and political order in dialectical relationship with what is now a crosscultural intersubjectivity, are at best emergent in our situation. Theology today is to mediate what Christians believe as true and value as good, not so much with a relatively stable set of cultural meanings and values as with an emergent and potentially more differentiated set adequate to a global social order. For a systematic theology to mediate Christian faith with the contemporary cultural matrix is for it to participate in the emergence of a new matrix informed by cultural values suited to the proportions of the global social relations that they are to order. The transformation of culture on a global scale is the condition of the possibility of a humane infrastructural order for a global society.

The needed transformation of culture will emerge in part from the retrieval, cross cultural communication, philosophic reference-specification, and dialogically achieved integration of our presently available, historically transmitted knowledge of, and attitudes toward the world, God, ourselves, and the sense of our lives. Following Eric Voegelin, I find these presently available patterns of cultural meaning and value to be threefold: cosmological, anthropological, and soteriological symbolizations of the primordial experience of participation in a movement with a direction that can either be found or missed. I propose that cosmological and anthropological constitutive meaning constitute a dialectic of culture whose integrity is grounded in neither of its internally constitutive poles, but in the soteriological differentiation of consciousness that theology is to mediate with cosmological and anthropological insight and truth in such a way as to promote an integral dialectic of culture.

Like the dialectics of the subject and of community, then, the dialectic of culture is a dialectic of contraries. Both poles are to be affirmed, each in its appropriate relation to the other. The dialectic of culture is another instance of the tension of limitation and transcendence, with the cosmological pole a limiting factor and the anthropological the promoter of transcendence. The integrity of culture is a function of the concrete unfolding of cosmological and anthropological insight and truth; the inauthenticity of culture is a function of the breakdown of this integral unfolding due to the displacement of the tension toward one or other pole.

Cosmological symbolizations of the experience of life as a movement with a direction that can be found or missed find the paradigm of order in the cosmic rhythms. This order is analogously realized in the society, and social order determines individual rectitude. Cosmological insight thus moves from the cosmos, through the society, to the individual. As such it is more compact than anthropological insight, where the measure of integrity is recognized as world-transcendent and as providing the standard first for the individual, whose ordered attunement to the world-transcendent measure is itself the measure of the integrity of the society. Anthropological insight moves from God through the individual to the society. The dialectic of culture, like every dialectic of contraries, is a concrete unfolding of these linked but opposed principles of change.

These two ways of experiencing and understanding the participatory engagement of consciousness in the movement of life are characterized by quite contrasting experiences of time. Cosmological constitutive meaning has its roots in the affective, biologically based sympathy of the organism with the rhythms and processes of nonhuman nature. Anthropological truth is, on the contrary, constitutive of history as the product of human insight, reflection, and decision. A first approximation to the relation between them would contrast cyclical and linear time; but in fact, cosmological time is not precisely cyclical nor is anthropological time linear. The issue is one of schemes of recurrence with greater or lesser probabilities of emergence and survival due to the relative constitutive contribution of insight, reason, and decision. Cosmological consciousness alone binds human schemes of recurrence too stringently to those that inform cosmic process, while anthropological consciousness alone is insensitive to its biologically based, rhythmic participation in nonhuman nature, and given the necessary technical skills will promote a relatively posthistoric mode of existence in contrast with the relatively prehistoric existence of the cosmological societies. The distortions of the dialectic would thus take the form either of anthropological consciousness losing affective sympathy with nature as it constitutes history, or of cosmological consciousness succumbing massively to a fatalism that it supposes is inscribed in cosmic rhythms. A contemporary soteriology must display the deliverance effected by the divinely originated solution to the mystery of evil, not so much from cosmological existence as from mechanomorphic perversions of anthropological truth. The integral dialectic of cosmological and anthropological truth under the higher synthesis of the soteriological differentiation would provide an ecumenically available set of meanings and values to inform the social infrastructure of a global communitarian alternative

to the imperialistic distortions of the dialectic of community. Because
such a set of cultural meanings and values is not yet an established feature of life, theology's mediation of the soteriological vector with the
contemporary situation will itself contribute to the crosscultural generation of the cultural values of a world-cultural humanity. In mediating
faith and culture, theology will be constituting the very meanings and
values of a new cultural order.

3.6   Conclusion

My hope is to construct or at least anticipate a systematic theology
that would understand Christian and theological doctrines in the light
of an understanding of historical process. Such a systematics would
have as central general categories those that I have expressed in this
paper.

It remains to be stated how such a systematics would be not only
academic and praxis-oriented, but also ecclesial. The academic and
praxis-oriented characteristics have been developed at some length in
this paper. I will conclude with some comments about the ecclesial
context of this systematic theology, hoping thereby to illuminate the
realm of religious values, whose integral functioning is the condition of
the possibility of the integrity of the entire scale of values.

From the discussion of cultural values, it is clear that the systematic theology that I have in mind would evoke remotely a transecclesial
world-cultural communitarian alternative to the totalitarian potentials
of the competing and escalating imperialistic systems. But it would
evoke proximately the church as a catalytic agent of this alternative.
The most satisfactory model of the church within this perspective is
that of the community of the suffering servant of God. Theology is
both an intellectual ministry to that community and a component of
that community's ministry in the world. Thus not only must theology as an intellectual enterprise satisfy criteria of rigorous method, so
that systematic theology is genuinely systematic and not a matter of
"rough coherence," and not only must theology as historically situated
receive its agenda from the exigencies of its contemporary situation;
it also must as ecclesial be radically pastoral, prophetic, and keryg-
matic, evoking the church as a community of witness, fellowship, and
service with a disclosive and transformative role to play in the con-

temporary historical situation. As such, it must be carried on within a horizon of Christian self-understanding that is articulately objectified in categories that are at once continuous with the tradition and pertinent to the ever new demands of the prevailing situation. These categories must articulate the constitutive intelligibility of the praxis of the kingdom of God that itself constitutes ecclesial ministry. That praxis, a matter of "doing as Jesus did," lies in a participation not only in Jesus' ministerial proclamation and enactment of the kingdom, but also in the paschal self-offering through which the alternative situation announced and evoked in Jesus' proclamation and praxis became embodied, however precariously, in a real historical community. As the principal catalytic agency of Jesus himself lay in his redemptive suffering, so the principal catalytic agency of the community called and empowered to do as Jesus did will lie in its participation in the law of Jesus' cross. The constitutive intelligibility of the community of disciples, that through which alone the church can be truly an incarnational sacrament of Jesus to the world and an eschatological sacrament of the world itself, lies in this innermost elemental feature of the divinely originated response to the human problem of evil.

The inner form of the catalytic agency of suffering servanthood lies in fidelity to the integral scale of values through which the distorted dialectics of the subject, culture, and community are transformed into the concrete unfolding of linked but opposed principles of change that constitutes an integral dialectic.[25] The categories of suffering servanthood name the religious values that condition the possibility of the personal integrity that in turn can promote the cultural values needed to inform a global dialectic of community capable of assuring the equitable distribution of vital goods to the one family of humanity under God in history.

---

[25] For a more extensive elaboration of this theme, see Robert M. Doran, "Suffering Servanthood and the Scale of Values," *Lonergan Workshop*, Vol. 4, ed. Frederick Lawrence (Scholars Press, 1983), 41-67.

Chapter 4

Systematics, Communications, Actual Contexts

Philip McShane

"Successive contexts have been formed only to provide the base and the need for forming a further, fuller context; and, as is clear from our final chapter, even several hundred pages have not brought us to the end of the process."[1]

The present essay points towards contexts, specifically the upper open blade of an actual context of adequate theology in future millennia. The essay stands in genetic continuity with a previous *Festschrift* essay on "The Actual Context of Economics": not an appendix, then, but rather a tale wagging the dog.[2] Where the previous essay centrally drew attention to the challenge of the achievement of the forty-eight year old Lonergan who wrote the initial quotation, the present essay

---

[1] Bernard Lonergan, S.J., *Insight: A Study of Human Understanding*, (New York: Philosophical Library, 1958) 731.

[2] McShane, "Generalized Empirical Method and the Actual Context of Economics," *Creativity and Method*, ed., M. Lamb, (Milwaukee: Marquette University Press, 1980), 543-71.

moves that challenge from the seemingly only personal challenge of *Circulation Analysis* and *Insight* to an historic role-full humdrum challenge of the vortex of functional specialization, a vortex which will impishly wag the sluggish individual quest.

In that same page of the work *Insight*, Lonergan remarks on "the inception of a far larger one." I suspect that none of us has real intimations of the lonely sick heroic climb of Lonergan to the mist-prints of the short work, *Method in Theology*. It certainly was the inception of a far larger one, and it is only by sifting through unpublished lectures, notes, and scribbles, that one can come to sense the dimensions of his reach for a methodical redemption, under grace, of history. I would hope to intimate a growing structured sense of that reach in a later book;[3] here I can only express clues, suspicions, map readings. There are four sections to follow. A first section gives some indication of my deep respect for, and long struggle with, Bernard Lonergan's meaning. It should be useful for young people who constantly feel pressured towards a mythic speedy growth in understanding. The second section, drawn from a presentation for the Santa Clara Symposium, places "the actual context of economics" in a new context. The third section here both enlarges that new context and fits genetically into my previous essay's discussion of "bridges of meaning." The fourth section places the clues to the enterprise of methodical redemption in the larger context of that vein of the Cosmic Word which is modernity's[4] genesis of an ongoing genesis of scientific humility and method.

4.1   Struggling with Lonergan's Meaning

I have had the privilege of writing in honor of Bernard Lonergan in various *Festschriften* since 1964, and in this essay, paying homage to him in his eightieth year, I find it difficult to know what further to say. I have, on occasion, compared Lonergan to Beethoven, Rembrandt, Galileo, Mendeleev, Joyce. Perhaps I might recall here the initial quotation of my contribution to *Creativity and Method*, regarding Joyce keeping

---

[3] A work in progress tentatively entitled *Process: A Paideia*. See the concluding page of McShane, *Wealth of Self and Wealth of Nations*, (Lanham, MD : University Press of America, 1981).

[4] For the meaning of "modernity" see the preface and chapter one of *Searching for Cultural Foundations*, ed. P. McShane, (Lanham, MD: University Press of America, 1984).

"the scholars busy for 300 years, so that anyone who has been working on *Finnegans Wake* for the past 20 years, still has 280 to go. Not every *Wake* commentator has accepted the full measure of the dedication, apparently, for some have paused for long respites along the way."[5] Lonergan's cultural profundity, in fact, goes far beyond the great men to which I have compared him. I have taken little respite along the way in reaching for his meaning and "that reaching has changed me profoundly."[6] But unlike Lonergan with Aquinas, I am no first rate mind chasing after another. So perhaps here I may write for lesser minds like my own in an honest biographic sense so that they may be less discouraged by "the murderous grotesque of our time",[7] as it effects the academy, from slowly stumbling round and up the mountain of meaning.

I was fortunate to discover both *Insight* and the *Verbum* articles in the late fifties. I had just come through four years of mathematics and mathematical physics and still regard it as a major turning point that I learned to read by struggling through such works as Whittaker and Watson, *A Course of Modern Analysis.*[8] In that particular work the chapters were short, but each ended with a substantial collection of problems. A first reading left one blank before the problems. Only after weeks of laboring through the problems did one arrive at the state that Lonergan describes in another context: "one has simply to read, and the proper acts of understanding and meaning will follow".[9] I mention this experience here because I see as central to present confusion in philosophy and theology the problem Lonergan points to in remarking that present culture does not teach people how to read. And of course one may take "read" in a larger sense: reading houses, attics, nests, etc., with Bachelard;[10] or, with Don Quixote and Lonergan, "reading the book of himself."[11]

---

[5] Bernard Benstock, "The State of the Wake", *James Joyce Quarterly*, 14 (1976-7), 237.

[6] *Insight*, 748.

[7] E. Voegelin, "Reason: The Classic Experience", *Southern Review* (July, 1974), 251.

[8] (Cambridge University Press, 1952, 4th ed.)

[9] B. Lonergan, S.J., *Verbum: Word and Idea in Aquinas*, ed. David Burrell, C.S.C., (Notre Dame: University of Notre Dame Press, 1967), 219.

[10] See Gaston Bachelard, *The Poetics of Space*, trans. Marsa Jolas (New York : Orron Press, 1968), 14, 21, 39, 47, 83.

[11] James Joyce, *Ulysses* (London : The Bodley Head, 1954), 175.

My first impression of Lonergan's achievement was of a massive paradigm shift, something like a shift from pre-Lavoisier chemistry to the context of the periodic table. This became painfully evident when I began to study theology in 1960 and found not a queen but a confused common sense eclecticism. The discovery forced me to express my early enthusiasm in such articles as "The Contemporary Thomism of Bernard Lonergan,"[12] and "The Hypothesis of Intelligible Emanations in God."[13]

That early enthusiasm and respect has not dwindled but grown over the years. I find, even after almost three decades, that I have only begun to glimpse the remote subtlety of Lonergan's discovery of subject and object, and in this I seem to be at odds with many of his "disciples." Yet I am not more than averagely slow-witted. That problem was ever-present to me as I edited the Florida conference papers and I expressed it briefly in the preface to Volume 2: "And so, while it is true that the verbal expressions of the minds of great men shorten our labours, that like pygmies we stand on their shoulders, there can be an element of illusion regarding just how much shorter our labours are to be, just how authentic we stand."[14]

Here I think it useful to illustrate the problem of reading Lonergan from personal experience. I recall three clear instances. The first instance comes from the book *Insight*. By 1963 I had some suspicion of what the book was initiating but I was acutely aware of being bogged down in chapter eight, which deals with the heuristic notion of the notion of thing.[15]. That chapter was a central preoccupation through the winter of 1963-64, and only in the spring was I satisfied that I had the beginning of an appropriation of the spontaneous notion. And certainly my experience leaves me out of sympathy with David Tracy's view of the distinction between "things" and "bodies": "The distinction (perhaps his best known one) is easy enough to grasp if the previous

---

[12] *Philosophical Studies*, Ireland, XI (1961-62), 63-80.

[13] *Theological Studies* 23 (1962) 545-568. I take the opportunity to note that the first two lines of 549 should be omitted.

[14] *Language, Truth and Meaning*, ed. P. McShane, (Notre Dame: University of Notre Dame Press, 1972), ii.

[15] The word "notion", which occurs regularly in headings and texts in *Insight*, has layers of meanings, paralleling the variety of ways of being "at home in transcendental method" *Method in Theology* [New York: Herder and Herder, 1972], 14

chapters have been understood."[16]

A second instance regards Lonergan's economics. In the late sixties he sent me the manuscript which had remained in his files since 1944. It was only in the seventies that I came to attempt a serious reading. After five years of persistent re-reading it became clear to me that Lonergan had done for dynamic economics something equivalent to a jump in astronomy from Tycho Brahe to Laplace. The meaning of Lonergan's economics is part of foundational theology. Yet that meaning is quite beyond the present perspective either of political theology or of standard economics. Its discontinuity with thinking in these areas warrants fresh starts free from comparisons either with contemporary faulty revisions in economic theory or with the hazy reflections of political theology in these past decades. One must read Lonergan's political economics over against the actual object—which centrally is subjects—of which he has conceived the normative heuristic.

A third instance of personal difficulty is a present one. I find the eighth functional specialty as elusive in *Method in Theology* as I found the eighth chapter in *Insight* twenty years ago. The following sections represent present gropings. What, for instance, is meant by the brief initial section of Chapter Fourteen, the 92nd of *Method in Theology*, the 199th of *Insight* and *Method* combined, entitled "Meaning and Ontology?" Could it be read profitably under an alternate title such as "passionate subjectivity in the lucid closed options of the finality of implementation?" Is it pointing towards what I will conclude to at the end of section three below, the mutual self-mediation of the actual contexts of mindful theology and meaningful history? What I write here will help, I hope, towards a communal search for the meaning of the executive reflection that crowns theology's withdrawal. What I write, then, is not summary but rather tentative pointers, map-readings, suggested directions for climbing.

As I grow older I believe less and less in summary expression, even when one has reached a worthwhile perspective. Too many people seem willing to attempt for Lonergan what Fichte attempted for Kant,[17] or what De Quincey attempted for Ricardo.[18] I have little faith in such

---

[16] David Tracy, *The Achievement of Bernard Lonergan* (New York: Herder and Herder, 1970), 121-2.

[17] Fichte's "Sun-clear Statement to the Public at large. An attempt to force the reader to an understanding" was published, in the English translation of A. E. Kroger, in *The Journal of Speculative Philosophy*, Vol. II (1868).

[18] "Dialogue of Three Templars on Political Economy, Chiefly in Relation to the

attempts, particularly if they have no content driving rhythmically from below upwards towards morning dreams and images. In their clarity they belong largely to undifferentiated consciousness in the later stages of meaning. They have no place in compact consciousness. They will, hopefully, dwindle as we come to the end of the horrors of modernity, the age of garrulousness, during the next millennium.

The fundamental issue is hierarchically-harmonious adult growth, particularly in that displacement towards heuristic system that is the foundational enterprise.

We live between the passionate passivity of the empirical residue and the dynamic passion[19] of infinite Persons. What is primary in history, even without sin, is silent darkness. Even late in life, or in history,[20] there cannot be more than illusory twilight, and the foundational search is an endless meta-empirical asking for greater depth in the same questions. It is a struggle against the terror of biography which parallels what Eliade names the terror of history.[21]

I have written biographically here, and while the writing may seem mainly descriptive it expresses a fundamental foundational stand. When I was 45 years old I wrote in agreement with Husserl, without foundational misery, "How I would like to live on the heights. For this is all my thinking craves for. But shall I ever work my way upwards, if only for a little, so that I can gain something of a free distant view? I am now forty-five years old, and I am still a miserable beginner."[22] I would hope, in the future, to remain in agreement with Bachelard: "Late in life, with indomitable courage, we continue to say that we are going to

---

Principles of Mr. Ricardo," *The Works of Thomas de Quincey*, eds. Adam and Charles Black (Edinburgh, 1862), Vol. 4, 176-257. More than two decades later he produced a more substantial work, "Logic of Political Economy", Vol. 13, 234-452.

[19] On the relation of Trinitarian passion to suffering and evil, see Lonergan, *Understanding and Being: An Introduction and Companion to "Insight"*, eds. E. & M. Morelli, (New York and Toronto: Edwin Mellen Press, 1980), 327-30.

[20] One must sublate, through Lonergan's view on emergent probability, inverse insight and mystery, what Voegelin has to say of history: "...history is discovered as the process in which reality becomes luminous for the movement beyond its own structure; the structure of history is eschatological", (Voegelin, *The Ecumenic Age*, [Baton Rouge: Louisiana State University Press, 1974], 304).

[21] Mircea Eliade, *The Myth of the Eternal Return*, (London: Routledge and Keagan Paul, 1955), 139-62.

[22] From a letter of Edmund Husserl to Franz Brentano, October 15, 1904; quoted in H. Spiegelberg, *The Phenomenological Movement*, Vol. I, (The Hague, 1965), 89.

do what we have not yet done: we are going to build a house."[23]

Burl Ives, at 74, spoke of his endless struggle against deficiencies in his voice: he was still, at that age, devoting two hours each day to singing scales.[24] The theologian and the philosopher, indeed the academic who would face the challenge of generalized empirical method in history, must endlessly return to the scales in a contemporary context, to the ABC[25] of the reality of the self, the historic world, the Absolute, all revealed only within the self in solitary quest.

4.2 Economics and the New Systematics

My primary intention here is to give some indication of the complexity of a new systematics of economics as a functional specialty. Secondarily, I wish to indicate the larger significance of the foundational conception of this systematics by relating the heuristic both to the last functional specialty, communications, and to the general task of theology. I will pass over Lonergan's contribution to the foundations and systematics of economics, the history of that contribution and its relation to other views: sufficient indications of which are already available.[26] I will attempt, rather, to give clues, analogies and random illustrations that will open the discussion towards later comprehension and functional specialist collaboration.

The conventional view of Systematic Theology is the one which contrasts a *Via Systematica* with a *Via Analytica*, best illustrated perhaps by the Trinitarian theology of Aquinas sublated by Lonergan's treatises of the 1960's. What I am suggesting as a possible third-stage heuristics of a New Systematics comes from Lonergan, but clues to it also come from the modern sciences that deal with genetic development—growth of plants and animals, and studies which deal with the dialectical development of humans. Sources in Lonergan for the notion are mainly two: Lonergan's discussion of systematic understanding in *De Intellectu et*

---

[23] *The Poetics of Space*, (Boston: Beacon Press, 1969), 61.

[24] An interview with Stereo Morning, CBC, November, 1983; repeated July 1984.

[25] I think of the triangle ABC of *Insight* (27, 504) as well as the "Transcendent Triangle" advancing as lover (see n. 18 above). There are the scales, too, of poetry, and the risks of integral presence in finitude (see 145, n.60, *Searching for Cultural Foundations*.

[26] Philip McShane, *Lonergan's Challenge to the University and the Economy*, (Lanham, MD: University Press of America, 1980), Chs. 6-8; and "Features of Generalized Empirical Method," 556-57.

Methodo,[27] and his own efforts during the past decade culminating in the 1982-83 version of his economics. A useful and available context for theologians is *Caput Primum* of Lonergan's *Conceptio Analogica Divinarum Personarum*[28] and its revised version in *De Deo Trino, Pars Systematica*.[29]

A first aid to the notion of the new systematics comes from reflection on the heuristics of the study of a growing plant or animal—*Insight*'s discussion of genetic method is relevant.[30] The understanding of such realities involves a seeking of the form of a sequence of integrations of varying lower manifolds. One may next complexify this notion by envisaging human development which adds a dialectical factor. Next, it is perhaps helpful to consider the difference between a reflective diary of such a development and a completed biography which, among many other things, may add the tonality of destiny, or "making something better than the reality."[31]

Next, a shift from the individual to history; indeed, specifically to a fourfold history: the history of economic fact, the history of economic theory (e.g., Schumpeter), the history of economic policy, and the more recently-emerged contrafactual economic history.[32] I would note here that these histories will be slowly and remarkably transposed by "the use of the general categories in all specialties,"[33] categories which will include the culture-invariant general economic analysis of Lonergan meshed into a heuristic of schemes of recurrence. So, for instance, a restructuring of research by the functional distinctions of the productive process will yield new patterns of statistics. Again, the same distinctions will ground fresh patterns of the rhythms of 19th century British, or 20th century Soviet, economics. This shift from individual to history brings us closer to an appreciation of the two struggles of Lonergan: his struggle in *De Intellectu et Methodo* to link history and systematics in a manner that, so to speak, would carry history forward "with minimal loss," and his struggle in this past decade, working with

---

[27] A 72-page typescript of a 1959 course given at Rome, produced at St. Francis Xavier College, Rome. Available at the various Lonergan Centres.

[28] Rome : Gregorian Press, 1957.

[29] Rome : Gregorian Press, 1964.

[30] Lonergan, *Insight*, 448-483.

[31] Lonergan, *Method in Theology*, 251.

[32] See, e.g., A. Fishlow, "The New Economic History Revisited," *The Journal of European Economic History* (1974).

[33] *Method in Theology*, 292.

Schumpeter and a few other books, to apparently "supplement, illustrate, etc.," his own basic systematics with insights and even rescued oversights, with the labours of economic innovators and "odd balls" alike. A key issue here is the task of "reversing the counter-positions" so as to carry forward into the genetic systematics any understanding possibly contributory to the practical understanding of some economic situation in some culture somewhere.

A further issue is the extent to which Lonergan's recent work was dominated by a praxis heuristics of such a genetic systematics. Certainly, he sought such a notion in the late fifties; also, early in his 1982-83 manuscript he takes a stand with Schumpeter: "Scientific analysis is not simply a logically consistent process that starts with some primitive notions and then adds to the stock in a straight-line fashion ...Rather it is an incessant struggle with creations of our own and our predecessors' minds."[34] At least one can say that, just as in *Insight* Lonergan was doing generalized empirical method not in the way he defined that method in *Insight*[35] but in the way he later defined it,[36] so in recent years he operated spontaneously towards the transposition of the content of a complex systematics in a way that brings together his pre-functional specialty reflections on systematics and the differentiation of his consciousness into functional specialist operations. Finally, I would suggest that a closer reading of the chapters on the fourth, fifth, sixth, and seventh specialties in *Method in Theology*—from the perspective, one might say, of the general categories of pages 286-87— would reveal a drive of the "universal viewpoint"[37] towards the present view of systematics.

Let us return to a final clue to the nature of the new systematics, reached by relating it to the eighth specialty which I here presume to call "Executive Reflection." For simplicity, consider the new systematics to yield a related genetic sequence of empirically-grounded understandings simply symbolized by U_{ij}. The i and j indicate the looseness of relation: unlike the connectivity of the sequence of "form and matter" in a plant, the "form" of an economic theory or policy of one time or place may have its "proper matter" at another time elsewhere. Executive reflection mediates between this complex ever-growing sys-

---

[34] *History of Economic Analysis*, (Oxford: Oxford University Press, 1974), p. 4.
[35] *Insight*, 72.
[36] See "Feature of Generalized Method," 545-56.
[37] See *Insight*, 564 ff; *Method in Theology*, 153.

tematics and the varieties of disciplines, cultures, and media of present and later times and places.[38] Clues to the particular praxis-relevance of U_{ij} can come from the i or the j or the position in the sequence: one might reflect on the Rostow school on "takeoffs" for illustrations. So, French agriculture-based theory-policy of an earlier century transposed by general functional economic categories, might be found relevant to a culture-sensitive economic transformation of a twenty-first century Indian province.

Theologians may note the manner in which, in their own field, such a "transposition of systematic meaning from a static to an ongoing, dynamic process"[39] would meet the challenge of providing "an understanding of the realities affirmed by doctrines,"[40] of being "at home in modern sciences, modern scholarship, and modern philosophy,"[41] and of providing a systematic objectification of religious interiority that is "historical, phenomenological, psychological, sociological,"[42] thus becoming adequate to the threefold task of communications. The pressure for such a demanding enlargement of systematic theology will come from the cultural matrix: so, to take an example other than economics, a systematics of anxiety is called for in present psychology, that, contextualized by the transcultural base of general categories, would bring into illuminating genetic coherence such apparently unrelated searchings as the description of *anxietas* in Cicero's *Tusculan Disputations* and the definition of anxiety in *The Neurotic Personality of Our Time*.[43]

Returning to economics, I would note that Lonergan's contribution of an invariant component to economic dynamics, within its context of general and special[44] categories, is profoundly discontinuous with present economics and present methodologies and philosophies of economics.[45] Moreover, as Alfred Eichner points out, present economics departments mainly represent not a science but a social system.[46]

---

[38] See *Method in Theology*, 132-33; and *Searching for Cultural Foundations*.

[39] *Method in Theology*, 304.

[40] *Method in Theology*, 349.

[41] *Method in Theology*, 350.

[42] *Method in Theology*, 290.

[43] K. Horney, *The Neurotic Personality of Our Time* (New York: Norton, 1937).

[44] See, e.g., F. Lawrence on Christian success in "The Human Good and Christian Conversation," in *Searching for Cultural Foundations*, 86-112.

[45] See *The Philosophic Forum* (1983), which contains a double issue on Philosophy and Economics.

[46] "Why Economics is Not Yet a Science," Working Paper no. 7, Centre for Economic and Anthropological Research (December 1982); see also A. Rosenberg,

Eichner, himself, represents a minority group with a different but still deeply limited perspective.[47]

A useful strategy in coming to some appreciation of the discontinuity of Lonergan's view with present work is to venture into the history of theories of distribution. Maurice Dobb's *Theories of Value and Distribution Since Adam Smith* is a convenient initial text.[48] Theories of distribution, right down to current debate, are bogged down in the *priora quoad illos vel hos*[49]of varieties of prices, and succeed only in regularly generating incoherencies regarding immeasurables.[50] Lonergan, in contrast, through a long struggle witnessed to by discarded manuscripts of the thirties, succeeded in thoroughly removing prices, etc., from the *priora quoad* through a theory of distribution and redistribution which compares to current theory as does q. 27 of the *Summa* to Tertullian's Trinity. It is a startling illustration of what Lonergan calls "the displacement towards system."[51] It leaves the meanings Lonergan attaches to prices, profits, etc. incomparable with current confused meanings.

There are, however, some, of a more open perspective, that are not mainstream economists. For example, Jane Jacobs in her new book[52] insightfully pinpoints the positively significant features of inter-city economic activity and the varieties of transactions of decline—military production, welfare programs, transplant investment, advanced-backward trade, VAT ...—in a manner that solidly contributes to a new systematics. She recognizes "patterns in economics history as so repetitious as to suggest that they are almost laws."[53] What she puts forward as a "radical intervention or discontinuity other than transactions of decline"[54] is a relevant dismantling of sovereignty and empire.[55]

"If Economics isn't Science, What is it?" *The Philosophical Forum*, vol. XIV, nos. 3-4 (1983), 296-314.

[47]See *A Guide to Post-Keynesian Economics*, ed. A. Eichner (New York: M. Sharp, 1979).

[48]See Maurice Dobb, *Theories of Value and Distribution Since Adam Smith* (Cambridge University Press, 1973).

[49]See Lonergan, *De Deo Trino II* (1964), 44-45.

[50]See Dobb, *Theories of Value*, 247 ff.

[51]*De Deo Trino I*, 10, n. 10.

[52]Jane Jacobs, *Cities and the Wealth of Nations*, (New York: Random House, 1984).

[53]*Cities and the Wealth of Nations*, 206.

[54]*Cities and the Wealth of Nations*, 214.

[55]See McShane, *Lonergan's Challenge to the University and the Economy, 196.*

She considers this only as a "theoretic possibility."[56]   However, if her reflections are sublated into the actual context of functional distinctions in economics,[57] microautonomy and lucidity of characters of intentionality,[58] then her theoretic possibility falls within the schedules of probability to be envisaged by the normative science, however inoperative[59] it may be in the present slums of mind.[60]

Again, J. J. van Duijn's *The Long Wave in Economic Life*,[61] points to a large-scale genetic systematics of the life cycles of innovation and infrastructural investment beyond politics: "policy makers are oriented toward directly-observable short-term fluctuations."[62]   But his assessment of other approaches[63] applies to his own: there is a tendency in him to lump together varieties of industries, remediable only by precisely and spontaneously operative functional distinctions.[64] Like the biologist at the zoo,[65] the economist must "see another manner" in which goods and money flow.

Causing in the economics community the horizon-shift necessary to see thus in another manner is the massive task of education of which Lonergan has written: "coming to grasp what serious education realizes, and, nonetheless, coming to accept that challenge constitutes the greatest challenge to the modern economy."[66] The genuinely contemporary theologian has the uncomfortable task of becoming educated in the relevant invariant macrodynamic heuristic if he or she, in any functional specialty,[67] is to contribute to the mediation of that transposition of economic culture. He and she "have to take a professional interest in the human sciences and make a positive contribution to their methodology."[68]

---

[56] *Cities and the Wealth of Nations*, 214.
[57] *Creativity and Method*, 556-71.
[58] McShane, *Wealth of Self and Wealth of Nations*, 53, 93; and A. Rosenberg, *The Philosophic Forum* (1983), 302-07.
[59] *Insight*, 223.
[60] *Method in Theology* 39-40, 99.
[61] London: Allen and Unwin, 1983.
[62] J.J. Van Duijn, 14.
[63] J.J. Van Duijn, 28.
[64] Compare van Duijn's long wave chronology, 142-43, with its equivalent in Lonergan's diagrammatic analysis.
[65] *Method in Theology, 83.*
[66] Lonergan, unpublished manuscript of the late 70's.
[67] *Method in Theology*, 292.
[68] *Insight*, 743. I would like to acknowledge my indebtedness to Nicholas Graham

4.3 Foundations and Bridges of Meaning

For further clues regarding the structure of the enterprise of systematics and communications we turn to the foundations specified by *Insight* and *Method in Theology*. It is perhaps necessary to draw attention to the fact that these writings are substantially Lonergan's contribution to the fifth functional specialty, to which may be added certain sections of his Latin works. So, in *Insight*, there is a drive towards what are later called categories, and while the book was written prior to the differentiation of consciousness which is functional specialization, it both provided Lonergan with data of consciousness for that distinction and is transposable without major change into the *oratio* of the fifth specialty. The changes are minor: so, for example, clarifications by contrast reach a new precision through the operation of counterposition-reversal, implementation as a character of metaphysics becomes distributed over different specialties, and Chapter Seventeen in particular calls for refinements and enlargements in ways that we will touch on presently.

I vividly recall Lonergan expressing a certain frustration, in the mid-sixties, regarding the beginning of *Method in Theology*: what was he to do? he couldn't repeat all of *Insight* in Chapter One. As an examination of *Method* shows, what he eventually did was to build the achievement of *Insight* into the task of *Method* in a discomfortingly unsubtle fashion. This is perhaps best noted through a careful reading of his sketch of the general categories on pages 286-88. So, one may note a complexification of the basic heuristic resulting from an enlargement of the contribution of Chapter Six of *Insight* under (2), while (1) and (3) place Chapter One of *Method* in that larger context; (4) and (5) point to an inclusion of the heuristics of Chapters Two and Three of *Method*; and (6) - (9) add the massive post-modern perspective of *Insight* to the foreground of *Method*. And at this stage one is normatively in a position to provide a developed account of Chapters Two to Four of *Method*. What is this developed account? It is the account that, for example, transposes the heuristic diagram of page 48 of *Method* into a properly explanatory heuristic, so that the theologian be no longer

---

of Toronto, who provided me with his texts of Lonergan's lectures of the past decade, kept me informed on current literature, and put me in touch with Jane Jacobs while she was completing her recent book.

"arriving on the scene a little breathlessly and a little late,"[69] in present times. Two examples may help. One may consider foundationally, in the context of the eighteen terms, the good of order. Since "what is good, always is concrete,"[70] that good has the complexity of an economic order. Again, one may consider, in a theology of hope, the capacity and need for hope. But what does one mean by "hope?" As there is a physics, chemistry, and biology of aggression powerfully pushed towards explanation and implementation by the needs of war, so there is an explanatory perspective on hope. Can the theologian rest content with a vague descriptive specification either of the economy or of hope?

The description of the general categories moves on to note the possible models of change, drawing extensively on *Insight* to lead the reader to the challenge of reaching towards a universal viewpoint. Here I recall an early point, that *Method* in its entirety is foundational. So, the fundamental models of change remain to be more fully determined by the discussions of contexts that occur further on, especially in Chapter Twelve.

One senses, then, a powerful heuristic basis, "a central nucleus that somehow could retain its identity yet undergo all the modifications and enrichments that could be poured into its capacious frame from specialized investigations,"[71] normative of the actual context of future theological enquiry, grounding a genetico-dialectic collaboration within each specialty and between specialties much as the periodic table grounds chemists' painstaking collaboration or an adequate evolutionary hypothesis would unify detailed biological enquiry.

"Changes in the control of meaning mark off the great epochs of human history,"[72] and this generalized data-based vortex control of mediating meaning opens towards an encirclement and confinement[73] in the finality of being that goes beyond the optimism of *Insight* to a patient reverence for large numbers and long intervals of time. So, the universal viewpoint is to be reached slowly by the larger community of second, third and fourth rate minds by a liberating entrapment

---

[69] *Insight*, 733.

[70] *Method in Theology*, 27.

[71] From the first, unpublished, Preface to *Insight* (reprinted in *Method: A Journal of Lonergan Studies*, vol. 3, no. 1 [March, 1985], 3-7).

[72] "Dimensions of Meaning", in *Collection: Papers by Bernard J. F. Lonergan, S.J.*, ed. F. E. Crowe, S. J., (Montreal: Palm Publishers, 1967), 256.

[73] *Insight*, 484, 521-22, 570-71.

in the cycles of functional specialization, and general categories can
emerge in the minds of regular theologians not by reading *Method* but
by the manifestation of the need for and use of such categories in all
specialties.[74] Thus, instead of present attempts to "apply functional
specialization" that are analogous to phlogiston enthusiasts dividing
the periodic table in eight after Mendeleev, there will emerge the elite
homeliness[75] of small controlled contributions to a respected science of
theology.

In Chapter Seventeen of *Insight* Lonergan remarks:

> [O]ne may grant readily enough that meanings form a ge-
> netically and dialectically related sequence of unknowns
> and that expressions develop from the undifferentiated to
> the specialized. The two basic assertions are sound but
> where do they lead? Though the actual implementation of
> a method cannot be tucked into the corner of a chapter on
> a more general topic, still some sketch seems desirable.[76]

The structure of an implementation based on a transposition of that
sketch, and the related canons, into functional specialization, certainly
cannot be tucked into a short article. It seems important, however, to
share clues that may carry forward Lonergan's foundational enterprise.

I have already spoken of Lonergan's struggle in the sixties, and I
would add here three further points preliminary to touching on aspects
of the required transposition.

First, I would note the relevance of Lonergan's Latin works for an
initial reaching towards components of the sixth and seventh functional
specialties. Secondly, there are not only sets of unpublished lectures
of method such as those referred to in Section II, but also a substantial collection of handwritten notes of the period which remains to be
investigated. Thirdly, there are sets of texts of *Method* both from Lonergan's summer courses through the sixties and from his attempts to
bring the book to completion. Of these texts, including *Method* itself,
I would note first that the full richness of his unpublished searchings
and contributions within his Latin treatises did not find their way into
them; secondly, that the last two specialties in particular suffer from

---

[74] *Method in Theology*, 292.
[75] *Method in Theology*, 14, 350-51.
[76] *Insight*, 579.

late condensed expression.[77]

So, from struggling with unpublished handwritten notes, I have been led to a notion of the eight specialties as a staircase climb of increasingly enriched contexts and to a conviction that I (and perhaps others) was misled by a more familiar image of *oratio recta* as a descent from Foundations. In these notes one finds such remarks as "synthesis is a doctrine about history" in relation to doctrinal theology, and in relation to systematic theology, "synthesis is a theory of history."[78] One gets a sense of the reach towards an adequate basis of pastoral theology from notes like the following: "understanding yields, not just one set of concepts, relations, but any variation for any purpose; ...theology 1) not a Platonic Idea 2) but the many species (not individuals, except as types, as dominating personalities) 3) in a genetically and dialectically differentiated genus."

The increasing complexification parallels, I suspect, that required for economic executive reflection that I noted in Section II.

Lonergan's summary indication of general categories ends with the statement, "the problems of interpretation bring to light the notion of a potential universal viewpoint that moves over different levels and sequences of expression."[79] One reaches basic clues to the use of this component of general categories in the last three functional specialties by bringing together, in a larger personal actual context, *Insight's* discussion of pure formulation and *Method's* later indications of contexts: ongoing, prior, subsequent, derivative, interacting, etc.

The brief treatment of pure formulations, and related hypothetical expressions, emerges from the posing of a problem of interpretation that transposes partly into problems of *oratio obliqua* but primarily into problems relating directly to Doctrines, Systematics and Communications.[80] The transposition of pure formulation would seem to lie within a theory of history, grounded fully in the explanatory con-

---

[77] I am indebted here to work done by N. Graham on the evolution of *Method in Theology* through various manuscripts and institutes.

[78] The quotations in this paragraph are from unpublished handwritten notes of Lonergan from the early sixties, Batch B, 8, 6, V. The notes were given by Lonergan to Fr. Crowe in June, 1972, and catalogued by McShane. They remain in the Regis College Lonergan Centre, as yet not publicly available.

[79] *Insight*, 288.

[80] The reference is to *Insight*, 580, but one should add the context of *Insight*, 738-42.

text of emergent probability,[81] in mutual self-mediation both with doctrines and communications.[82] There are the actual expressions, high points of doctrinal development, that mediate the systematic quest. But there is also the genesis of hypothetical expressions within a systematic reach that home in, through probabilities and possibilities, on actual expressions in Doctrines. Further, there is the genetic relation of Systematics to Communications in a reach for hypothetical expression that could become relevantly actual, in tune with the expression of the finality of being in particular cultures. Finally, the collaborative operation of the mutual self-mediation of theologians of *oratio recta* has a set of normative controls briefly indicated by Lonergan in the sketch of interpretation and in the related canons. To the powerful threefold controls indicated in the sketch[83] there are added the demands of the canons for a withdrawal in systematics from description into differentiations of the protean notion of being and for the operation of four principles of criticism that would shift positively the statistics of the ongoing process of listening and speaking of theologians. Systematics becomes transcultural, even if still perspectival,[84] looking back to the Hebrew/Christian expression and meaning in its world context, looking back and forward to the benign communication of the saving message to all people of all times.[85]

In the final section, some indications will be given of natural analogies for this quest from such fields as biology and medicine. It is useful to conclude the present section, however, with familiar illustrations.

Consider the first five theses of Lonergan's *De Verbo Incarnato*.[86] A close analysis of these theses would yield illuminating contributions to the specialties of *oratio recta*. So, for example, the discussion of

---

[81] See K. Melchin, *History, Ethics and Emergent Probability* (Lanham, MD : University Press of America, 1987).

[82] On mutual self-mediation, see Lonergan, "The Mediation of Christ in Prayer", *Method: Journal of Lonergan Studies*, vol. 2 (1984), 12-14. I am indebted throughout this section to discussions with Sinead Breathnach who is writing a thesis on "Communication and Communications" at Trinity College, Dublin, Ireland.

[83] *Insight*, 580-1.

[84] On perspectivism, see *Method in Theology*, 216-18, 224, 246.

[85] One aspect of this, with emphasis on China, is treated in McShane, "Middle Kingdom, Middle Man," *Searching for Cultural Foundations*, 1-43.

[86] References will be to the 1961 edition (Gregorian Press, Rome) which differs substantially from the 1964 edition only in later pages, due to changes in the thesis on the knowledge of Christ. The 1960 edition has differences in pagination due to changes of print-size.

schemata in thesis one not only relates back to New Testament interpretation but relates forward through the "analytik"[87] of immanent
sources of meaning[88] to pastorally relevant differentiations under the
canon of relevance.[89] Again, reflections on deviant viewpoints have the
color of counterposition-reversal: thus, attention is drawn not just to
the error but to the significance of Apollinaris.[90] But, above all, there
is a recurrent reaching for pure formulations not just for themselves
but for controlled mutual self-mediation of Doctrines and Systematics: *"ex reali difficultate ad difficultatem terminologicam fere a priori
concluditur,"*[91] and indeed vice versa.

Right through these theses there is the general categorial use of "the
integral heuristic structure which is what I mean by a metaphysics,"[92]
qualified by a perspective on mystery,[93] on contingent truths about
God,[94] and on the non-reducibility to the metaphysical elements of
the reality of such truths.[95] As Lonergan pointed out in his reply to
the second Florida volume, he can take his stand on such metaphysics.[96]
What was needed was the enterprise of *Insight* to ground it adequately,
to sublate and extend it. The following five theses of *De Verbo Incarnato* move vigorously and comfortably in that actual context. Only
then do issues of subjectivity emerge. There is a strategy here worth
noting. I see no point in discussing God with Anthony Flew if he
doesn't know what a dog is; I see little value in discussions about sub-

---

[87] The proposed title of chapter one of the book referred to in n. 3 above was
"Procedural Analytiks", an attempt to twist words towards subjects in line with
Method in Theology, 88, n. 34: "At a higher level of linguistic development, the
possibility of insight is achieved by linguistic feed-back, by expressing the subjective
experience in words and as subjective." An Analytik is a person, just as an Actual
Context is a person or group of persons. But one must, in fact, envisage a much
more radical linguistic shift in the third stage of meaning.

[88] *Insight*, 580.

[89] *Insight*, 587.

[90] *De Verbo Incarnato*, 109-10.

[91] *De Verbo Incarnato*, 108.

[92] *Method in Theology*, 287.

[93] See Thesis 5 of *De Deo Trino I*, particularly, 274; see also *Method in Theology*,
index under Mystery.

[94] Lonergan, *De Constitutione Christi*, (Rome: Gregorian Press, 1956), 49-53.

[95] *Insight*, 734.

[96] "Bernard Lonergan Responds," in *Language, Truth and Meaning*, 310-12.

jects with theologians like Schillebeeckx[97] and Hamilton[98] if they do not know what objects are.

My main wish here, however, was to draw attention to Lonergan's Latin works for light on *oratio recta*. I chose to emphasize *De Verbo Incarnato* over the more complex *De Deo Trino* because it more evidently leans on pure formulations within proportionate metaphysics, such as minor real distinctions that are culturally invariant in humans,[99] that fruitfully illumine mysteries of an incarnate divinity, that provide a bridge to expressions of those mysteries suited to persons for whom Greek expression of minimal[100] systematic religious meaning may sound like alien profundities.

The bridge slowly to be provided is part of a complex network of salvific mediations finalized in a gentle providence.[101] Within that network it will invite, cajole,[102] the monocultural mind, locked in some translation of Greek expressions and Hebrew morality, to a larger patience and tolerance. One may recall at this stage Lonergan's comments on the Kimbanguist Church[103] and perhaps find here a fuller context for those comments.

There are some six thousand African Christian churches,[104] not all, indeed, of the high religious tone of "The Church of Jesus Christ on Earth through the Prophet Simon Kimbangu." How is one to envisage the dynamic of their origin and growth through the mediation of

---

[97] Lonergan, "Christology Today: Methodological Reflections," *Le Christ hier, aujourd'hui et demain*, eds. R. La Flamme and M. Gervais (Quebec: Laval University Press, 1976), 45-65 (reprinted in *A Third Collection: Papers by Bernard J. F. Lonergan, S.J.*, ed. F. E. Crowe, S. J. [Ramsey, NJ : Paulist Press, 1985]).

[98] See F. E. Crowe, S.J., "Christologies: How Up-to-Date is yours?", *Theological Studies* 29 (1968), 87-101.

[99] *Insight*, 490.

[100] *Method in Theology*, "slight tincture" (279), "slight dose" (309).

[101] *Insight*, 665. For a complementing component see P. McShane, *Shaping of the Foundations*, (Lanham, MD: University Press of America, 1976) 207, n. 136, where Whitson's *The Coming Convergence of World Religions*, (New York: Newman Press, 1971) is linked with the progress of science.

[102] The cajoling of *Insight*, 398, is transposed by the slow rounding of the vortex of *Method in Theology*.

[103] "Prolegomena to the Study of the Emerging Religious Consciousness of Our Time," *Studies in Religion/Sciences Religieuses*, 9 (1980), 3-15 (reprinted in *A Third Collection: Papers by Bernard J.F. Lonergan, S.J.*, ed. Frederick E. Crowe, S.J. [Ramsey, N.J.: Paulist Press, 1985], 55-73).

[104] David B. Barrett, *Schism and Renewal in Africa: An Analysis of Six Thousand Contemporary Religious Movements*, (Nairobi: Oxford University Press, 1968).

functional specialization?

The integral pure formulation, a psychological presence[105] of a contemporarily full theory of history, is crowned by the reach of Communications for historico-geographic sets of hypothetical expressions.[106] The specialists in Communications must envisage, through the complex genetic perspective of the fuller actual context of Systematics mediated by scholarly sensitivity to local cultures, the dynamics of nations, tribes, villages, to move towards reflective conditions of the cultivation of a symbiosis of faith and locally-grounded actual, probable, possible expressions.

One may view the crowning task of functional specialization in terms of a full notion of actual contexts. There is the actual context that is the community of subjects having questions and answers within functional specialization, the community of those who have suffered "displacement towards system"[107] for the sake of the salvation of history. Then there are the actual contexts that are the communities[108] of the globe in the actuality of their strange symbiotic quests.[109] These latter contexts are overlapping, derivative, prior, etc: one may think concretely of the role[110] of Irish and English Jesuit communities in the Christianization of the complex set of communities of the two Rhode-

---

[105]The basic text here is *Method in Theology*, 177. For a fuller perspective see McShane, *Searching for Cultural Foundations*, 147, n. 85.

[106]Expressions are not limited to linguistic expressions. See *Method in Theolog*, index under "Expression."

[107]*De Deo Trino I*, 10, n. 10.

[108]*Method in Theology*, 78-81.

[109]One must keep sensitive to quests in spatiotemporary discontinuity that are still symbiotic. "More than ever before, the present-day religions of Africa are an exercise in cultural encounter and mutual influence. In this regard, many scholars simply gloss the similarities in contemporary Afro-American and African religions. These similarities do not develop from a unidirectional cultural diffusion. Instead, similar processes of cultural change and contact within the respective societies have taken place simultaneously, and the influence of New World black churches on the new African religions is also felt. The parallel expressive forms in music, dance, and oratory represent creative combinations of indigenous cultural patterns with external media for representing them." (B. Jules-Rosetta, "The Arcadian Wish," in *The New Religions of Africa: Priests and Priestesses in Contemporary Cults and Churches*, ed. B. Jules-Rosetta (Norwood, NJ: Ablex Publ. Corp., 1979), 221-222. So, for example, in the case of Rhodesia mentioned in the text, two Irish Jesuits in the mid-century worked on the potential of African rhythms, but they, in fact, belonged to a wider musical context.

[110]Recall, *Method in Theology*, 48, and note the relation of our discussion to the "grasp of virtual resources" in *Method in Theology*, 362 ff.

sias, remembering always that the eighth functional specialty involves
a transposition of history carrying forward error, and indeed malice,
salvifically.[111]

One can thus come to see the crowning task of theology as the
mutual self-mediation of actual theological contexts and actual cultural
contexts. So, we arrive, like *Finnegans Wake*, "by a commodius vicus
of recirculation," back at the first sentence of *Method in Theology*: "A
theology mediates between a cultural matrix and the significance and
role of religion in that matrix."

The task envisaged is far from present possibilities: theologians
scarcely glimpse, much less share, the actual context of the general
categories; studies of religion are solidly truncated and regularly ab-
stractive; actual evangelization remains substantially in the mode and
haste of classical culture.

No doubt evangelization has come some distance from the arrogant
colonialism recounted and expressed by Sir Harry Johnson, who concluded his classic history with the forecast that "the eventual outcome
of the colonization of Africa by alien peoples will be a compromise—
a darkskinned race with a white man's features and a white man's
brain."[112]

But essays such as "The Resistance of the Nyau Societies to the
Roman Catholic Missions in Colonial Malawi"[113] bear witness to a
continuity of mentality through this century.[114]   So, "the struggle
at village level to maintain a socio-cultural identity against pressures
from planter, administration and mission"[115] continues. An evangelization mediated by a third-stage meaning scholarly differentiation of
consciousness, "a sympathetic openness to the village strangeness of

---

[111] *Method in Theology*, 251; *De Verbo Incarnato*, Theses 15-17.

[112] Sir Harry H. Johnston, G.C.M.G., K.C.B., Hon.Sc.D.,Cantab, *A History of the
Colonization of Africa by Alien Races* (New York: Cooper Square, Publishers,1966),
451. Earlier editions were 1898, 1913, 1930.

[113] Matthew Schoffeleers and I. Linden, in *The Historical Study of African Religion*,
eds. T. 0. Ranger and I. N. Kimambo (Berkeley: University of California Press,
1972), 252-73.

[114] The first Roman Catholic black bishop, in the sixteenth century, was educated
at Lisbon and Rome. The first Protestant black bishop, in the nineteenth century,
Samuel Crowther "was an Egba slaveboy from Lagos, who by education acquired
the intellect and outlook of a European" (Johnston, *History of the Colonization of
Africa*, 243). Rome and cricket still remain significant.

[115] Schoffeleers and Linden, *The Historical Study of African Religion*, 252.

a universe of differentiated persons,"[116] sharing God's patience with history, remains remote.

Again, modern studies in the sociology and the history of religions are increasingly empirical and complex. But they have no basis in generalized empirical method. They may claim freedom from paradigm: "while there is no unified theoretical paradigm imposed upon each of these essays, they all employ original field research and a data-driven model for the development of theories of symbolism and collective behaviour."[117] Yet throughout there is a massive blind commitment to the paradigm of truncation. Furthermore, elements of the cultural matrix that are symbiotic with religious tradition and expression can be regularly bypassed. So, the editors of a book related to the Dar es Salaam conference of 1970 concede in their introduction that "The Dar es Salaam Conference on the historical study of African religion was consciously taking part in an artificial, even a distorting enterprise. It separated the topic of African religion from the topics of African politics, economics and social institutions. And it separated the topic of African 'traditional' religion from those of African Islam and Christianity."[118] What is not only absent in the body of modern studies, but systematically excluded, is the open metaphysics of the actual context, deeply grounded in a subjectivity isomorphic with history and Mystery.

Finally, that actual context in its functional specialist perspective is not remotely constitutive of any present theological community. What, then, are the probabilities and possibilities of adequate theology in the twenty-first century?

4.4 The Actual Context of Theologies and the Middle Sciences

This final short section parallels the first section in pointing up the need to overcome terror, or the inner monster;[119] and where the first section

---

[116] *Searching for Cultural Foundations*, vi.

[117] Bennetta Jules-Rosetta, "Symbols of Power and Change: An Introduction to New Perspectives in Contemporary African Religion," *The New Religions of Africa*, 1.

[118] Schoffeleers and Linden, *The Historical Study of African Religion*, 1.

[119] "If a man is a hero, he is a hero because, in the first reckoning, he did not let the monster devour him, but subdued it not once but many times," C. G. Jung,

focused on Odyssey as against ontogenetic immaturity, this last touches
on Iliad as against phylogenetic immaturity. The issue is a terror of
history excluding a procedural revelation of finitude's evolution in triple
darkness.

It seems that theology has something to learn from the analogy
of nature that is the emergence, development and growing humility of
natural science. The optimism of the 19th century is gone.[120] Physics,
dealing with a cluster of curiously named particles, is, in its search for
coherence, subtly trapped by a Euclidean imagination. Chemistry, despite Mendeleev and the emergence of quantum chemistry, still lacks a
clear identity.[121] The genetic and evolutionary sciences, to which we
will return presently, are bogged down in a reductionist lack of aggreformic perspective yielding to the demands of their empirical object.
But yield they will under the pedagogic dynamics of history, with the
slowness that is the character of history.

This is no place to attempt a procedural analysis of the history
of sciences. What I wish to do is to focus briefly on one key and
illuminating instance of the struggle of science, the area of the middle
sciences that can be brought into isomorphism with Lonergan's analysis
of genetic method.

The reason for this focus is perhaps already obvious. Attention
was drawn at the beginning of Section II to genetic method as a basic natural procedural analogue in searching for the methodology of
an adequate systematic theology, and Section III moved towards the
notion that what the theological community must reach for in Communications is the integrated proximate grounds of the mediation of
"the cumulative, historical process of development in a multiplicity and
succession of individuals,"[122] that successive multiplicity being normatively conceived explanatorily: "while common sense relates things to
us, our account of common sense relates it to its neural basis and re-

---

"The Relations between the Ego and the Unconscious," *Two Essays in Analytic
Psychology*, trans. R.F.C. Hull, *Collected Works*, (Princeton: Princeton University
Press, 1966), vii, 173. There is a need for a heuristic transposition of metaphorical
talk of terror and monsters into an explanatory perspective on adult repentance.

[120] Science is not, of course, "pure knowledge" nor is it only in supporting war
that "scientists have known sin", J. R. Oppenheimer, *The Open Mind* (New York:
Simon and Schuster, 1955), 88.

[121] On the topic, see W. Danaher, *Strategies of Chemistry* (Lanham, MD: University Press of America, 1985).

[122] *Insight*, 741.

lates aggregates and successions of instances of common sense to one another."[123]

A central communal unknown of the total heuristic is clearly the meaning of development both in relation to a historic totality and to individual plants, animals, and men. That development is thus an unknown may be glimpsed by reflecting on the section of *Insight* which starts with the words "study of an organism begins from the thing-for-us."[124] The organism is evidently developmental, and its study is presently trapped in various ways at this beginning. Newman's "common sense contributions"[125] includes a notion of development that is also opaquely present in the mind of the modern botanist or zoologist, and the situation is honestly summed up in the words of the biologist Paul Weiss: "Does not everybody have some notion of what development implies? Undoubtedly most of us have. But when it comes to formulating these notions they usually turn out to be vague."[126]

Moreover, this vague spontaneous notion is ground into irrelevance by a present reductionist culture in the middle sciences. This is massively evidenced, for instance, by the volumes of The Society for Developmental Biology,[127] where the predominant tone through thirty years of work is that of a cybernetic mythmaking regarding information storage and sharing in and between molecules, cells, stages, etc. Furthermore, this cybernetic tone regularly warps the reductionism into a microvitalism: truncated subjects are just as likely to overrate the cognitive performance of macromolecules as they are to exaggerate the intelligence embedded in a microchip. But what is fundamentally excluded is that transposition of Aristotle's view of potency to be found both in Lonergan's heuristics of finality and development[128] and in the objective correlative, the organism.

Nor are there saving features in the broader ecological context of

---

[123] *Insight*, 244.

[124] *Insight*, 464.

[125] *Method in Theology*, 261.

[126] P. Weiss, *Principles of Development: A Text in Experimental Embryology*, (New York: H. Holt and Co.,1939), 1.

[127] There are 25 volumes and several supplements running through the years 1939-1968, brought out by The Society for Developmental Biology as the fruit of 27 symposia, published under the general title Developmental Biology.

[128] *Insight*, 444 ff.

such studies.[129] Whether one looks to studies internal to the field,[130] or to broader works such as those originating from von Bertalanffy,[131] one finds no grounding perspective for a coherent theory of the hierarchic structure of the object of the middle sciences that would contextualize developmental studies. "Whereas the inverse problem of analytic resolution of a system into subsystems is readily treated by such top-down approaches as deduction, and single level systems are amenable through induction or statistical procedures, there is no corresponding technique for vertical bottom-up organization. This lacuna is a task for a new epistemology."[132] Lonergan's filling of the lacuna through aggreformic third-stage comprehension of the world of science, available for more than forty years,[133] has had no impact on twentieth century science.

Now such a situation in that part of the Cosmic Word which is man's understanding of the genetic realities of the middle sciences is itself a revelation to the theologian.

In its broadest sense, the situation is continuous with, and contributory to, the complex providential warping of the fundamental questing that is human subjectivity. Meshing with the massive folly and malice of the drive of modernity towards empire and state, which blossoms in the neurotic control structures of modern government and business, is a pseudo-theoretic of microcontrol which seeds patterns of experimentation and implementation, of mindset and lifestyle, of research and relaxation, of farming and foodprocessing, that cuts man out of the

---

[129] Such features are treated in McShane, *Randomness, Statistics and Emergence* (Dublin: Gill Macmillan and Notre Dame: University of Notre Dame Press, 1971). On botany and zoology, see, respectively Chs. 1 and 3 of McShane, *The Shaping of the Foundations.*

[130] A recent effort is T.F.H. Allen and Thomas B. Starr, *Hierarchy: Perspective for Ecological Complexity* (Chicago and London: University of Chicago Press, 1982). The book is of value, not for any positive advance, but for its explicitness regarding epistemological confusion (see 5-11; 37-46; 129-31), and in bringing the reader into the middle of the erudite muddle.

[131] L. von Bertalanffy, *General System Theory* (New York: Braziller, 1968); *Hierarchy Theory: the Challenge of Complex Systems*, ed. H.H. Pater (New York: Braziller, 1973).

[132] Albert Wilson, "Systems Epistemology" in *The World System*, ed. Ervin Laszlo (New York: Braziller, 1973), 125-26.

[133] Lonergan, "Finality, Love, Marriage," *Theological Studies* 4, 1943), 477-510; reprinted in *Collection*. While *Insight* greatly enriches the perspective, both emergent probability and the underpinning aggreformism are already there: "A concrete plurality of lower entities may be the material cause from which a higher form is educed or into which a subsistent form is infused" (481; *Collection*, 20).

genetic throbbing of history.

Generically, what is revealed is a phylogenetic immaturity of such pre-adolescent proportions that I am tempted to characterize modernity in its full sense as the Age of the Tadpole.

Present theology is part of this age. If the dreams of children can be warped by a brutalized culture,[134] the visions of theologians cannot be considered secure. Certainly, there is nothing mature about recent erroneous and monocultural papal pronouncements on sexuality,[135] no more than there is anything mature about present preaching on the Christian Trinity.[136] Perhaps, as Joan Robinson said with regard to economics, "It is time to go back to the beginning and start again."[137]

That beginning, I am convinced, lies in the discovery and expression by Lonergan of the eightfold empirical way, in so far as that discovery is operatively accepted in some suspicion of the lack of three basic differentiations in the theological community, all three being "quite beyond the horizon of ancient Greece and medieval Europe."[138] Nineteenth century theologians may be partly forgiven for not noticing that the self-energy of God is more complex than the self-energy of the electron, that the development of daisies is simpler than the development of doctrines. Present times relentlessly reveal the density of the forms of electrons and daisies: do they not also reveal the remoteness of adequate theological meaning?

To the negative side, then, of present sciences' struggle with such realities as plant and animal growth, one must add a positive side. Whatever the muddles regarding the objects of inquiry, subjects in science are forced to humble open particularity in their searchings. When one asks in that context, what is development, one must answer in terms of this or that particular development. One struggles as best one can, in the absence of an adequate actual biological context, towards a verifiable perspective on such realities as "Nuclear and Cytoplasmic Control

---

[134] See E. G. Schachtel, "On Memory and Childhood Amnesia," *Psychiatry* 10 (1947), 1-26.

[135] A main issue, of course, is that raised by the encyclical *Humanae Vitae*. Very simply, "the ordination of intercourse to conception is not a natural law." (Lonergan, "Finality, Love, Marriage," *Collection*, 47, n.79).

[136] Basic flaws here mar the insightful book, *The Passionate God*, by Rosemary Haughton, (London: Chapman, 1976).

[137] Joan Robinson and John Eatwell, *An Introduction to Modern Economics*, (Maidenhead: McGraw-Hill, 1973), 51.

[138] *Method in Theology*, 317.

of Morphology in *Neurospora*," "Development and Control Processes in the Basal Bodies and Flagella of *Chlamydomonas reinhardii*."[139] So, in functional specialist theology, totalitarianism has to yield to a particular empiricism that still strives to remain open to the heuristics of subject and object. "What formerly was supposed to lie within the competence of a single dogmatic theologian, now can be undertaken only by a very large team."[140] The systematic theologian would aim, not at a total organism, but at the genesis of some relevant cell. And, as Galileo's seeding of empirical method brings forth in this century a shaky sapling, so generalized empirical method is now an acorn in search of air.

A more basic positive aspect of the evolution of science is that associated with the First Vatican Council's pointing to the significance of analogies of nature,[141] and indeed with Aquinas' frequent use of the word *"sicut."* That aspect is laced through the present paper, but I would make two brief final points.

First, if it is to be an analogy relevant to an explanatory systematics, then it must be cast within an explanatory heuristic. So, one may draw analogies from studies of the foetal and infant eye, and from study of such studies to further one's understanding of development of dogma, genetic systematics, growth-communications. But such analogies must sublate contemporary studies of the stages of normal and abnormal foetal and infant eye development so that, for example, strabismus is not just a described squint but a heuristically contextualized abnormality related both to the present lower molecularity of chromosome and muscle and to later higher patterns of the flexible circle of ranges of schemes of recurrence of adult life. From such a perspective one can view specializations with regard to the developing eye in a manner that throws light from the middle sciences on the last three functional specialties. A developing eye can be studied to discover just what is there, in a manner that is not unrelated to finding "the meaning of the dogma in the context in which it was defined."[142] The growing eye can be viewed from the fullest contemporary explanatory perspec-

---

[139] Both these papers are in *Developmental Biology* (26), 1967. The first is the work of E.L. Tatum and D.J.L. Luck; the second involved a team: Sir John Randall, R. Cavalier-Smith, Anne McVittie, J.R. Warr and J.M. Hopkins.

[140] *Method in Theology*, 315.

[141] DS 3016.

[142] *Method in Theology*, 325.

tive to arrive at a transcultural understanding of its place in the actual, probable, possible schemes of biography and history. The (abnormally) growing eye can be envisaged in the cultural context of parents and kin in a sensitive therapeutic fashion: an envisagement analogous to that of communications. Finally, I would note that this searching for the fullness of natural analogies not only is an internal fidelity in theology but leads to the real possibility of cultivating in scientists "the high office of the scientific spirit."[143]

Secondly, I would note that the analogies centrally relevant in the third stage of meaning are the procedural or methodological analogies, analogies that focus on the evolution of mind. Nor should this be surprising. The whole drive of *Insight* and *Method* is towards procedural lucidity, and this would seem to dovetail with a fundamental orientation of history to reveal, not content, but process.

In conclusion, I would note then an evident, highly visible aspect of modern science is its tradition of journals and conferences remote from public discourse. A visit to a zoological library with adequate journal holdings would, I suspect, be a sobering experience for a theologian with the standard literary education.[144] He or she is faced with a massive array of incomprehensible specialized efforts. In contrast, many theological journals offer general eclectic sweeps, regularly eminently readable for the wrong reasons. Again, one may contrast conferences of chemists—indeed, they are usually already specialist within the science—with conferences of theologians. Whatever the deficiencies of present chemical perspective, participants are expected to be comfortable in a contemporary actual context of Mendeleev's advance.

What will the actual context of theologians be, in a hundred years or so?

---

[143] *Insight*, 746.

[144] The genesis of an adequate actual context requires massive changes in the schemes of recurrence of present education. One may think, for instance, of the non-overlapping contexts of, on the one hand, a literate theological community talking vaguely of alienation and, on the other, a business community hastening down blind alleys of high technology.

Chapter 5

Historicity and Philosophy: The Event of Philosophy, Past, Present, and Future

Thomas McPartland

The event of philosophy shatters the rock of relativism even as it simultaneously challenges every total system, every finished viewpoint, every frozen dogma.[1] For philosophy has both an existential dimension and a systematic dimension, each bearing a normative relation to the other. Philosophy, on the one hand, is the love of wisdom, the way of life of one committed to the unrestricted search for truth; the love of wisdom carries with it a faith in the intrinsic intelligibility of being and a hope that the search will not be in vain. Precisely because of the philosopher's orientation to complete intelligibility, on the other hand,

---

[1] For an enlargement of the remarks in these introductory paragraphs, including discussion of Hellenic philosophy, see Thomas J. McPartland, "Historicity and Philosophy: The Existential Dimension," in Timothy Fallon, S.J., and Philip Riley eds., *Religion and Culture: Essays in Honor of Bernard Lonergan, S.J.* (Albany, N.Y.: State University of New York Press), 107-122.

philosophy has its systematic exigence, the demand to expand and formulate its insights in accord with the norms immanent in the desire to know. Thus arising from the existential disposition of the philosopher are the very norms which overcome the specter of historical relativism and which specify the objective pole of philosophy with its systems, sets of propositions, and arguments; at the same time, these norms charge philosophy with the task of perpetual renovation, reformulation, and development to match the unrestricted sweep of the desire to know. Indeed, this becomes a task quite pertinent to a critical culture and to a progressive civilization. Philosophy is an inherently historical project.

Unique among contemporary philosophers, the late Bernard Lonergan has emphasized both the subjective and objective poles of philosophy. Perhaps this emphasis is best captured in his contention that "genuine objectivity is the fruit of authentic subjectivity."[2]

Implicit in Lonergan' treatment of philosophy, we believe, is the recognition of its distinctively historical character and its historical responsibility. In this essay, as we utilize key categories of Lonergan's thought and seek to develop some of his salient themes, we shall explore the historicity of philosophical experience. A few further introductory remarks will serve to locate our topic.

The event of philosophy first happened in the historical circumstances of ancient Greece in the person of such figures as Parmenides, Heraclitus, Socrates, Plato, and Aristotle. These Hellenic lovers of wisdom saw themselves as engaged in a sacred mission through their attunement with the Divine Mind; they were indeed participants of divinity in their intellectual quest; they were drawn to philosophical inquiry by a divine pull. This experience of divine-human encounter, constitutive of the history of philosophy, was expressed in the Greek words for reason (*nous*) and theorist (*theoros*), which continued to echo their root meanings. The original meaning of *nous*, associated with the revolution of the sun god, evoked a sense of returning home from darkness and death to light and consciousness. Likewise the *theoros* was a person on a journey, having been sent on a religious mission to oracles or to such festivals as the Olympic games; gradually *theoria* (theory) came to be connected with travel inspired by the desire to know; and eventually it referred to the knowledge acquired while travelling. Thus philosophers were *theoroi* on the noetic road of inquiry.

---

[2]Bernard J.F. Lonergan, S.J., *Method in Theology* (New York: Herder and Herder, 1972), p. 292.

Ever since philosophy first made its appearance on the stage of history in Hellas the imperative to continue it has posed a number of strategic questions that revolve around the historicity of the event of philosophy: If the meaning of the original philosophical tradition—with both its existential depth and cognitive standards—is to be appropriated, what are the respective roles of the philosophical community and of the individual philosopher? What is the relationship between the historical tradition and the concrete situatedness of the philosopher in the present? Do the dynamics of this relationship also inevitably extend to carrying forward the event of philosophy into the future? Does the association of feeling, image, and symbol with heuristic insights and the momentum of inquiry embrace in a substantive way the appropriation, communication, and historical development of philosophy? What is the precise relation of philosophy not only to its own future but also to the future of mankind? We shall now attempt to address these issues informed by the ideas of Bernard Lonergan.

5.1   Engaging the Philosophical Past

The continuation of philosophy is an ongoing historical achievement embracing the dialectic of community and person in their historicity.

5.1.1   Dialectic of the Philosopher and Philosophers

Historical existence in general witnesses a dynamic, complex, and dialectical relation between individual and community. The communal reality is more than the sum total of its individuals' ideas and deeds; it is precisely the horizon, the organization, and the pattern of what is common to many individuals; it has its own historical life that persists over time (though not apart from individuals); and its historical destiny is a linking of successive situations by a set of decisions that is greater than the sum of the individual wills of its participants.[3] But it is not a collective will that questions, gains insights, and judges. It is not a collective will that deliberates, decides, and acts freely. There is no group entity or substance existing in itself above and beyond individuals, as

---

[3] Bernard J.F. Lonergan, S.J., *The Philosophy of Education*, eds. James Quinn and John Quinn (Cincinnati, 1959) (transcription of lectures given at Xavier College), 313-314.

idealists and essentialists allege. The person cannot be reduced to a mere function of the technical, social, or cultural milieu. Individuals cooperating together constitute the nucleus of the community, and the perduring communal life, in turn, becomes the objective historical situation in which individuals are born, are reared through socialization and acculturation, and are nourished by education.[4] There is, then, an historical circuit in which subjects create community and community creates subjects.[5]

The historical existence of philosophy, too, shares this dialectic. On the one hand, the outer word of philosophical tradition carries the expression of philosophical meaning and mediates personal philosophical self-appropriation. The existential truth of philosophy is conveyed in the memory of such representative philosophers as Socrates; the life of Socrates, as portrayed in Plato's magnificent dialogues, is a vivid instance of incarnate meaning, where the entire personality of Socrates evokes the spirit of the love of wisdom. Without the recollection (*anamnesis*) of the exemplary philosophers the spark of philosophy may not be lit or may only flicker.[6] The most precious literary treasures of philosophy, both existential and systematic, are the great classics, works of impenetrable depth and amazing richness, which are perpetual challenges, inexhaustible fonts of questions that invite the interpreter into ever fuller exploration of the subject matter. Without the philosophical classics the ship of philosophy would flounder adrift in a wild sea, having lost its venerable charts. The horizon of the interpreter is always at risk in meeting the classics; the enterprise opens the interpreter up to the possibility of self-transcendence, to more profound self-knowledge; he may have to lift his horizon up to the level of that of the author of the text, for an existential condition for understanding the ideas of

---

[4] *Method*, 79; *Collection: Papers by Bernard Lonergan,S.J.*, ed. Frederick E. Crowe, S.J. (Montreal: Palm Publishers, 1967), 245-254.

[5] On the individual origin of meaning, see *Method*, 255-256; Bernard Lonergan, S.J., *Verbum: Word and Idea in Aquinas*, ed. David B. Burrell (Notre Dame: University of Notre Dame Press, 1967), 23-24; on the communal basis of meaning, see *Method*, 41-47, 79, 90-92, 257-58, 269; Bernard J.F. Lonergan, S.J., *Insight: A Study of Human Understanding*, rev. ed. (New York: Philosophical Library, 1958), 535, 703-13; *Collection*, 245-54; *A Third Collection: Papers by Bernard J.F. Lonergan, S.J.*, ed. Frederick E. Crowe, S.J. (Mahwah, N.J.: Paulist Press, 1985), 196-97.

[6] On *anamnesis*, see Plato, *Meno*; on the encounter of a "Zeuslike soul," see *idem.*, *Phaedrus*, 252c-253a; for a brief allusion to the passing on of tradition, see *idem.*, *Timaios*, 20d-21a.

a thinker of the caliber of a Plato or an Aquinas is that the interpreter must initially reach up to the mind of Plato or Aquinas.[7] This is a never-ending task."A classic," wrote Schlegel, "is a writing that is never fully understood. But those that are educated and educate themselves must always want to learn more from it."[8] The classics, Lonergan argues, "ground a tradition, creating the milieu in which they are studied and producing in the reader through the cultural tradition the mentality, the *Vorverständnis*, from which they will be read, studied, interpreted."[9]

On the other hand, the outer word of the philosophical tradition in and of itself is merely the carrier of the expression of meaning; the insights behind the expressions can be grasped only by the creative art of interpretation; the mind of the individual philosopher must come into play. To be sure, the interpretation will have its necessary compliment of communal collaboration but it will also have its irreducibly personal dimension: the self-appropriation of the individual philosopher. In addition, the tradition itself is forged and constantly replenished by the influence of those philosophical geniuses of the ilk of Plato, Aristotle, Aquinas, Descartes, and Kant who mark decisive turning points in the history of philosophy, either by inaugurating bold new lines of inquiry (Plato, Descartes, and Kant) or by synthesizing previous developments through masterful overarching insights (Aristotle and Aquinas). The original genius fashions new linguistic usage, molding philosophical culture.[10]

The particular circumstances behind the flowering of genius provide a most striking illustration of the dialectic of person and community. The genius does not operate in a vacuum; he profits from the human cooperation that supports vital cultural institutions; and he ordinarily relies on the largely unnoticed work of countless lesser figures. "For the genius," Lonergan observes, "is simply the man at the level of his time, when the time is ripe for a new orientation or a sweeping reorganization."[11] The path of philosophical genius must have been cleared by the intellectual efforts of predecessors. Furthermore, the genius is implicated in the general movement of the *Zeitgeist*. The cross-

---

[7] *Insight*, 748; *Method*, 161.

[8] Quoted in *Method*, 161.

[9] *Method*, 161-62.

[10] *Verbum*, 23-24.

[11] *Insight*, 419.

fertilization of ideas, the raising of questions, and the repercussions
of discoveries can generate certain intellectual currents that define the
general assumptions of an age; these assumptions, born by philosophical communities, schools, and sects, are probably unknown, or not very
well known, by most contemporaries, even geniuses, since, for the most
part, they are taken for granted and function behind the scenes; and
precisely because they direct, foster, or impede inquiry, these pervasive
assumptions deeply affect contemporaries, even geniuses. The genius,
of course, may challenge the *Zeitgeist* with reflective awareness, or he
may use the categories of the *Zeitgeist* as a springboard to leap to intellectual heights heretofore beyond the reach of the dominant horizon.
But, in either case, he will be responding to the general assumptions
of the age and, consequently, will be decisively influenced by them.
Still, however propitious the time may be for a wholesale redirection
of thought, it nevertheless requires the mental force, the creative edge,
the singular dedication of genius to exploit the situation.

5.1.2   Historicity and Relativism

Having outlined the dialectic of philosophical community and philosophers, we must now examine in more detail the historicity of each
element, keeping in mind the dynamic interrelationship of each to the
other. The achievements of philosophical community—and thereby of
individual philosophers—are severely conditioned by the general historical situation, with its technological, economic, political, and cultural
components.[12] Thus the development of philosophical culture in Hellas was prompted by the technological invention of writing and was
contingent upon sufficient economic differentiation to allow for leisure
time.[13] The philosophy of Plato was as much colored by the crisis of the
polis as the philosophy of such contemporary existentialists as Marcel,
Jaspers and Heidegger is affected by the crisis of modern technologi-

---

[12]Lonergan suggests that cognitive self-appropriation is conditioned by what
Hegel called "objective spirit," the historical objectification, manifestation, and
embodiment of subjective processes. Bernard Lonergan, S.J., *Understanding and
Being: An Introduction and Companion to "Insight"*, eds. Elizabeth A. Morelli
and Mark D. Morelli (New York: Edwin Mellen Press, 1980), 270-71.

[13]Eric Havelock, *Preface to Plato* (Cambridge, Mass.: Harvard University Press,
1963).

cal civilization and political bureaucracy.[14] Greek and medieval philosophy typically labored under the assumption of a hierarchical, and
oftentimes cyclical cosmos, whereas twentieth century philosophy has
had to take account of an emergent universe and historical consciousness. The most telling historical conditions, however, reside within
philosophy itself. There is an historical movement internal to philosophy. If philosophy is like a four-story structure, with metaphysics
at the top built upon epistemology, and epistemology resting upon
cognitional theory, and cognitional theory grounded upon the performance of the authentic lover of wisdom at the foundation below—if, in
other words, philosophy is based on performance, not premises—then
it follows that as cognitive performance develops so will philosophy,
in its systematic form, be able to advance. Lonergan, for example,
sees progress in modern mathematics, empirical science, depth psychology, and historical method as supplying new, precise evidence for
philosophy.[15] New data on the operations of the human mind stimulate new insights and breakthroughs in philosophical understanding.[16]
Accordingly, any theory of the human mind "is bound to be incomplete
and to admit further clarification and extension."[17] Philosophical interpretation can never totally capture the richness and elusive movement of philosophical performance. This is historicity but not historical relativism. Philosophical formulations are framed within horizons,
networks of interlocking questions and answers, usually relying upon
partially unacknowledged presuppositions.[18] Neither the formulations
nor the horizons are final and definitive.[19] The living act of philo-

---

[14] On the crisis of the *polis*, see Werner Jaeger, *Paideia: The Ideals of Greek Culture*, trans. Gilbert Highet, 3 vols. (New York: Oxford University Press, 1943-45), II, chap. 1; Gabriel Marcel, *Man Against Mass Society*, trans. G. S. Fraser (Chicago: Henry Regnery Co., Gateway Edition, 1962); Karl Jaspers, *Man in the Modern Age*, trans. Eden and Cedar Paul (Garden City, N.Y.: Doubleday and Co., 1957); Martin Heidegger, *The Question Concerning Technology and Other Essays*, trans. William Lovitt (New York: Harper and Row, Colophon Books, 1977).

[15] *Insight*, 386.

[16] *Insight*, 388.

[17] *Method*, 19. Philosophical positions invite development. *Insight*, 388.

[18] *Method*, 163-164; *Collection*, 213-14.

[19] Bernard J.F. Lonergan, S.J., *A Second Collection: Papers by Bernard J.F. Lonergan, S.J.*, eds. William F.J. Ryan and Bernard J. Tyrrell (Philadelphia: West-minister Press, 1974), 15, 25, 199, 207-08, 233, 259; *Method*, 325; *Third Collection*, 186-88, 193-94.

sophical insight is not necessarily exhausted by linguistic expressions.[20] The intention of philosophical truth does not rest content within any historically given philosophical horizon. Philosophical understanding can advance within established contexts and then move beyond those contexts to effect a genetic sequence of philosophical horizons perhaps available only to the retrospective glance of the historian. Indeed the historian can frequently apprehend philosophical interconnections and similar paths of questioning better than the original contributors.[21] By submitting to the norms of the pure question—the identity amid historical difference—genuine philosophers extend the import of their work beyond their own particular horizons and enter into the philosophical dialogue of the basic horizon of inquiry.[22] While truth does not exist apart from minds and the context of their operations, the basic horizon of inquiry establishes both the link among those contexts and the criteria by which to judge them.[23] Philosophical positions that, on the surface, seem incompatible may, in fact, be revealed as complementary, consonant, or sequences in a line of progress. Upon closer scrutiny, differences in philosophical positions may come about because different questions were raised, or the same questions were raised in different contexts, or the same questions were answered in compatible, though not equally penetrating, manners. The march of philosophy, of course, is not along a smooth road. Philosophers have been many, disparate— and contradictory.[24] The fragmentation of philosophical worldviews, not to mention rancorous squabbling of antagonistic philosophical sects, all too conspicuously occupies the pages of the history of philosophy. No doubt, psychoneurosis, egoism, group bias, common-sense obscurantism, and neo-gnostic exploitation of metaphysical profundities can poison the love of wisdom. But the products of such corruption belong to the history of ideology, in its pejorative sense, not to the history of philosophy, as conceived in this essay.[25] The history of philosophy must rather contend with the disturbing fact that dialectical opposition among philosophical horizons occurs in spite of fidelity to the intention

---

[20] See the Lonergan-influenced article of Norris Clark, "On Facing the Truth About Human Truth," *American Catholic Philosophical Association Proceedings* 43 (1969), 4-13.

[21] *Method*, 178-79, 192, 250; *Insight*, 387,587.

[22] *Insight*, 387.

[23] *Method*, 325-26; *Second Collection*, 207-98.

[24] *Insight.*, 386.

[25] Lonergan defines ideology as rationalization of alienated existence. *Method*, 55.

of truth. Does relativism triumph after all? Not if the norms of inquiry are rigorously and thoroughly applied to expose any contradictions between a given philosophical interpretation and the actual performance of philosophizing.[26] In other words, the failure to attend to the complexity of cognitional operations and, in particular to differentiate the confrontational element of biological consciousness from the more sophisticated activities of the mind generate philosophical errors, what Lonergan calls the "counter-positions."[27] Still, counter-positions can be profoundly helpful as they ruthlessly hammer out the inevitable implications of dubious assumptions; they can also be intimately tied to fruitful insights.[28] Can the battle of philosophies play an ultimately positive role in the drama of philosophical understanding? Continued fidelity to the desire to know entails reversing the counter-positions, separating insights from oversights, and extrapolating genuine discoveries from the constricting framework in which they were embedded. The very struggle with rudimentary philosophical misconceptions leads to a further enrichment and strengthening of authentic philosophical positions which could not have been so clarified otherwise. Beneath the myriad conflicts of doctrine, then, the history of philosophy displays a startling unity of program, goal and intention.[29] Yet the aim can be sought only by participating in the historical drama of philosophy.

5.1.3   Historical Consciousness and Functional Specialties

Coming to grips with the historical tradition of philosophy, therefore, is not merely an antiquarian interest of the historian; it is an integral moment of the project of philosophy, which demands that the insights of the philosophical tradition be appropriated and developed—cognitively and existentially. In order to appropriate the tradition, philosophers must first know it; but, conversely, in order to know it well, they must also appropriate it; and in order to add to its capital, they must have

---

[26] *Collection*, 214-15.

[27] On the problem of "biological extroversion," see *Insight*, xx-xxiii, 182-84, 250-54, 385, 389, 496, 412-16, 423-25, 581-83; *Method* 28-29, 238-40, 263-65; on counterpositions, see *Insight*, 388.

[28] *Insight*, 389.

[29] *Insight*, 386-87. "The historical series of philosophies would be regarded as a sequence of contributions to a single but complex goal." *Insight*, 389.

first appropriated its substance. We must explore this hermeneutical circle of a philosophical community.

Now Lonergan has implicitly demonstrated how this encounter with the philosophical tradition is precisely a community endeavor, requiring the specialized efforts of its members.[30] To encounter the past philosophers must know it, and philosophers know the past the same as they know anything: through the cognitional pattern of experience, understanding and judging.[31] Suppose, to pursue Lonergan's ideas of functional specialties, that specialists would focus in particular on one cognitional stage in this process. Some specialists would assemble the relevant philosophical data by preparing manuscript collections, critical editions, indices, tables, repertories, bibliographies, handbooks, dictionaries, and encyclopedias;[32] other specialists would interpret the meaning of philosophical texts, producing commentaries or monographs on an author's treatment of discrete topics, on the single opus of an author, or on an author's entire corpus;[33] and still others would judge the historical links among authors, schools, and eras by tracing genetic and dialectic sequences, by detailing the major horizon shifts, and by identifying the unique turning points, the transcending breakthroughs, that irrevocably alter the pattern of philosophical thinking.[34] Each kind of specialist, to be sure, would employ the full range of cognitional operations of experiencing, understanding, and judging. But by paying primary attention either to the experiential basis of the sources, or to understanding the texts, or to assessing historical trends each kind of specialist would functionally cooperate with experts in other domains: history would be mediated by interpretation and interpretation, in turn, by research; conversely, interpretation (through an extension of the hermeneutical circle to the *Zeitgeist*) would be influenced by the conclusions of history and research, in its turn, by the conclusions

---

[30]The structure of the appropriation of tradition by a religious community—thematized by Lonergan in one of his more profound and original ideas—can, he suggests, be applicable to the other cultural communities. *Method*, 364. Compare with James Collins, *Interpreting Modern Philosophy* (Princeton: Princeton University Press, 1972), 24-34, 406-17; Collins, in his "working hypothesis," sees the components of historical investigation as the sources, historical questions, the interpreting present, and the teleology of historical understanding.

[31]*Method*, 133.

[32]*Method*, 127, chap. 6, *passim.*

[33]*Method*, 127, chap. 7.

[34]*Method*, 128, chaps. 8-9.

of both interpretation and history.[35] Only the dedicated cooperation of these functional specialists, each combining philosophical sensitivity with professional skill, would be able to promote a sophisticated, open-ended knowledge of the philosophical past. While the overriding goal of these researchers, interpreters, and historians would be that of objective knowledge of the philosophical past, already their philosophical perspectives would necessarily enter into the picture: for researchers must rely upon principles of selection and organization; the horizon of the interpreter, as Gadamer has so brilliantly demonstrated, is an integral part of the hermeneutical circle; and historians have, as their proper commission, not mere doxographical description of reified ideas and sectarian dogmas, but an explanatory account of the historical unfolding of the desire to know.[36] Once, however, an explanatory account has been rendered, the subjectivity of the philosopher becomes more intensely engaged. The history of philosophy is the drama of the multitude of philosophical horizons, some apparently irreconcilable. And the multitude of philosophical horizons in the history of philosophy seems only matched by the multitude of philosophical horizons operative in the historians, interpreters, and researchers themselves.[37] The philosophical past hurls its challenge at the philosophical present. The conflicts among philosophies and among historians of philosophy have the salutary effect of further clarifying basic philosophical issues.[38] It is incumbent upon philosophers to analyze the nature of the dialectical oppositions, to discern ultimate philosophical assumptions, to classify the crucial differences, to pronounce upon which assumptions are compatible with self-appropriation and which are not, to draw out implications of true "positions," and to correct false "counter-positions."[39] The functional specialty of what Lonergan calls "dialectic" seeks to safeguard dialogue with the philosophical tradition from the indiscriminate onslaught of blatantly a priori assumptions.

The challenge of the past impels the philosophical community to penetrate anew to the foundations of philosophy in the meaningful concreteness of the present, posing a series of pointed philosophical questions about objectivity, truth, reality, and the good that calls for

---

[35] *Method*, 141.

[36] *Method*, 161, 220-24, 246-47; *Insight*, 587.

[37] *Method*, 246-47.

[38] *Method*, 253.

[39] *Method*, 249-50.

the response of self-appropriation. As philosophical tradition is an ontological dimension in the life of philosophy, so the scholarly and dialectical mediation of the history of philosophy is an intrinsic component of philosophy. Reflectively articulate philosophical thinking originates through such an encounter with the past.[40] While the past must be open to criticism, it can never be erased or eliminated by a program of universal doubt; it can never be dominated as a Cartesian object.[41] The act of philosophizing is indeed a communication situation, in the words of Paul Ricoeur, "someone saying something about something to someone."[42] This is a situation in dialogue, where the partner in philosophical discourse, the "someone" in the horizon specified by the logic of questioning, is equally the self, the Wholly Other (the divine Nous), the other "sons of Zeus," and the patrimony of tradition. The outer expression of philosophical meaning, however, can be integrated satisfactorily only by philosophers involved in self-appropriation. The communal prerequisites of philosophy notwithstanding, this is, in the final analysis, a personal task, where performance of the philosopher as an incarnation of the desire to know becomes data for self-interpretation. The horizon of philosophy is the horizon of the philosopher. Fidelity to questioning the question entails a threefold philosophical conversion: a religious conversion, the experience of unrestricted love of being, inspiring a faith in being's intrinsic intelligibility and a hope in the efficacy of inquiry; a moral conversion, the passionate commitment to the love of wisdom as a worthy mode of life; and an intellectual conversion, the identification of truth, objectivity, and reality with the directional tendency of inquiry.[43] Such a profound transformation of horizon requires a "vertical exercise of freedom," the selection of a new concrete synthesis of conscious living.[44] Intellectual conversion, with its "startling strangeness,"[45] no less than the existential transfigurations,

---

[40] Extrapolated from *Method*, 130, 246-47, 250, 365.

[41] On the role of tradition, see *Insight*, 703-18; *Method*, 41-47, 182, 223, 244; on the fallacy of the Cartesian program, see *Insight*, 409-11, 716.

[42] Paul Ricoeur, *The Conflict of Interpretations: Essays in Hermeneutics*, Northwestern University Studies in Phenomenology and Existentialist Philosophy (Evanston: Northwestern University Press, 1974), 83-88; for a Lonergan-influenced commentary, see Emil J. Piscitelli, "Paul Ricoeur's Philosophy of Religious Symbol: A Critique and Dialectical Transposition," *Ultimate Reality and Meaning*, vol. 3 (1980), 288.

[43] On religious, moral, and intellectual conversions, see *Method*, 237-44.

[44] *Method*, 40, 237-38, 269.

[45] *Insight*, xxviii.

leads the philosopher on a journey, the journey of the *theoros* away from the homeland, only to return someday. The journey of philosophical self-appropriation, as a radical expansion of horizon, means that the philosopher must face the dread of his new possibility in the universe of being: dread, that is, in the Kierkegaardian sense of a "sympathetic antipathy."[46] The prisoner leaving Plato's cave is blinded by the bright rays of the *agathon* and can acclimate himself to its luminosity only by stages.[47] The budding philosopher is simultaneously attracted to the radiance of the *agathon* and disoriented by the loss of his cave mentality in the shadow world. Hence the personal intellectual history of the philosopher is decisive.

The uniquely subjective effort of self-appropriation, issuing in what Lonergan describes as "a decisive personal act," is the foundation of philosophy.[48] This self-knowledge can then be formulated in theoretical terms, and with these theoretical tools philosophers can address the future through functional specialties that reverse the cognitional pattern of experiencing, understanding, and judging. The philosophical community can critically affirm the essential truths of the philosophical tradition.[49] Beyond that, philosophers can seek to develop its salient themes through systematic understanding.[50] Finally, philosophers can communicate to diverse audiences what they have systematically understood and developed, affirmed, and selected from out of their encounter with the past tradition.[51] The performance of developing the authentic patrimony of the philosophical tradition becomes part of the tradition itself; it becomes data for future interpretation of the past. Thus the philosophical community recovers, renews, and carries forward the event of philosophy, thereby displaying its historicity.

5.1.4 Mythopoesis

The communication of the meaning of a philosophical tradition legitimately utilizes all the dynamic resources of art, symbol, myth, drama,

---

[46]Soren Kierkegaard, *The Concept of Dread*, trans. Walter Lowrie, 2nd ed. (Princeton: Princeton University Press, 1957), 38.

[47]Plato,*Republic*, 515c-516b.

[48]*Insight*, xix.

[49]On the functional specialty of "Doctrines," see *Method*, 132, chap. 12.

[50]On the functional specialty of "Systematics," see *Method*, 132, chap. 13.

[51]On the functional specialty of "Communications," see *Method*, 132-33, chap. 14.

and narrative—and there is something inherent in philosophy that even demands such expression.[52] This pronounced affective character of philosophy, represented in its most mature form in the dramatic artistry and mythopoesis of Plato, however, has rarely been given due recognition since the time of that Hellenic genius.[53] If philosophy is, above all else, the love of wisdom, then philosophical communication must have as its task, above all else, the issuance of an invitation to philosophize, a call with all the subtlety, richness, and power of image and affect.

Philosophy itself is a drama of the *psyche* of the lover of wisdom against the counterpulls of inauthenticity and disorder, and the journey of the *theoroi* over the ages, constituting the grand tradition of philosophy, is part of an ongoing, still open, still unfinished story. The art of reappropriating the meaning of a philosophical tradition must necessarily recast the story of its origins and development, its trials and struggles. From the perspective of the present the drama of the past assumes new proportions—unbeknownst to the earlier actors. To borrow a metaphor Lonergan was so fond of using when he spoke of historical movement in general, there is to the history of philosophy a transpersonal dimension analogous to the course and outcome of a battle, which is not determined by the conduct of individual soldiers simply as individuals, nor necessarily known by them, nor inevitably in accord with the plans of the generals, the philosophical geniuses.[54] To encounter the philosophical past is to gain a retrospective glimpse of the destiny of the philosophical tradition. For destiny, in Lonergan's estimation, is the linking of successive situations by a set of decisions by the participants in the drama that is not the decision of anyone in particular.[55] Destiny is not only a fact but also a mystery because abiding in the drama of the philosophers on their voyage of inquiry there is the presence of the divine partner, experienced in the attraction to truth, the gift of the generic openness of questioning, and the participation in the divine thrust of unrestricted love.

---

[52] *Method*, 356.

[53] See Eric Voegelin, *Order and History*, 4 vols. (Baton Rouge: Louisiana State University Press, 1956-74), III, 10-14, 151-57, 183-94; John Sallis, *Being and Logos: The Way of Platonic Dialogue*, Duquesne Studies, Philosophical Series 33 (Pittsburg: Duquesne University Press, 1975), Introduction; Hans Georg Gadamer, *Dialogue and Dialectic: Eight Hermeneutical Studies on Plato*, trans. P. Christopher Smith (New Haven: Yale University Press, 1980), chaps. 1, 3.

[54] *Method*, 179, 199.

[55] *Philosophy of Education*, 313-14.

The drama of philosophy is an orientation to the mystery of the known unknown and must, therefore, have its complement of seemly myths and symbols. Why? Because the desire to know has its psychic infrastructure, its disposition of images and symbols impelled by the teleological drive of recurrent archetypes arising from the unconscious cosmic depths and by the spiritual energy released in anagogic symbols at the border of transcendence.[56] Approximating Bergson's élan vital, these images and symbols, and the meanings they bear, are suffused by the experiences of call, openness, and unrestricted love.[57] This is to say that philosophical symbols, along with their narrative accompaniment of myths and stories, carry heuristic insights, pointing philosophy, with a majestic power, in the direction of intrinsic intelligibility. The love of wisdom generates the understanding of faith and the affect-laden wings of hope. The philosophical triad of eros, faith, and hope have as their primordial expressions those carriers of meaning whose very form keeps intact the heuristic nature of the philosophical enterprise.

To be sure, the functional specialty of Communications will play its distinct role of bringing the message of the new tale of philosophy. It has the crucial mission of telling the story. But does it create the story? Is telling the tale simply a matter of translating into myth what is, after all, clearly definable and intelligible in conceptual language: Would this not be to reduce myth to either allegory or mere pedagogy? The appropriation of philosophical tradition, we can suggest, spawns a philosophical artistry and a philosophical mythopoesis. Most significantly, for the purpose of this essay, we can discern three elements in the process, each corresponding to a mode of historicity: the past, the present, and the future.

First, the encounter with philosophical tradition supplies the evidence for a narrative of the story of philosophy. Indeed since the history of philosophy is the drama of the *psyche*, historiography must convey that sense of drama. The historian of philosophy must have the

---

[56] See Robert Doran, *Subject and Psyche: Ricoeur, Jung, and the Search for Foundations* (Washington, D C: University Press of America, 1979), 210-252; *idem.*, "The Theologian's Psyche: Notes toward a Reconstruction of Depth Psychology," in *Lonergan Workshop*, ed. Frederick Lawrence (Missoula, Montana: Scholars Press, 1978), I, 107-11, 120-21; *idem.*, "Subject, Psyche, and Theology's Foundations," *The Journal of Religion* 57 (July 1977), 279-80.

[57] Bernard Lonergan, S.J., "Reality, Myth, Symbol," in *Myth, Symbol, and Reality*, ed. Alan M. Olson (Notre Dame: University of Notre Dame Press, 1980), 33-34, 37.

requisite combination of philosophical sensitivity to the "serious play" of philosophy and artistic talent to portray it. Striking examples are Werner Jaeger's *Paideia*, an explanatory account of the development of Greek cultural ideals, particularly those of Plato, often painted in a powerful epic stroke, and Voegelin's *Order in History*, an existentially engaged presentation of the epocal struggle of the Hellenic lovers of wisdom against the disorder of their age.[58]

Philosophical biography likewise has a similar dramatic and artistic obligation; namely, to capture the incarnate meaning of a philosopher revealed in his personal fidelity and passionate devotion, his patient frustration and rapturous delight, on the road of inquiry. The incarnate meaning of a philosopher can also inspire art-forms that transcend biographical narration per se, Plato's dialogues about the life and death of Socrates being the supreme illustration. Perhaps bearing some likeness to Plato's dialogues—because it exhibits the mode of what Kierkegaard called "indirect communication"[59]—would be an evaluative intellectual history of the stripe that would render judgment in that peculiar style in which form becomes, or enters into, content: its judgments would come in the dramatic arrangement of themes, the juxtaposition of prominent thinkers, and the focus on the historical consequences unfolding from rudimentary philosophical assumptions; highlighting the challenge of possibility, it would be a powerful invitation for personal philosophical reflection on foundational issues.

Secondly, the activity of self-appropriation in the present plunges myth into the creative vortex of the psyche purged of bias and blind spots, opening up the directed dynamism of the élan vital. This energy must be co-opted by philosophy in a critical philosophical hermeneutic with real poetic, mythic, symbolic depth.[60] For philosophy is not the wisdom of divine omniscience but the love of wisdom, a process of inquiry, which has no immediate access to the idea of being, no total understanding of all there is to be known.[61] Nor will it ever have. The contours of the known unknown may be constricted but the mystery never eliminated. The whither and whence of the drama of existence,

---

[58] Werner Jaeger, *Paideia*, I-III; Voegelin, *Order and History*, I-III.

[59] Soren Kierkegaard, *Concluding Unscientific Postscript*, trans. David F. Swenson and Walter Lowrie (Princeton: Princeton University Press, 1941), 68, 74, 246-47, 319-21.

[60] Lonergan seems to applaud Plato's recourse to myth and Aristotle's attraction to it in his later years. "Reality, Myth, Symbol," 33.

[61] *Insight*, 348-52, 259-62.

the boundary situations, existentially at the center of our concern, cognitionally at the border of our horizon, will remain ever shrouded in mystery.[62] To be sure, philosophy can pronounce on the great truths of the self, world, and God.[63] But these affirmations of philosophy do not exhaust our questioning. Philosophy maps out the boundaries of reality but still leaves open vast territory to be explored. Myth is a genuine, if unique, form of understanding, which, as an expression of the generic openness of inquiry, precisely explores that territory. It thereby becomes a constitutive element of philosophy. Accordingly, philosophy must negotiate along the strange paths at the border of the dynamic unconscious, bringing its own critical acumen, its own differentiated awareness, into the depths to determine the adequacy of myths that express philosophical truth. Far from being an exercise in romanticism the enterprise must be one of philosophical appropriation. The treasure of symbols must be carried back to fund the project of philosophy. Myth would not only be a prior historical condition of the emergence of philosophy, not only a prior occasion for philosophical inquiry, not only a pedagogical device for artistic communication, but a genuine moment within philosophy, a reservoir of heuristic insights at the very foundations of inquiry.

Now philosophical appropriation must therefore reflect the inherent historicity of myth itself. The teleological outpouring of the energy of the élan vital anchored by the demands of the nervous system is an a priori component of mythopoesis counterbalanced by two a posteriori components relevant to our concern here: first, the store of traditional themes and motifs, circumscribing the range and substance of myth, and, secondly, the personal life drama of the individual philosopher. This last point suggests implications of an earlier remark. If the intellectual biography of the philosopher is crucial, then the philosopher must appropriate that intellectual history. What intellectual interests shaped the entry into the philosophical life? What were the cardinal intellectual shifts along the journey of inquiry? What experiences were a springboard to philosophical conversion? What wisdom figures inspired the enterprise? What symbols, dreams, and life scenarios played, and continue to play, a formative influence on philosophizing? Thus philosophical self-appropriating entails a venture of *anamnesis*, a recollection of the concrete symbols and narrative episodes that under-

---

[62] *Insight*, 546-49; *Method*, 110, 113-14, 321-23, 341-45.

[63] *Insight*, 339-42, 458-83, 509-20, 669-86.

pin the desire to know in the philosopher's personal drama of life. It is within this context that William Mathews has applied the seminal work of Ira Progoff's journalling of one's life story.[64] Philosophical training, insists Mathews, should include an introduction to the skills required to write the story of one's philosophical search.[65] The whole project of cognitional appropriation is rooted in the story of one's intellectual development, a personal wisdom story.[66] To reinforce philosophy as a way of life—to take up existentially the truth of philosophy—one must articulate one's conversion story.[67] Along similar lines, Voegelin has maintained that systematic reflection is never "a radical beginning of philosophy or can lead to such a beginning."[68] Rather the beginning lies in the "biography of consciousness," "the experiences that impel toward reflection and do so because they have excited consciousness to the 'awe' of existence."[69] Voegelin then conducts "anamnetic experiments" to recount such experiences, some conspicuous for a long time in his memory, some readily recalled but without clear meaning, some remembered only after having been long forgotten.[70]

Thirdly, there is the dimension of the future. Mediated by critical scholarship, rooted in the psychic foundations of the love of wisdom, myth can be linked to the affirmation of the basic truths of the philosophical traditions. Moreover, isomorphic with systematic development of that tradition can be further exploration of foundational symbols, myths, and poetic themes. Might we even anticipate that the rich exploration by such metaphysical poets as Rainer Maria Rilke and T.S. Eliot would herald subsequent, more systematic treatment of philosophical problems?

The *theoroi* must navigate the wide ocean of basic horizon from their barks of homebound relative horizons. They must attain a distance

---

[64] William Mathews, S.J., "Journalling Self-Appropriation," *Milltown Studies* 7 (1981), 96-184; *idem.*, "Personal Histories and Theories of Knowledge," *Milltown Studies* 8 (1981), 58-73; Ira Progoff, *At a Journal Workshop: The Basic Text and Guide for Using the Intensive Journal Process* (New York: Dialogue House Library, 1975); *idem.*, *The Symbolic and the Real: A New Psychological Approach to the Fuller Experience of Human Existence* (New York: McGraw-Hill Book Co., 1973).

[65] Mathews, "Journalling Self-Appropriation," 105, 129.

[66] Mathews, 106; see also *idem.*, "Personal Histories."

[67] Mathews, "Journalling Self-Appropriation," 106.

[68] Eric Voegelin, *Anamnesis*, trans. Gerhard Niemeyer (Notre Dame: University of Notre Dame Press, 1978), 36.

[69] Voegelin, 36.

[70] Voegelin, 36-37.

from tradition only to renew it. And must not this renewal contain a story—and a myth—of the theorists themselves on their awesome, risky voyage of inquiry?

5.2 Philosophy and Praxis

Philosophy indirectly, but decisively, is concerned with the future conduct (praxis) of human affairs. Indirectly: it offers neither conceptualist generalities nor blueprints. But decisively: through the existential example of the philosopher and through systematically developed insights on the long-term perspective and on the eclipse of reality it addresses the issues of greatest import for the human good. It urges assumption of historical responsibility. In so doing it devotes itself to pressing concerns of religion and of culture.

5.2.1 Philosophical Therapy and Existential Deformation

Philosophy, as a variety of religious experience, offsets the enervating effects of historical decline at the roots. As Lonergan has so lucidly demonstrated, the principle of historical decline is the poison of bias, which can take on the shapes of neurosis, individual egoism, group egoism, and common-sense shortsightedness. [71] We can suggest, however, that bias has existential sources; that if we penetrate beneath the biases adumbrated above we can uncover radical precipitates of existential deformation; and that such radical factors, always subsisting in an explanatory relationship with each other, are dread, concupiscence, and *ressentiment*. Let us examine this existential complex, which ravages both individuals and societies and of which it is the mettle of philosophy to combat.

Self-transcendence engages the authentic self in a continuous process oriented to absolute transcendence. The pure desire to know is unrestricted in its search for intelligibility; the intention of the good is unreserved in its attraction to what is worthwhile; the love of God is both the otherworldly pull of the Wholly Other and the experience of participation in infinite divine reality. Thus self-transcendence,

---

[71] *Insight*, 191-203, 218-42.

even as it is always limited by its concrete human, historical, and personal situations, likewise always displays what Lonergan calls "vertical finality."[72] By raising the existential issue of future possibility, the pure question challenges the self as presently constituted, occasioning the experience of dread.[73] Accepting the challenge gracefully, one may expand one's horizon in accord with vertical finality. Rejecting the challenge out of hand, one may hover in the abysmal depths of despair. Fleeing the challenge, one may attempt to flee dread as well by various time-tested escape routes. Chief among the avenues of flight is the way of *divertissements*—including money-making, status-seeking, philandering, overeating, and wine-tippling—catalogued by the ancient Stoics, explored perceptively by Blaise Pascal, dramatically illustrated, in its most refined species, by the notorious *fin-de-siècle* movement of Decadence, and portrayed, in a more pervasive form, by the banality of modern consumer society.[74] A related road of escape, frequently linked to *divertissements*, but one more nefarious because it bears the signpost of vertical finality, is what Saint Augustine named concupiscence, the concentration of infinite craving on a finite object, usually power, fame, or sex;[75] this is a disease of the spirit that can perniciously attack religion itself or, deflecting its unrestricted drive, can corrupt it, whence anxious flight from reality parades, with the various biases, under the banner of the sacred; this same disposition is what Kierkegaard called the "sickness unto death," the self's relation to itself whereby the self defines itself in terms of some finite relationship, object, goal, destiny, or fate, pouring into this frail vessel of a definition all of its infinite concern.[76] It is here that another deformation joins concupiscence, namely, *ressentiment*; for concupiscence, hiding, as it does, the infinite in the finite, must protect itself from an outburst of the dreaded

---

[72] *Collection*, 18-22.

[73] Bernard Lonergan, S.J., "Horizon and Dread," in *Notes on Existentialism*, (Author's notes for lectures given at Boston College, Summer 1957; reprinted by Thomas More Institute, Montreal), 9-10.

[74] On the psychopathology of the Stoics, see Voegelin, *Anamnesis*, 47-103; on Pascal, see Voegelin, *From Enlightenment to Revolution*, ed. John H. Hallowell (Durham, N.C.: Duke University Press, 1975), 51-59; on the consumer society, see *Conversations with Eric Voegelin*, ed. R. Eric O'Connor (Montreal: Thomas More Institute Papers, 1980), 139-40.

[75] *Collection*, 50-52.

[76] Soren Kierkegaard, *The Sickness unto Death: A Christian Psychological Exposition for Upbuilding and Awakening*, trans. Howard V. Hong and Edna H. Hong (Princeton: Princeton University Press, 1980).

infinite, which threatens to break its feeble chains, and must also lash out at the boredom and anomie inevitably accompanying the loss of a true relation to the infinite by finding an appropriate scapegoat. This it can strive to accomplish through *ressentiment*, the state of mind, identified by Nietzsche and then Scheler, that belittles the value of a superior and eventually distorts the whole hierarchy of values.[77] Would not the values most immediately in the firing line of the allied forces of *ressentiment* and concupiscence be those of the sacred, truth, and philosophy?

This triad of dread of transcendence, flight into concupiscence, and collusion of *ressentiment* has its unmistakable, ominous parallel in the history of communities. Every society bears a relation to transcendence, symbolizing this orientation to the mystery of being in a civil theology, which expresses a legitimation of the society as an actor in the drama of history. Every society faces historical challenges to its horizon of cultural expressions, traditions, and social practices and may indeed experience dread at these threats from beyond and the concomitant awareness of its own finitude, if not of its possible demise. Every society may respond to the dreadful challenge by a dazed willingness to be seduced by the wily bias of common sense with its short-sighted, narrow practicality, by excursions into the sweet land of *divertissements* on a mass scale, or—in the extreme—by collapsing its symbols of ultimate concern, representing the known unknown, into decidedly finite projects, interests, and compulsions: always with a dreaded, and infinite, earnest. When concupiscence thus becomes the pied piper of a society, the blind leading the blind, it is because that society has already brought on itself an eclipse of reality, a refusal, fortified by anxiety, to be open to the horizon of being. Is it, therefore, surprising that a Western civilization marked by anomie, decadence, hedonism, stilted behavior, and dogmatic adherence to social conventions should, at the same time, suffer from periodic outbursts of nationalism breaking all bounds of rationality, as in the heady days of August 1914? Can one not perceive beneath the foreign policy preoccupations, diplomatic procedures, and international crises of European nation-states the boiling cauldron of infinite concern, the fever of the sickness unto death? Why, in truth, do we witness modern obsession with the nation, or the class, or the race? Clearly concupiscence can deftly nurture group bias,

---

[77] *Method*, 33, 273; Max Scheler, *Ressentiment*, trans. Lewis A. Coser (New York: Schocken Books, 1972).

substituting the nation, the class, or the race for ultimate reality and value.[78] This process of deformation is only accentuated when group bias is tied to the inflammatory pronouncements of neo-gnostic revolutionary movements that would beguile their followers into an apocalyptic dream where the imminent victory of a class or a race would herald its apotheosis and the veritable resurrection of history. Every society in the grip of concupiscence, however, would have to defend its intoxication against the call of being by belittling openness to reality; increasingly, this *ressentiment* would distort the hierarchy of values, assaulting religion, authentic selfhood, and the unrestricted desire to know. Following in the train of *ressentiment* would come benumbed social conscience, the host of biases, and then a regressive cycle of ever more fragmented and incoherent cultural viewpoints.[79]

We have been depicting here what Lonergan has termed an "existential gap,"[80] an operatively limited horizon in which an atrophied interpretation of human reality is fundamentally at odds with what human beings can be and ought to be. The philosopher has the imperative to close such a gap, to expose by his very life of commitment and fidelity the blind spots of the dominant horizon.[81] Specifically, the philosopher counters the antipathetic aspect of dread with the sympathetic attraction of eros, the deceitful closedness of concupiscence with the openness of the spirit of questioning, and the deep-seated weakness of *ressentiment* with the strength and integrity of living the truth. The issue at stake is not ultimately a proper set of propositions (which can be repeated without any understanding) nor a defective system of philosophy in its isolated conceptual splendor; the issue is ultimately a transformation in the mode of life, in the drama of existence, in the pattern of thinking, a leap beyond the present horizon (including any defective philosophy) insofar as it is at odds with the spirit of inquiry—

---

[78] These modern forms of social concupiscence are usually tied to the goal of a universal, or ecumenic, empire; as Voegelin argues, the idea of an ecumenic empire is the idea of a "concupiscential exodus from reality," an unlimited drive to expansion, which was proclaimed in its purest form in the Melian Dialogue, recorded by Thucydides. Whereas the modern drive of imperial concupiscence is couched in the language of world-immanent ideologies, ancient empires, confronting their own finitude, began to associate themselves with ecumenic religions. See Eric Voegelin, "World Empire and the Unity of Mankind," *International Affairs* 38 (1962), 170-88; *idem.*, *Order and History*, IV, chaps. 2-3, 260-71.

[79] On the cycle of cultural decline, see *Insight*, 226-32, 237.

[80] "The Existential Gap," *Notes on Existentialism*, 9.

[81] "Horizon and Dread," *Notes on Existentialism*, 12.

a conversion.[82] The philosopher of any era can profit from the example of Plato in this regard; Plato in his youth had experienced the convulsions of the Peloponnesian War, a conflict diagnosed by the historian, Thucydides, as an infection of Hellas by the "lust for power;"[83] for Plato, in his dialogue, *Charmides,* the antidote to this existential malady was certain, the charm of fair words, the words of philosophical discourse that would cure such a "headache."[84] While the remedy of philosophy, of course, is not guaranteed to be successful on the stage of historical events, at least in the short run—as the fate of Socrates ironically attests—its religious therapy is nonetheless vital. The therapy of philosophy meets the inevitable resistance of the existential gap by appealing to the desperateness and hopelessness of the situation and by cutting down its pretentions through the signal importance of satire and humor.[85] The philosopher does not offer enforced dogmas nor even theoretically compelling assent but an invitation to self-awareness and openness to being, an appeal to dwell in the Heraclitean *koiné cosmos* permeated by the divine logos.[86]

5.2.2   Philosophy and Intellectual Culture

The religious task of philosophy is also a cultural task. Philosophy must carry out a cultural mission to promote the responsible direction of history. Philosophy, in its existential sense, infuses cultural life, institutions, and politics with its spirit. While it thus permeates culture, institutions, and politics, it has no utopian commission; for it does not create ideal institutions; it does not spawn a bureaucracy, which would equate policy with the definitiveness and universality of concepts;[87] it does not consider politics as technique (as it does not consider academics as technique).[88] In a word, it does not act directly on social policy. But, more importantly, it acts indirectly. Through its imprint on cultural ideals, through education, and through the arts of communication it reaches down to the proverbial "man on the spot,"

---

[82]"The Existential Gap," *Notes on Existentialism,* 9.

[83]Thucydides, *The Peloponnesian War,* Crawley trans. (New York: Random House, Modern Library College Editions, 1951), 190.

[84]Plato, *Charmides,* 156d-157c.

[85] "Horizon and History," *Notes on Existentialism,* 13-14; *Insight* 624-26.

[86] "Horizon and Dread," *Notes on Existentialism,* 11-12.

[87]*Insight,* 234-235; *Third Collection,*60-61.

[88] *Third Collection,* 103-104.

the person familiar with the classroom, the economy, or international affairs, guiding and inspiring such a person to grasp the fuller relevant insights into the concrete situation that only he or she can grasp while, at the same time, cultivating an appreciation of the long-term perspective.[89]

If the sway of the love of wisdom indirectly touches a large circle of people, it extends more directly to the much smaller number preoccupied with higher intellectual culture, though one still greater than those engaged in philosophy strictly in its systematic aspect. The love of wisdom is, in fact, the origin of the sciences, scholarly disciplines, and literature, even as they differentiate themselves from philosophy in its systematic sense. To separate themselves completely from philosophy would be to cut themselves off from their existential source, and this would be to court cultural disaster. Why? It is the love of wisdom that creates the nucleus, and the only nucleus, of a true academic community by creating a common field of experience, understanding, judgments, and commitments.[90] We can breathe new meaning into the old Platonic idea of the *polis* by conceiving it as a cultural community informed by the love of wisdom or, perhaps, more accurately, we can impart contemporary significance to that ancient term by identifying it with, to employ Lonergan's language, borrowed from the Stoics, a cosmopolis.[91] Those persons engaged in true *paideia* would acknowledge as their horizon the horizon of the pure question with its immanent norms: this is the substance of a real sense of community embracing all academic and scientific pursuits. Undoubtedly this *polis* must first reside in the formative efforts of a creative minority.[92] And in a time of cultural fragmentation, philosophical illiteracy, and antiintellectual intellectuals, when it may often seem that among one's immediate contacts the only member of such a community is oneself, then the advice of the Platonic Socrates stands across the ages: incessantly build the *polis* in oneself.[93]

The cultural task of philosophy, however, does topple over into its objective pole. The systematic aspect of philosophy exerts a method-

---

[89] *Insight*, 234-35.

[90] For Lonergan's discussion of community, see *Method*, 79, 356-57.

[91] *Insight*, 238-42.

[92] *Philosophy of Education*, 62-63; *Third Collection*, 10, 103-04.

[93] Plato, *Republic*, 591e-592b; Jaeger, *Paideia*, II, 354-57; see Voegelin, *Anamnesis*, 3-6, for his personal struggle against the "school philosophies" of his youth.

ological influence over higher culture. Philosophy, after all, is the "basic science of human living" as it thematizes the norms of authentic human living and systematically articulates metaphysical principles. A properly validated metaphysics challenges every restricted cultural viewpoint that would eclipse reality. Avoiding reductionism as well as any monocausal interpretation, metaphysics comprehends the nuanced reality of human being as a synthesis of matter and spirit.[94] Because of the isomorphism of knowing with the object of inquiry metaphysics can thereby promote the integration of the various scientific and academic fields that investigate the many-sided nature of human reality.[95] Philosophy can also unify itself, historical scholarship, and social policy on the level of methods; it can lay the foundations for intellectual collaboration by demonstrating how these fields are fundamentally related specialties in the ongoing appropriation of historical tradition by higher culture as it encounters the past, explores substantive philosophical problems, and decides on essential policy and doctrines for future development. Philosophy, above all else, can emphasize how human studies must be critical, normative, and evaluative;[96] how the current technical, social, and cultural situation can contradict authentic human possibility and objectify the existential gap;[97] how present turmoil and breakdown can be traced to past errors;[98] and how, given new ideas, feelings, and decisions, historical agents can alter the historical situation.[99] Such an appreciation of the critical role of historiography can spur healthy cooperation among fields in the history of thought so that psychohistory, history of culture, history of ideas, intellectual history, and history of philosophy can be organized together to stress the increasingly explicit presence of philosophical assumptions.

The task of philosophy, then is both diagnostic and therapeutic.[100] The philosopher can neither succumb to the *Zeitgeist* by devaluating the intellectual currency nor speak in vague generalities that ignore concrete historical circumstances.[101] The philosopher must address the issues of maximum import for human welfare and for human dis-

---

[94] *Insight*, 469-779, 514-20.
[95] *Insight*, xi, 390-91, 564-68, chaps. 7,15.
[96] *Insight*, 235-36.
[97] "Horizon and History," *Notes on Existentialism*, 13.
[98] "Horizon and Dread," *Notes on Existentialism*, 12.
[99] *Notes on Existentialism*, 12.
[100] See Voegelin, *Order and History*, I, xiv.
[101] "Horizon and Dread," *Notes on Existentialism*, 12.

aster in the given historical situation.[102] Philosophy must unveil the true springs of progress. As Lonergan has so precisely stated, its basic function is to illuminate the effort of intelligent, reasonable, free, fully responsible self-constitution.[103] Philosophy, therefore, rather than fleeing historical consciousness must support it by its own species of religious experiences and its own decisive role in culture. Here Lonergan's lifelong work itself can serve as guide and exemplar of such a fusion of the existential, the historical, and the systematic.

In the meaningful concreteness of the present historical situation philosophy, we would urge, has two main tasks:

First, it must recover the fullness of the existential pole—cognitive, moral, religious, and affective—along with recognition of historicity. This essay has alluded to the intimate relation between noetic consciousness and religious consciousness as well as to the historically constitutive nature of the eruption of philosophy in Hellas; it has stressed the existential significance of the philosophical tradition, the foundational character of the philosopher's personal biography, the integral relevance of symbol, myth, and poetry to philosophy, and the moral and cultural imperatives of philosophical praxis—all as a propaedeutic contributing to that goal.

But, secondly, this endeavor must foster a renewal of systematic philosophical thought, carrying it beyond materialism, positivism, scientism, naive or dogmatic realism, and transcendental idealism. The philosopher's religious experience is not merely a subjective illusion, and the hope for intrinsic intelligibility is not a forlorn hope. Yet to raise these issues is, in part, to enter the terrain of epistemology and metaphysics. To wrestle with these issues is, in part, to work out the epistemological and metaphysical implications of the normative process of inquiry. Far from eschewing epistemological and metaphysical matters, our conclusion of this essay must be that historical responsibility demands that we take up these ancient concerns—albeit divorced from deductivist proofs and dogmatic apologetics—in order to regenerate contemporary culture.

---

[102] *Notes on Existentialism*, 12.
[103] *Notes on Existentialism*, 11.

Chapter 6

Language as a Carrier of Theological Meaning

Nancy Ring

The methodological work of Bernard Lonergan, based as it is on the praxis inherent in human consciousness, has provided theologians with a normative criterion for their work. Since, however, Lonergan's work is concerned primarily with method rather than with specific theological content, it has encouraged theologians to test their "bright ideas," their "hints and guesses" by enlarging upon them and by assessing them within the parameters of method. That is what I have attempted to do in this contribution to Lonergan Studies.

I have long entertained the "bright idea" that theological language is more than, or should be more than, theoretical. It should also be transformative of human living. The following essay is an attempt to unfold this "guess" within the theological method of Bernard Lonergan. It is not presented as a finished piece of work, but rather, in the spirit of Lonergan, is offered to the theological community in the hope that it will evoke further discussion, collaboration and refinement by others interested in the question of theological language.

I proceed with this topic, then, both cognizant of and warned by Lonergan's statement that

[a] little learning is a dangerous thing, and the adage has, perhaps, its most abundant illustrations from the application of logic to the tasks of interpretation. A familiarity with the elements of logic can be obtained by a very modest effort and in a very short time. Until one has made notable progress in cognitional analysis, one is constantly tempted to mistake the rules of logic for the laws of thought.[1]

The position developed in this paper is that language, as a carrier of meaning, functions not only as the expression of meaning, generally, and theological meaning, particularly, but that language also delimits or shapes the images born in the imagination, images in which meaning has its elemental source, insight its image; from which knowledge reaches its term, and deliberation and decision, their convincing evidence. Further, language can function metaphorically, thereby giving rise to new images, new insights, new knowledge, new decisions. Finally, language as both a carrier and a source of meaning is neither univocal nor equivocal, but is analogous. Its meaning depends upon the realm of meaning in which it is functioning. Thus, language, while retaining its basic functions of expressing meaning and shaping and recombining images, also gives us entrance into the worlds of common sense, theory, interiority and transcendence.

What is the value and function of language? Lonergan states that language is that which frees us from the necessity of immediate sense experience in order to know.[2] Here we must be very careful to understand that Lonergan does not mean that language separates us from our sense experience. Indeed, sense experience is probably the source of both language and religion.[3] Without its sensate base, language would be a totally artificial construct.[4] But language does free us from the

---

[1] Bernard Lonergan,S.J.,*Insight: A Study of Human Understanding* (London: Darton, Longman and Todd, 1957), 573.

[2] Bernard Lonergan,S.J., *Method in Theology* (New York: Herder and Herder, 1972), 76.

[3] Both Ernst Cassirer in *Language and Myth* (New York: Harper Brothers, 1946) and in *An Essay on Man* (New Haven: Yale University Press, 1944) and Giagranco Cantelli in *Giambattista Vico's Science of Humanity*, eds. Giorgio Tagliacozzo and Donald Phillip Verne (Baltimore: The John Hopkins University Press, 1976), 57, put forth this view.

[4] Such is, in part, the position of at least some deconstructionists. See Louis Mackey, "Slouching Toward Bethlehem: Deconstruction Strategies in Theology," *Anglican Theological Review* 65 (1983), 255-272.

limitations of speaking and writing of (as well as knowing) only those things in the presence of which we are temporally and spatially situated. Thus, rather than separating us from sense experience, language enables us to experience vicariously that which is absent.

In freeing us from the necessity of being spatially and temporally present to that which is known, the development of our language initiates us into the world of common meanings attained by our language group over generations. It makes available for human consideration the wisdom of the past and the present. Because of this, we can consider language as a type of institution. It transmits a shared communal experience to persons who, in turn, receive their identity from membership in the language group. In this way, Lonergan can say that language is a carrier of the meaning both of fact and of value; it expresses the communal impulse toward self-transcendence located in a particular group, and it expresses this in an objective manner through the articulation of the meanings and values which inform the group's culture.[5] Language, freed from spatiality, specificity and externality, expresses the objectivity of fact and value attained by a particular group. Once we have introduced the notion of objectivity, though, we are led to the question of the subjectivity of language and the relationship existing between subjectivity and objectivity.

The instrumental, expressive and transforming qualities of language must be understood as more than a naive or superficial conformity of words to thought, or as the merely coherent and logical material expression of the terms of judgment and decision. If objectivity is self-transcending subjectivity,[6] then it is fair to say that meaning not only expresses its terms in language, but that the experience of language is the necessary condition for thought. Until language develops, neither conceptual thought nor full objectivity in the realms of theory, interiority and transcendence is possible.

So, language does carry meaning, but in so doing, it also gives rise to new meaning. Just as, according to Lonergan, the mature fruit of objectivity can be plucked from the tree of human subjectivity,[7] so too language; for the objectivity achieved by language can never be had

---

[5] Lonergan, *Method*, 87.

[6] Bernard Lonergan, S.J., "An Interview With Fr. Bernard Lonergan, S.J." in *A Second Collection: Papers by Bernard J.F. Lonergan, S.J.*, eds. William Ryan, S.J., and Bernard Tyrrell, S.J. (Philadelphia: The Westminster Press, 1974), 214.

[7] Bernard Lonergan, S.J., "The Subject," *Second Collection*, 71.

independently of human subjectivity.

Now, to appropriate truth, insight into an image arising from data is necessary.[8] But, we may ask, from whence does such an image arise? Of course, from the imagination, but the imagination is not a playground of amorphous and unrelated images and symbols; rather, it is an element of human thought shaped and contoured by one's language, language shared with a specific, historical group. So, insight itself is shaped and limited by linguistically formed images. Because the imagination is flexible, however, it is capable not only of presenting and representing images that correspond to a single reality, but it can recombine images to a seemingly infinite degree until one image or group of images seems to "collect" the data of experience better than another. Thus, imagination is the basis of language appropriate to the different realms of meaning. The new language, though, shapes and reshapes the imaginal. The development is spiral. That is the reason we can say that language is not only an expression of meaning, but, also a source of new meaning. We can infer, as well, that if the conscious process of experiencing, understanding, judging, deciding and loving is to be developmental, an on-going process of self-correction, then the imagination, shaped by language, is one primary source of such development. Lack of such development of the imagination inevitably leads to personal and social decline. This is so because we spontaneously and consistently act out of the meanings and values arising in the imagination. If the flow of images, including their recombination, is stopped, so is development.[9]

Rather than such a spontaneity being termed prereflective, I prefer the term "postreflective" because the reflective experience of the community which is the source of the imaginative structure of the personal and communal imagination is, in the first instance, a received meaning, a meaning transmitted by the language structures of the communal imagination. Such a spontaneity, although perhaps personally prereflective, is the result of reflection, judgment and decision which has preceded the action of the person and the immediate community.[10]

Just as there is a certain reciprocity existing between knowledge and

---

[8] *Insight*, 8.

[9] *Insight*, 193-94.

[10] In developing this understanding on the received tradition, I am indebted to Frederick Crowe, S.J., *Old Things and New; A Strategy for Education. Lonergan Workshop*, vol. 5, suppplement (Atlanta: Scholars Press, 1985).

the act of judgment,[11] there also is reciprocity between meaning and its linguistic expression. That which can neither be spoken nor written, is not known in the full sense of the term as understood by Lonergan. That which can be articulated must be in consonance with its experiential base, but in the process of development and self-correction it also broadens or modifies the experiential, imaginative base out of which further expressions of meaning are formed and shaped.[12]

Lonergan has assured us that the process of conversion, culminating in or characterized by human self-transcendence consists in the dynamism of the moment to be transcended (one's present state) and the transcending moment, the state arrived at by judgments of fact and decisions for value that situate one in a new place—either greater horizontal freedom or entrance into a new horizon resulting from an exercise of vertical freedom.[13] The process consists in the negotiation of limitation and transcendence.[14] It would seem that this same dynamic is both operative in and integral to understanding the movement generated by language. Language both limits what we can see, forms our horizons, and at the same time provides a basis for the enlarging of our horizons. That is, it limits as well as frees. An example may be in order: our perspective changes according to whether we speak of "broken families" or "single-parent" families. Such language shapes the contours of our imagination which provides the images and symbols which constellate our experience, feelings and meanings, issuing in the myth or story out of which we spontaneously act. If we act out of a "broken family" story, our actions will be different than if we act out of a "single-parent" story. So, our actions, which on one hand provide us with experience upon which we reflect in order to understand and conceptualize, on the other hand incorporate the decisions by means of which we constitute ourselves and our world as originating values.[15]

Thus, a primary source of our attention to experience should be our use of language. In the terms of hermeneutics, we should apply the hermeneutics of both suspicion and recovery to our personal and communal language. We should suspect that our language system is

---

[11] Lonergan, *Second Collection*, 71.

[12] There is a correlative, here, with Lonergan's explication of the inner word of religious experience and the outer word of scripture, sacrament and church (*Method*, 112-113).

[13] *Method*, 237.

[14] See *Insight*, 627-630.

[15] *Method*, 50-51.

not only structuring our imaginations, forming the concepts and, ultimately, the worldviews out of which we act, but doing so in a restrictive
way which reinforces our flight from self-transcendence and prevents us
from living, imaginatively, in a world of emergent probability. Thus,
possible schemes of recurrence which could lead to self-transcendence
wither and die, and stultifying ones are allowed to solidify. In such
a case, the conscious project of self-transcendence is subverted at its
imaginative source.

Language, though, is also part of the hermeneutics of recovery, because it can present us with a range of new possibilities. To the extent
that we suspect our language of restricting our worldviews, of becoming
inappropriate to our experience, to that extent we can enter a process
of re-languaging and thereby reconstruct our imaginations which give
rise to new worldviews and consequent horizons, personal and social.
A radical re-languaging could issue in an exercise of vertical freedom.
Lest this be understood simply as manipulative technique or an example of behaviorist conditioning rather than of change, more attention
must be given to the process of how personhood develops within the
linguistic community.

Development is understood to occur in the experience of the other.[16]
The experience of the other, however, is registered in three "moments"
of development. The first moment is localized in the *experience* of the
other. This is an aesthetic experience. The second moment is realized
in the experience of the *other*. This is a psychological experience. The
third moment is the experience of the *OTHER*. This is an experience
of the Transcendent. In every case, the community precedes the individual, and one comes to personhood during a process in which the
duality of the symbiotic relationship of child to mother, the first moment, gives way to the triadic relationship of mother, father, child (the
second moment). It is in this moment that the child first recognizes the
mother as separate from itself, and, therefore, recognizes itself as an individual. In this process, the aesthetic experience of oneself is sublated

---

[16] This section on the development of the other is a partial result of research funded
by the Committee on Faculty Development at Le Moyne College, Syracuse, New
York, during the summer of 1982. It is largely based on the work of Jacques Lacan
and Suzanne Langer. However, it is even more a development of original reflection,
indeed based on these authors, but carried further by conversations between me
and Charles E. Goldsmith, Ph.D., Milwaukee, who is himself a developmental psy-
chologist in clinical practice. Thus this section is a somewhat original contribution
which, I believe, is consonant with the work of Lonergan and his commentators.

by the psychological experience of an *other*. It is only at this moment, when the child can say, "I," that it is established in its own beginning uniqueness. The child is freed from the immediacy of physical need, and that need is sublated by desire, desire for the absent (the mother), the absence which was produced by psychological separation. It is in this "space" created by separation that creativity is born, a creativity that posits acts to fill the distance created by the separation.

Developmentally, the symbol is a sublation of image. It arises from the experience of the *other*. In this mediated relationship, need is sublated by desire which characterizes and informs all subsequent development. Desire is a function of an imperative experienced on the imaginal level rather than the physiological level; it closes the distance between one's self and the other. It is distinguished from need by its symbolic permanence which gives birth to feeling rather than to emotional response.

Feeling is the vehicle which reveals to one the state of one's psyche, the context which gives contour to the meanings and values out of which one lives. Insofar as feelings function in the psyche, their presence does not necessarily evoke physiological changes; but insofar as they sublate the aesthetic which manifests itself in images, there is an emotional substratum to desire which registers itself in memory traces as needs, needs that provide a consistent reference point of that which produces pleasure and displeasure.

Now, out of this quasi-permanent context of feeling and desire, one acts to diminish the pain-causing effects of subjectivity and to augment and increase the pleasurable effects of the distancing occasioned by entrance into the symbolic order. In so doing, the dynamism of creativity unfolds, and the acts performed enable one to transcend present limitations and to actualize possibilities.

When this second moment is enacted, the developmental focus shifts from image-producing activity. Symbols differ from images in that they are multivalent, and contextualize and constellate feelings. The relationship of symbol and feeling is so implicit that one does not exist without the other. Symbol cannot be discussed in the absence of feeling, nor can feeling be discussed in the absence of symbol. Symbols focus the meaning of the lived experience of lack. The symbolic activity of the imagination is the specific ordering of the experience of the *other*.

In the discursive process, the symbolic representation of desire is understood theoretically. Creative acts of meaning are concretized in forms available to the public forum. Such forms are susceptible to evaluation and critique by others. Mathematics, science and religious creeds are examples of creative symbolic activity ordered by the discursive process.

The second moment of the experience of the *other* prepares for and leads to the experience of the *OTHER*. The intentionality of desire leads one to the knowledge that no other can fulfill one's desire, psychologically; and, therefore, this desire for the other is sublated by the desire for the *OTHER*. In the language of symbol, the psychological symbol is sublated by the anagogic symbol: God revealed in Christ Jesus.[17]

Just as the psychological symbol is characterized by the temporal, the generic, and the existential, so is the anagogic symbol. And although image is sublated by symbol, image remains foundational to symbol, even to the anagogic symbol, just as the level of experience remains foundational to understanding, judgment and decision. Consequently, to allow new images to enter into the process of symbolization is to eventually allow the reinformation of the Symbol par excellence. We can thus speak of God in Christ in new ways, ways that will give rise to new understandings of Symbol, ways that will eventually provide a new context or paradigm of God-talk, one that is controlled by authentic development.

But the symbol is not free-floating. It is given meaning and value by the story, the narrative of the community. Even the symbol of Christ is contextualized out of the operative construct of the community. Thus, the meaning of the dying and rising Christ and, therefore, of God's meaning for the world,[18] is given meaning within the interpretive story of the community. It is within this interpretative context that development or decline takes place. If the community places the symbol within a context of domination and control, decline takes place because desire is diminished or subverted. If the symbol is placed within a context of theoretical control, decline may occur because the open-endedness of the self-correcting process, founded in praxis, is restricted. If, however, the symbol is placed within the context of dialogue and participation, the symbol of the dying and rising Christ can give rise to social, historical, theological development because the intentionality of the symbol

---

[17]Robert Doran, S.J., "Christ and the Psyche," in *Trinification of the World*, eds. Thomas Dunne and Jean-Marc Laporte (Toronto: Regis College Press, 1978), 138.

[18]Lonergan, *Method*, 119, 363.

is controlled by the demands of authenticity unrestricted, at least partially, by preconceived understandings of the good that are abstract rather than concrete.[19] Thus, a new theological language can develop.

Now, theological language presents us with a unique situation because it is a function of the transcendent realm of meaning. Since faith is knowledge born of love,[20] a theological reflection upon faith must respond both to the demands of symbol and of rational discourse. Symbol is the language of religious experience, personal and communal, because the faith born of religious experience cannot be contained by theory. Yet, rational discourse is the language of the public forum within which and for which the theologian speaks. It must be coherent and controlled by the normativity of method.

In what has been previously stated, it may seem that symbol, because it is contextualized by a particular story, does not have the final word. But I would argue to the contrary. The critical and methodical exigences do give rise to judgments of fact and value. It is in this context that we can understand Ricoeur's statement that symbols give rise to thought.[21] With this I agree.

Because of the transcendent exigence, however, I would go further. Since the normativity of method[22] controls the meaning of judgments of fact and value, such judgments are freed from both relativism and absolutism. Thus, such judgments are never unalterably final, but rather can open onto the realm of the transcendent. Now, if symbol is that by means of which we are related to the other, even more so is it that which unites us to the *OTHER* which we have experienced in love. The articulation of the Symbol, though, will be methodically and thus normatively controlled and linguistically expressed.

In theological language, thought is sublated by symbol—the symbol which appropriates but goes beyond judgments of facts and values into the known unknown. It assumes facts and values within its process of

---

[19] For the articulation of the various social paradigms—dominative control, theoretical control, and participation—I am indebted to Charles Goldsmith, Ph.D. For a fuller elaboration, see his article, "The Pastoral Care Movement and The Pastoral Model," in *The Saint Luke's Journal of Theology*, 25 (1982) : 122-135.

[20] Lonergan, *Method*, 115.

[21] Paul Ricoeur, *The Symbolism of Evil*, trans. E.Buchanan (Boston: Beacon Press, 1967), 19.

[22] Here, I use "method" as described by Bernard Lonergan, "... a normative pattern of recurrent and related operations yielding cumulative and progressive results." *Method*, 4.

relating to the transcendent, but it is also capable of revaluing facts and recontextualizing value and meaning, just as religious conversion, the unconditional falling in love with God, sublates intellectual and moral conversion. By such sublation, religious conversion provides a new criterion by which one arrives at value and meaning as well as the worth of facts.[23]

Symbol does this to an eminent degree because it both gives rise to thought and sublates thought by allowing itself to be open to re-information by new images to which it repeatedly returns for "re-sourcing." These images provide the material for new insight, issuing in new language, and with the new language, a new contour for the imagination. And so the process continues.

No one has expressed this search for new images and words better than T.S. Eliot in "Burnt Norton":

> Words move, music moves
> Only in time; but that which is only living
> Can only die. Words, after speech, reach
> into the silence. Only by the form, the pattern,
> Can words or music reach
> The stillness, as a Chinese jar still
> Moves perpetually in its stillness. ...Words strain,
> Crack and sometimes break, under the burden,
> Under the tension, slip, slide, perish,
> Decay with imprecision, will not stay in Place,
> Will not stay still.[24]

Thus, theological language, even when appearing to be theoretical, that is, coherent and relating terms to one another, must be appropriated symbolically. In that way, what is being explained may also be rendered experientially present. Theology is, consequently, not only discursive but transformational. A theological language which fulfills the demands of rational discourse and of symbol will transmit a tradition authentically; it will provide the context which will facilitate the self-transcendence of persons and their communities. Such communities and persons will be characterized by on-going development and conversion. Increasingly, the doctrines and teachings of faith will be marked

---

[23] Lonergan, *Method*, 105.
[24] T.S. Eliot, "Burnt Norton," *The Four Quartets* (New York: Harcourt, Brace and World, 1943), 19.

by dialogue rather than debate, participation rather than hierarchy, and freedom rather than control. That so many of the ecclesial, civil and social groups to which we belong do not evidence these character-istics is symptomatic of decline. In regard to religious communities, it is indicative that theological language has become inappropriate to the experience of the transcendent exigence of many in the community, and that such language impedes rather than promotes self-transcendence.

Particular instances of the demand for new theological language can be found in both the religious experience of contemporary women and the religious experience of both women and men who live in an historical situation marked by the necessity of cooperation rather than competition if the planet is to survive. Regarding women's experience, we can say that, with few exceptions, the male experience of faith has been coupled with the western philosophical tradition to produce the present state of theological imagination, which as we have suggested may be leading to decline. When women hear and read such theology, they are many times co-opted into reading and hearing as males.[25] In such cases, they either disregard their own experiences or adapt these to the male paradigms of power and hierarchy. (In fact, they are told such is God's will.) Other women's reactions are to disregard the tradition as unrelated to their experience, because, in the language of intentionality analysis, such an expression of doctrine is not an objectification of their religious experience—*not* because they don't understand philosophy, but because they *do* understand oppression and the dominative power of hierarchy relative to the marginalized. A similar application can be made relative to those women and men who see that collegial leadership must replace dominative power if the planet is to survive.[26]

To conclude, theological language which, although theoretically ad-equate, fails to express the values of collegiality, mutuality and coop-eration as manifestations of grace, for example, is an inadequate and truncated expression of the transcendent. When one's experience in prayer is allowed to produce new images and new language, one's the-ological language must also change so that new symbols can usher the community into a renewed experience of the Transcendent.

Most of all, a restructuring of the imagination must incorporate the

---

[25] Jonathan Culler, *On Deconstruction* (Ithaca, New York: Cornell University Press, 1982), Ch. 1.

[26] Matthew Lamb, "Christian Spirituality and Social Justice," *Horizons: Journal of the College Theology Society*, 10/1 (1983), 32-49.

experience of Christ, God's Word of Meaning. In Christ, the power of redemption and transformation is located in the helplessness of the Babe of Bethlehem and the Crucified of Calvary. The appropriateness of both expressions of God's meaning is endorsed and glorified in the experience of Resurrection.

Chapter 7

The Faces of Evil and Our Response: Ricoeur, Lonergan, Moore

Vernon Gregson

"The facts of good and evil, of progress and decline raise questions about the character of our universe."[1] These opening words of Lonergan's chapter on Religion in *Method in Theology* set the stage not only for the intellectual but also for the existential question about God. And not only for the existential question of whether I will believe in God, but also the existential question of whether I will collaborate with God to overcome evil and ensuing decline. In other words "the facts of good and evil" raise the soteriological question and raise that question in very personal terms, but with broad social implications. For Lonergan, soteriology is not primarily a doctrine addressed to the mind but a precept addressed to the heart, a heart which in the presence of God's love needs to acknowledge its complicity in the evil which calls for redemption, as well as its power, by God's grace, to collaborate in the redemptive process.

---

[1] Bernard Lonergan, S.J., *Method in Theology* (New York : Herder and Herder, 1972), 101.

This foundational inquiry will explore the subjectivity of the sote-riological project, enlisting in its aid Freud, Ricoeur, Moore and Lonergan. A significant contributing factor to the shifting foundation of theology is the intentional and symbolic recovery of subjectivity which has been occasioned by the transition from classical to historical consciousness. This essay employs the resources made available by the turn to subjectivity to reflect on the faces of evil and the dynamics of salvation.

Paul Ricoeur suggests that reflection best advances when it explores and interprets the narrative symbols which culture has formed. We will follow his lead at this point and reflect with him on the narrative structures which treat of the abundance of evil in our experience. What we hope to gain from this exploration is understanding of the concrete alternatives which our cultural and religious history offer us as we attempt to come to terms with the faces of evil.

For Ricoeur, the complex fact of the evil which we suffer and the evil which we do has given rise in human culture to four distinct types of symbolic narrative structures.[2] These narrative structures or myths individually and together serve to give at least a modicum of intelligibility and emotional plausibility to the origin and destiny of evil and to our response, as well as to God's response, to it. Three of these myths imaginatively explore the meaning and consequences of the primary locus of evil lying outside of our human will. They discover it either in the struggle of the gods before our creation, or in an indifferent or even malicious divine will, tragic to us, or in confining flesh in which we, as spirits, are seen to be imprisoned. The fourth myth uncovers the locus of evil in our own incomprehensible choices not to become who we might be, by not responding to or creating the values we might either foster or form. Ricoeur discovers this typology of symbolic narratives within our Western religious, philosophical, dramatic, and cultural traditions. The historian of religions, Wendy Doniger O'Flaherty, in her *The Origins of Evil in Hindu Mythology* confirms that this typology is pertinent to India's traditions as well.[3]

The first three myths find us to be either victims, as in the tragic myth; mere imitators of the gods, as in the Babylonian creation-out-of-conflict myth; or prisoners, whose destiny is to escape in knowledge

---

[2] Paul Ricoeur, *The Symbolism of Evil* (Boston: Beacon Press, 1969), 166-346.

[3] Wendy Doniger O'Flaherty, *The Origins of Evil in Hindu Mythology* (Berkeley: University of California Press, 1976).

and in fact from our bodies, as in the gnostic myth. Only in the fourth, the Adamic myth, are we primarily actors but where our action is seen to be uncreation, the choice of nothingness over substance, of vacuum over plenitude.

There is no doubt, if Ricoeur is at all accurate, that our religious, philosophical, dramatic, and cultural myths take evil, its origins and its dispositions seriously. But lest one imagine that those who originated the myths or who are in touch with the originating creativity of these myths, those in Ricoeur's "first naiveté," would through these myths either express or achieve a full sense of wholeness and unity with and within the cosmos, Ricoeur starkly reminds us otherwise.

> It is only in intention that the myth restores some wholeness; it is because he himself has lost that wholeness that man re-enacts and imitates it in myth and rite. The primitive man is already a man of division. Hence the myth can only be an intentional restoration or reinstatement and in this sense already symbolical.
>
> This distance between experience and intention has been recognized by all authors who have attributed to the myth a biological role of protection against anxiety. If myth making is an antidote to distress, that is because the man of myths is already an unhappy consciousness; for him, unity, conciliation, and reconciliation are things to be *spoken of* and *acted out*, precisely because they are not *given*.[4]

Ricoeur discovers the reason for the multiplicity of myths, then, in the fact that no single act of signifying "is equal to its aim."[5] No single act can accomplish even symbolically the unity we desire.

The recent work of Sebastian Moore[6] can serve at this point to shed at least some light on the bracing fact that not even our myths bring us wholeness except in intention. According to Moore, we are caught between memory and desire. We are caught between the memory, if it can be spoken of as such, of our unconscious union with the cosmos, a union which as a species we have left behind in becoming self-conscious

---

[4] *Symbolism of Evil*, 167-168.

[5] *Symbolism of Evil*, 168.

[6] Vernon Gregson, "Revisiting An Experiential Approach To Salvation," Seminar Report in *The Catholic Theological Society of America: Proceedings of the Thirty-Seventh Annual Convention* (June 10-13, 1982), 173-175.

and therefore human, and our desire for a now conscious union with all and with the All, which we can only long for either as gift or as achievement. The myths therefore both express our longing and structure it imaginatively and emotionally.

In the tragic myth, as it comes to expression in *Oedipus Tyrannus*, there is no release from the devious, capricious and malevolent will of the gods except the aesthetic one of recognition and tears, as we see our own fate acted out before us in the person of Oedipus. There is an undeniable truth in this tragic narrative. Our own experience, and that of others, too often seems perilously close to its portrayal. At times it would seem that we can do no more than honestly acknowledge a god who is wicked, and bemoan our fate. The god of tragedy, although "unthinkable," yet seems invincible at a certain recurrent level of our experience. Our bittersweet tears of recognition do not lie, nor do they necessarily capitulate. In the Babylonian creation-out-of-conflict myth, the *Enuma Elish*, there is on the other hand a triumph over evil, but that triumph is at the price of the sword of destruction. As Marduk triumphs over his chaotic progenitor Tiamat, so we too can be victorious over the evil that would devour us. But the God whom we ritually celebrate, and the gods over whom he has conquered, seem in the conflict to have lost in a decisive sense what divinity might be. There remains, however, a striking honesty in the conflict-creation myth. It speaks the truth about the existence of evil, particularly that aspect of evil of which I am not aware of being the author, and it dares to locate that evil in God. But God becomes diminished in the process and it is power rather than goodness which triumphs. Furthermore the evil of which I am author is not addressed, and therefore, ultimately, I am not addressed. I imitate in act and in cult Marduk's triumph, but I originate neither evil nor good and I am never face to face with God. I neither directly accuse nor am I accused. I do not ever pray for healing nor do I receive it. Our own bloody victories which participate in Marduk's indeed echo the past but they do not open to a future. There is to be no new creation, only identification with the original conflict-ridden one. Under the sun, there is to be nothing new.

For Ricoeur, the myth of conflict among the gods, in its truthful acknowledgment of our experience of evil outside us, is a brilliant attempt to make the tragic vision minimally intelligible. It almost achieves that, but it does not make the God that it uncovers worthy of worship.

In the gnostic myth of the evil body, we again find the evil that is outside us, the evil that is experienced as the other side of us, truthfully acknowledged. But now it is located not in the gods, but in the otherness of our bodies. The body and its passions are at war against us. The price of this "truth" is the conceptual reification of the divided self, forever in combat with itself, forever seeking in vain to escape from itself. We are "exiled souls," imprisoned in our bodies. Further, our body-prisons would entrap and seduce us into believing we are nothing more. We are tempted, then, either to ecstatically escape from our bodies or to ecstatically identify with them. Our memory of an original wholeness is obscured and our desire for final wholeness is rendered impossible. The ultimate, horrifying price of the "intelligibility" of our experience of evil which would be gained here, is eternal and recurrent fragmentation.

We have explored with Ricoeur three imaginal and intellectual scenarios which have served to give expression to and to shape our human experience of evil. We have tried with him to identify the elements of truth they contain and to suggest where they are less than adequate to the fullness of our experience and certainly to the fullness of our longing. But they are not the only expressions of our Western experience; and perhaps, if Ricoeur is correct, not even the focal one. That privileged position belongs to the Judaeo-Christian experience of an encounter with a demanding, a consoling, and ultimately a transcendent God. It is a myth which calls itself, and is, a history. In it we are, have been, and will be encountering God. That encounter is doubly revealing. We are unmasked in our power to act, in our powerlessness to act, and in our refusal to act and God is discovered to be accuser and friend. Freud is not off the mark in seeing in this encounter the contours of our parental relationships. The vis-à-vis with God finds us the accuser as well. The complaint of Job is not an aberration in the encounter with God. The accusations are mutual and we are deepened and humbled and made truthful in the process. *"Sunt lacrimae rerum"*—reality brings forth tears—holds for our encounter with God as well. Yet finally accusation can give way to truthfulness, and truthfulness to acceptance, and acceptance to wisdom and the possibility of joy. From the voice in the garden until the moment when all things are made new, a relationship is unfolded in the process of which it would not be rash to say that both parties are changed.

Ricoeur suggests that only a Christology can finally make the goodness of God credible in a world of our own and others' evil, in a world of our own caused and suffered evil. Only God's engagement in our struggle could make the goodness of God credible. We await the occurrence of that Christology either in fact or in recognition and manifestation. Ricoeur daringly, but I believe truthfully, also suggests that only when we ourselves have personally achieved the capacity for offered suffering will the world not be too wicked for God to be good, and even then, there remain the little children.[7] Evil then receives a face in the Judaeo-Christian symbolic narrative of history. That face is our own, and for Job and those who know his experience, that face is God's as well. Yet it is to that God that one pleads against that God. The encounter itself holds the promise that accusation is not the last word.

The projective character of at least the early stages of the Judaeo-Christian encounter with God ought not to obscure either the longing which it manifests on our part or the reality which is breaking through to us on God's part. For in the address by God we discover ourselves taken with new seriousness. There is in us the power to act and the call to act. If what is discovered is indeed our failure to act either wisely or well, still the manifestation of our own personal consciousness which occurs is a religious and cultural advance of decisive importance. We "are" before God. If the other myths speak the truth of the evil we suffer, the Adamic myth utters as well the truth of the evil we do. I say "as well" because Job persists to cry out in the face of the evil we suffer. As Ricoeur suggests, the parental accusation and consolation is pierced by Job's insistent complaint. After Job, consolation will not do, only a new wisdom and a new transcendence.

That new wisdom and transcendence Ricoeur discovers in the suffering servant and in the Christ. The complaint is still made. "My God, my God, why have you forsaken me," will always echo in Christian hearts as it echoed in the theological memory of the Gospel author. But the graced receptivity of Jesus turned that cry into a mercy for those who inflicted the pain and into a loving reconciliation with the Father who "required" it, not for his own sake but for ours. The evil that was *undergone* by Jesus became through his consent "an *action* capable of redeeming the evil....committed,"[8] even the evil inflicted by God. How that might be faces us with perhaps the profoundest mystery of the God-man encounter, a mystery which Ricoeur with characteristic daring yet with no less characteristic reverence seeks to explore.

---

[7] *Symbolism of Evil*, 325-326.

[8] *Symbolism of Evil*, 324.

Some would discover in the cruel suffering of Jesus—and their words echo in our memories and in our fears—the fitting capitulation of mercy to justice. The accusing and injured deity is at last assuaged, assuaged indeed by his own self-gift in the gift of his own dear son, but assuaged nonetheless. Paul Ricoeur expresses the point clearly and pointedly:

> ...there is no lack of "juridical theologies," which have understood substitutive suffering as a supreme way of salvaging the law or retribution. According to that schema, the suffering which is a gift would be the means by which mercy would give "satisfaction" to justice. In this mechanical balancing of the divine attributes, justice and mercy, the new quality of the offered suffering is swallowed up again in the quantitative law or retribution. [9]

Put simply, the death of Jesus paid back to the Father the penalty owed him for our sins. Mercy assuaged the demands of justice. One doesn't have to go as far as Freud who concluded that since the penalty Jesus paid to the Father was death, the crime must have been a primal murder of the Father, to see a rough approximation of retribution to offense operating here. Evil is strangely triumphant here even as it is vanquished. An eye remains the penalty for an eye, a tooth for a tooth.

Both a Jobian and a Christic complaint must be made at this point, and transcendence must be invoked to save a too vivid and, yes, a too timid immanence. If evil is the penalty for evil, then God is not God. Let us bring back Marduk and Oedipus. Or rather let us realize that we have never really left them. Goodness surely cannot and will not capitulate to evil, but rather, as Ricoeur suggests, it will itself humbly and through our own wills, transform evil into good. That at least is the Christian hope and that is the Christian prayer. It is as well both the vision and the expectation we have of God and, through his grace, of ourselves.

The mystery, and the little children, remain; but our experience of evil and of good achieves here an emotional plausibility which has both meaning and direction. The Adamic myth not only speaks truthfully about evil, both that which we suffer and that which we inflict, but it suggests, and through the suffering servant and the Christ, it can

---

[9] *Symbolism of Evil*, 325.

actually empower, the transformation of evil into a mysterious and redemptive good. The Adamic myth is rightly called revelation, because
it reveals who we are and who we may yet become, who God is, and
what mystery he is bringing to birth within the human family. The
symbol does give rise to thought, and can give rise to action.

It is this last Adamic myth which will be the focus of the remainder
of this paper. We will seek to explore its dynamic power and the
questions it raises about our human condition. I wish to attend in
particular to the question of the *lex talionis* and what it reveals about
human subjectivity. Why does that pattern of an eye for an eye, a tooth
for a tooth, tend to characterize so much of our moral, legal and even
our religious thought? Ironically, as we have noted, even that area of
theology, soteriology, whose precise goal would seem to be to reveal the
dynamics of a mercy which would break the *lex talionis* pattern is in
fact itself characterized by retributive thinking. Rather than breaking
that pattern, it succumbs to it. What is there about us that has led
our theological reflection to interpret the death of Jesus in penal terms,
that has given rise to theologies of compensation and satisfaction?

Here I am not raising the question of whether there are scriptural
warrants for these retributive interpretations. There surely are. But
why should the scriptural authors and later tradition use such categories to speak of the event of Jesus' death, particularly in the light of
Jesus' own attitude in his living and in his dying, which so obviously
breaks those categories? It is surely compassion, mercy and forgiveness
which are much more centrally manifested in the scriptural presentation
of Jesus' attitude even to those who betray him, kill him, or run away,
and, of special note, in Jesus' presentation of his Father's attitude.

Perhaps Freud and Ricoeur are correct in affirming that our God
concept is at base a projected God of "consolation" and "accusation,"
that we are all somehow haunted by a primitive feeling of nameless
guilt which seeks and even demands punishment. Perhaps that feeling, and the projected God which is in concert with that feeling, is so
strong that we will interpret even an event such as the death of Jesus,
which bears no obvious relationship to divine punishment, especially
to a punishment actually willed by God, as being in fact precisely a
substitutionary penalty. It is as if the possibility of a God beyond "consolation" and "accusation" is too frightening to bear, or to hope for.
And perhaps it is. For to suggest breaking the pattern of the equality of
justice, the *lex talionis*, is to suggest two frightening possibilities. The

first is that justice does not rule our cosmos, with the concomitant fear, such as Job experienced, that in fact something less than justice rules. And the second, moving in the opposite direction, is that if justice is not the law, then mercy is, and we ourselves will be called upon to respond, to personally respond, beyond justice and with mercy. Both are substantial and apparently justified fears. No wonder we hang on to old patterns. I take this to be the meaning of the statement Ricoeur referred to earlier. "The tragic vision always remains possible for all of us who have not attained the capacity for offered suffering. Short of this holiness of suffering, the question remains: Is not God wicked?"[10] In other words, the evidence in the world is that evil abounds or at least that it often bears little relationship to merit or blame, yet the challenge in face of that is not only to work for justice in human affairs but to go beyond justice to "offered suffering." Surely a challenge that we might well wish to avoid if at all possible! If we reflect on our own experience and that of others we can see how deeply the law of primitive equality and justice operates in each of us. Look at how we generally respond or at least want to respond to real or imagined injuries. Don't we, if we are honest with ourselves, find a deep-seated *lex talionis* in our bones and in our psyches? And when we see others or ourselves not responding with retribution, cannot our actual milder or even forgiving response at least sometimes be understood as reaction formation, as a denial of our real impulse and an unconscious substitution of a more socially acceptable emotion? Surely justice is the supreme law at least of our desires and we deceive ourselves if we deny it. The Hindus were surely convinced of this, although few of us are willing to follow their karmic speculation and conclude that a young child burned to death in a flaming house is merely suffering the consequences of his or her evil actions in a previous existence. Fortunately or unfortunately their in many ways courageous and speculatively elegant attempt to save justice doesn't emotionally wash. Closer to home, justice received a blow in the book of Job. Job's comforters comfort us for our losses as little as they comforted Job. Or rather they infuriate us as much as they infuriated Job when they attempted an adequation of loss with sin. The reality is that the character of our universe does not frequently call forth from our hearts a song to laud justice.

In this somber light, Ricoeur's formulation, and indeed affirmation

---

[10] *Symbolism of Evil*, 325.

about the need for offered suffering, is particularly striking, not least
because it appears to turn much of classical soteriology on its head.
Only the personal capacity for offered suffering can give us the perspective and indeed the courage to affirm that God is not wicked. The
cash value of Ricoeur's statement is that unless and until we ourselves
act as "suffering servants" our vision of God will be marred by an
insistent and nagging doubt about the goodness of God.

Can Ricoeur mean this? Is he saying that the priority is not the
realization that God is good and merciful and that therefore we have
been redeemed, but rather that we ourselves must be redeeming persons
before we can really believe that God is good and merciful? Not that
we are redeemed by Christ, but that unless we are redeeming persons,
we apparently cannot believe in the redemption?

I put the formulation in this pointed fashion because it highlights
the crucial subjectivity of Ricoeur's soteriological focus and formulation. But how do we become redeeming persons? Do we do so by our
own efforts of will? Or is it gift and freedom at once? And if it is gift
and freedom at once, what are its dynamics?

Ricoeur suggests a resolution to these questions in his presentation
of three scriptural figures who reveal human possibilities. We are Adam
who commits evil and is justly exiled as punishment. We are Job
who suffers unjust deprivation. And we can be the "suffering servant"
who turns the passivity of being victim into the activity of redemptive
consent to the evil that is undergone. These three alternatives exist for
our human condition. Adam represents the failure to act, at least the
failure to act wisely or well. Job represents the innocent victim who is
tempted to resentment and even greater passivity. And the suffering
servant represents the voluntary power to transcend the role of victim,
the power to "make of suffering, of the evil that is undergone, an *action*
capable of redeeming the evil that is committed."[11]

But how are we empowered to that action? Isn't the suffering servant a Bodhisattva or an Avatar, namely, a mythic figure, a symbolic
possibility? Or is it historical, either the Jewish people themselves
or, for Christians, the person of Jesus in his dying and in his rising?
And if the "suffering servant" is historical, how are we, how is our own
subjectivity affected by him?

It is here that Sebastian Moore in his explanation of the dynamics

---

[11] *Symbolism of Evil*, 324.

of the Christian in the presence of the Crucified [12] and of the disciples in the presence of their Master and Friend [13] can come to our aid. Some introduction to his analysis is in order.

Moore's explorations rely on the insights of depth psychology and of the Christian mystical traditions. But they are informed as well by a sensitivity to the scriptural texts. His inquiries serve in the first place to move Christian reflection beyond a "juridical soteriology" in which Christ merits "objective redemption" for us, which we by God's grace accept. And secondly his work serves to move reflection beyond alternative "moral" theories in which Jesus is effectively reduced to a model to be imitated. Moore takes Jesus' subjectivity, God's subjectivity, and our own subjectivity seriously and illuminates the dynamic interplay among them. In doing so he shows a possible working through of *our own* expectations of "consolation" and "accusation" as well as our view of God as characterized by those features.

Central to Moore's analysis is his understanding of sin. This understanding, which relies heavily on Lonergan, illuminates at the same time a question which has run throughout our inquiry; the question of the goodness of God. What is the relationship of the Transcendent to evil?

The key to understanding the precise character of the evil which is called "sin" is to understand *in what sense* it actually is *unreal* and yet has devastating reality as its consequences. Moore affirms that sin has "no being. The only kind of being it can have is the sight of itself in its ultimate effect, the crucified."[14] This view corresponds to and arises out of Lonergan's understanding of what he calls "basic sin,"[15] namely that failure of character, where, face to face with an obligatory moral good we fail both to bring about the good and, in fact, effect an evil, and in the same act, or rather non-act, we do not become who we might be. In my own terms, sin is the choice of vacuum rather than value, and that vacuum destroys. But what and how has this to do with Jesus? The refusal of Jesus' crucifiers of the personal transformation to which they were challenged by his message and by his person is precisely what

---

[12] Sebastian Moore, *The Crucified Jesus Is No Stranger* (New York: The Seabury Press, 1977).

[13] Sebastian Moore, *The Fire And The Rose Are One* (New York: The Seabury Press, 1980); Sebastian Moore, *The Inner Loneliness* (New York, Crossroad, 1982).

[14] *The Crucified Jesus*, 8.

[15] Bernard Lonergan, S.J., *Insight : A Study of Human Understanding* (New York: Philosophical Library, 1958) 666.

effected the crucifixion. Put simply, to respond to him they would have
had to break through the categories which bound them, and they chose
not to. Lonergan writes, "...basic sin is not an event;...it consists of
failure of occurrence, in the absence in the will of reasonable response
to an obligatory motive."[16] And, as evidenced in the death of Jesus,
that which "could and ought to be but is not"[17] has powerful effects,
the destruction of Jesus. The death of Jesus is the consequence of sin.

In Moore's study of human evil and the Crucified, he is searching
for the "linchpin,"[18] the intelligibility, not only, as we just suggested,
of the relationship between Jesus and his crucifiers but likewise of the
symbolic intelligibility of the transformation which occurs in the believer who allows the challenge of Jesus crucified to enter into his own
heart. In the crucifixion, the believer is faced with the irrational act,
the basic sin, of Jesus' crucifiers. Their irrational refusal to transcend
themselves results in the destruction of the Innocent one. But in the
objective destruction of Jesus, we the believers are also confronted with
what is our own "basic" sin, our own destructive rejection of the "fullness of life...which our own being dreads."[19] In the crucifixion, we see
lived out in history the drama in which each of us engages in our own
lives, our refusal to break the chains on our hope, our refusal to respond
to challenge and to value. "The art of contemplating Jesus crucified is
to come to understand...that the cross that I always first experience
as life's crucifixion of me is in reality my crucifixion of life."[20] In the
historically crucified we believers then are faced with the consequences
of the self-crucifixion which our own narrow ego inflicts both on others
and on itself. We crucify the resources of life, resources with which we
might have created not only ourselves but a world with others to the
praise of God. The death of Jesus makes explicit the persistent death
man inflicts both upon himself and upon others. Yet, paradoxically,
the very explicitness of the effects of the sin in the death of Jesus, and
God's response to it, entail not the victory of sin but its transformation. Moore suggests that there is deep fear within us that if we were
really known by God for the evil that is actually in our hearts we would

---

[16] *Insight*, 667 (Emphasis mine).

[17] *Insight*, 667.

[18] *The Crucified Jesus*, x ; cf. Vernon Gregson, *Lonergan, Spirituality And The
Meeting Of Religions* (Lanham, MD: The College Theology Society and The University Press Of America, 1984) 83-91.

[19] *The Crucified Jesus*, x.

[20] *The Crucified Jesus*, xii.

be rejected. With the crucifixion of Jesus, God's chosen Son, the evil in us is made manifest; the worst has been realized, the ultimate sin committed. And we await the inexorable *lex talionis*, we await retribution. But there is none. The act which would most surely provoke the talion law reveals it in fact to be ultimate illusion; God is not bound by any such supposed law. And the power of the illusion is broken. Three particularly illuminating passages from Moore develop this theme.

> The ultimate truth, which is God's unique embrace, is that the essential effect of sin—the crucified —is, identically, the healing. What sin ultimately *is*, is seen in the crucified. What sin ultimately *is*, is forgiven. For sin brought to its ultimate succumbs to God's love. It cannot be otherwise. It suffices for God to make our elusive evil explicit in crucifixion, for it to be no more.[21]

> What I have, in the sight of Jesus on the cross, is not the *motive* for believing in God's love so that this belief will *then* overcome my self-hatred, but the actual *process*, made visible, dramatized in the flesh, whereby my self-hatred reaches its climax of realization, avowal, confession and surrender. Man's self-hatred is not only the *obstacle* to his acceptance of God's love. It is the *medium* in which God's love is revealed to him as it transforms it. I meet God's love not be turning away from the hatred of myself to another motif, but as a climax of my self-hatred, its crisis and resolution. God does not just give me *reason* not to hate myself. He transforms my self-hatred into love. That is the meaning of the cross.[22]

> This is the ultimate mystery of us: that even our evil, even our tendency against wholeness, exposes us to the love of God. And it exposes us to that love in a way and at a depth to which even our desire for wholeness does not expose us. Jung insists that evil has to enter into our integration and charges Christianity with leaving it out. Jung is right about evil. It has to enter. In an unfathomable way it *desires* its own transformation. But evil enters in the total transformation only through crucifying Jesus.[23]

---

[21] *The Crucified Jesus*, 8-9.

[22] *The Crucified Jesus*, 37.

[23] *The Crucified Jesus*, 55.

The worst that our self-hatred and our hatred of others can do, the killing of God's anointed, has been done, and in the doing of it we are not condemned but forgiven.

Evil becomes the *felix culpa* not only of Adam's sin but of the sin of Jesus' crucifiers and of our own sin. Through the process of coming to terms with it we are redeemed. For Moore, evil is turned into sin and sin into grace.

This explanation of Moore's presents a symbolically and emotionally plausible dynamic of the believer's personal transformation in the presence of the Crucified. Seeing the effect of one's action or inaction so tragically and vividly expressed and yet seeing it responded to not with retribution but rather with mercy and forgiveness delivers a decisive rebuke to *lex talionis* and opens up the possibility of a confidence in God's love beyond "consolation" and "accusation". But so challenging and hence frightening is that possibility that it is no wonder that the event of Jesus' death finds resistance in our hearts to this new call to life and finds itself relentlessly interpreted in the psychically older and more comfortable terms of actually fulfilling the *lex talionis* rather than shattering it. There is something terribly resistant in us to spiritual maturity.

Moore's most recent writings[24] suggest a second symbolic dynamic which would lead to the stance of offered suffering and hence to that vision from which "the world would not be too evil for God to be good." This explanation focuses on the disciples and the desire for God which was awakened in them by Jesus. That desire for God which we almost dare not let surface because of our fear that it will not be fulfilled would have been aroused in the disciples by the person of Jesus and by his own intimacy with the Father. That very desire which had been brought to life by Jesus experienced a mortal crisis in the execution of Jesus, for that desire had been focused on and radically dependent on him. With his death therefore their desire was also thrown into the darkness of death. It dies with him. All that makes life significant had been brought to consciousness by Jesus and then brought to death by his death. The reality of the resurrection is that these dead men, those who were closest to him, passed through death, his death and their own, into new life. They were brought to life by the risen Jesus.

---

[24] *The Fire And The Rose Are One* (New York: Seabury, 1980) and *The Inner Loneliness* (New York: Crossroad, 1982); cf. Gregson, "Revisiting An Experiential Approach To Salvation."

For Moore, the criterion of the realism of our resurrection doctrine lies precisely in this. It was real enough to conquer the death of that desire and to bring it to life again with a confirmation and confidence it had never had before. The disciples had tasted psychic death and now they were alive again in a world made new to their eyes. Alive now not only with assurance but also with a mission to bring others alive by spreading the good news about Jesus.

This reading of the disciples' experience is most assuredly only a reading, but its emotional plausibility reveals a possible dynamic for our own confident emergence of our desire for God and the confirmation rather than destruction of our desire in the death and resurrection of Jesus.

Notice then in this last scenario what sin would be. It would be our holding on to our fears, our not allowing the release of our hope and our desire. It is there that the *lex talionis* would be found. We would not hope that we could get beyond retribution, would not hope that we could actually encounter either all the forgiveness we need or all the love we long for.

In conclusion, our exploration has sought to uncover elements in our cultural myths on the problem of evil, its origins and its disposition. We have taken a hard look at our own intransigence, at our own reluctance to let go, in Freud's and Ricoeur's terms, of the primal God of "accusation and consolation" and to search for and to discover the real Father, the transcendent divinity of love, of hope, and of desire.

Moore's rendering of the dynamics of our relationships with the Crucified brings our explanation to a close. As Ricoeur, Lonergan and Moore suggest, soteriology is not only or even primarily a doctrine for the understanding, but rather a grace to be received, an action to be lived.

Chapter 8

The Hermeneutic of Greek Trinitarianism: An Approach Through Intentionality Analysis

Eugene Webb

The hermeneutic challenge in the study of the history of Christian thought is a complex one. To the extent that this tradition of thought is an authentic expression of both spiritual experience and rational intelligence, it demands of the interpreter not only a sensitivity to the experience in question but also a willingness to insist upon the maximum of analytic clarity. Bernard Lonergan has developed what can hardly be doubted the most fully explicit analysis of theological method currently available, and it is also one that does not evade either of the demands just mentioned. I would like in this paper to discuss the theological applicability of Lonergan's "intentionality analysis" to the interpretation of the idea of the Trinity as it was developed in the fourth and fifth centuries by Greek Patristic thinkers.

The question of the meaning of Greek trinitarianism is a problem well worth studying in a Lonerganian perspective for two reasons: first, because renewed dialogue between the Eastern and Western churches will lead to a need for careful explication of basic concepts; and second, because Catholic theologians have so far given the distinctively Greek line of thought comparatively little study and have made little effort to relate it to systematic theology as subsequently developed. Though all subsequent trinitarian thought in both East and West has been founded on the conceptual and terminological distinctions made in the East in the fourth and fifth centuries, the focus of Catholic theologians has tended predominantly to bear on the western line of development from Augustine through Aquinas. Lonergan himself, in the last lines of that portion of his *De Deo Trino* translated into English as *The Way to Nicea*, has said, "Given that later systematization, however, it is only with the greatest difficulty that we who have inherited it can come to understand how the ante-Nicene authors could in fact have said what in fact they did say."[1] One might add that the same could be said of the post-Nicene Greek authors through Chalcedon. To discuss the terms and statements that were developed in this centrally formative period of the orthodox tradition through a consideration of what they could have been intelligently intended to mean by inquirers whose minds share with our own a common structure of intentionality should offer a valuable contribution to the hermeneutics of dogma, and perhaps also some useful preparation for the type of dialogue that would need to precede an actual rapprochement between the Eastern and Western Christian communions.

The method of intentionality analysis as I intend to employ it con- sists of the analysis of propositions into references to the particular types of object that may be intended by the various types of intentional operation analyzed by Lonergan in *Insight* and *Method in Theology*. One of the major potential contributions of this method to theology, I believe, is that it enables one to address questions of precise mean- ing without reductionism. It can seek specificity of reference without falling into the difficulties that have tended to beset the type of ana- lytic philosophy founded on empiricist psychology (with its tendency to assume a perceptionist epistemology) or on "ordinary language" (with its tendency to canonize what Lonergan has termed "commonsense"

---

[1] Bernard Lonergan, *The Way to Nicea: The Dialectical Development of Trini- tarian Theology*, trans. Conn O'Donovan (Philadelphia: Westminster Press, 1976), 137.

meaning). It can also seek specificity without ruling out the presence in religious experience of the unspecifiable. In fact, one of its advantages, as I hope to show, is that it can make clear the exact place and significance of the indefinable and unanalyzable in theological reflection without begging questions or letting enthusiasm for the numinous become an excuse for intellectual casualness in the areas in which analysis of meaning and critical verification have their own necessary role to play.

Briefly described, intentionality analysis involves specification of the objects of the four basic types of intentional operation as analyzed by Lonergan: attention, understanding, judgment, and decision. This categorization of types of human intentionality is, of course, familiar to any reader of Lonergan as is the reasoning by which he derives it from experience of cognitional process and reflection upon the basic questions of what we are doing when we are knowing and what we know when we do it. To explain Lonergan's analysis and his arguments for it in detail and to lead the reader through the process of experiential and critical self-appropriation of intentionality that a full understanding of its terms requires would take more space than an essay allows. It must suffice, therefore, simply to indicate that the method I mean to apply here consists of inquiry into the ways theological statements could be logically intended as references to the objects of the first three operations listed above: to objects of attention (data of sense and of consciousness), objects of understanding (ideas or intelligible possibilities), and objects of judgment (the real or actual, considered as that which may be known through correct understanding as determined by critical reflection upon both interpretation and evidence). These operations will sometimes be referred to in what follows as level 1, level 2, or level 3 operations respectively. They are related as levels of operation in that understanding presupposes some experiential data that can be construed in some pattern, and a judgment of truth presupposes that there is an interpretation that can be judged adequate or inadequate to the data it construes.

The intentional object proper to a level 1 operation will be referred to as an "empirical" object and is meant to encompass both data of sense and data of consciousness in so far as the latter are in any sense objective. A feeling, for example, can be noticed and brought to focal awareness by the act of attention; this renders it objective in the sense in which the term is used here. This is not to suppose, however, that all experience can be rendered objective. The actual performance of intentional operations is immediately experienced and therefore irreducibly subjective.

The object of a level 2 operation will be referred to as a "theoretical" object, by which it is meant that the object is theoretically conceivable even if its reality may remain questionable. What can not only be considered as a possibility but also critically verified will be called a "real" object.

Because the theological doctrines with which this essay will be concerned have to do not with world-immanent objects but with the personal and the transcendent, it will be helpful, in the case of an object known through critical judgment, to make a terminological distinction Lonergan has not himself made between a "real" object and an "existential" one. A "real" object, as was just explained, is that which can be not only understood but also judged real on the basis of evidence. By an "existential" object, on the other hand, I will mean the objective presence of a subject or, to be more precise, of the subject's manifestation in operations. By the term "subject" Lonergan referred to the performer of intentional operations.

The importance of the distinction between real and existential objects lies in the fact that subjectivity as such cannot except indirectly and analogously be the object of any intentional operation and is therefore "unspecifiable" in the sense mentioned above. One can inquire about a subject, and one can judge that there are sufficient signs of consciousness and purposefulness to warrant the judgment that observed behavior has its source in subjectivity, but strictly speaking one cannot focus attention on an objectively present subject, nor can one understand a subject through analysis of it into elements and their relations. One can analyze the operations in which subjectivity manifests its presence, but the subject as such is not directly observable or intelligible and therefore cannot, I would suggest, be "known" in the strict sense, although it can be "known about" through inference and its presence can be experienced immediately in the performance of intentional operations.

To speak of operations as "intentional" implies that they involve both a subjective and objective aspect. The "subject" is the one who does the intending. The "object" is what is intended. The term "intentional" implies the presence of both subjectivity and an object. An operation may be termed "intentional" in that its subject consciously performs it, i.e., experiences immediate self-presence in the operation and by this experiential self-presence controls its performance and directs it toward what is intended. The term "consciousness" will be used in this paper to refer to the experiential self-presence of a subject in the performance of intentional operations—his awareness, that is, of his intending and of what he intends.[2]

It will be useful for the purposes of the present analysis to distinguish between the subject as "immanent" and the subject as "transcendent." The subject is self-present in each operation; in this sense the subject may be referred to as "immanent" in the operation, i.e., the subject experiences immediate self-presence as consciously performing the operation. If a single subject performs more than one operation, then the subject is "transcendent" in relation to each of the operations. The term "transcendent" as used here does not mean that the subject stands beyond or apart from operations but rather that one and the same subject can be immanent in a variety of individual operations. This distinction between the subject considered as immanent and as transcendent can be helpful, as I hope to show subsequently, in interpreting the relation between the Patristic conceptions of *ousia* and *hypostasis* in trinitarian theology.

Kierkegaard was more directly concerned than Lonergan with the question of what it means to speak of transcendent subjectivity. It may therefore prove helpful to consider him briefly in connection with the present theme, since what he had to say has a bearing on theological as well as psychological and epistemological issues. In his *Philosophical Fragments* Kierkegaard speaks of the paradoxical character of the drive to know objectively the subjective, and he suggests that this concern is the moving force of all fully conscious inquiry:

> ...for the paradox is the source of the thinker's passion, and the thinker without a paradox is like a lover without feeling: a paltry mediocrity. But the highest pitch of every passion is always to will its own downfall; and so it is also the supreme passion of the Reason to seek a collision, though this collision must in one way or another prove its undoing. The supreme paradox of all thought is the attempt to

---

[2] Bernard Lonergan, *Method in Theology* (New York: Herder and Herder, 1972), 7-10.

discover something that thought cannot think.[3]

The goal of discovery Kierkegaard refers to here is subjectivity, which thought cannot think because thought cannot reduce it to an idea, i.e., to an object of intellection. But he also has something further in mind, as he makes clear a few pages later, where he identifies the paradoxical object thought seeks with God, who for Kierkegaard is pure, transcendent subjectivity.

> But what is this unknown something with which the Reason collides when inspired by its paradoxical passion, with the result of unsettling even man's knowledge of himself? It is the Unknown. It is not a human being, in so far as we know what man is; nor is it any other known thing. So let us call this unknown thing something: *the God.*[4]

The relevance for theology of this conception of God—as transcendent subject who manifests his presence in operations but who cannot himself be objectified for thought—should be clear when one remembers the role that the apophatic emphasis has played in Christian theology. Kierkegaard's thought on this matter virtually echoes that of St. Basil of Caesarea as quoted and commented upon by the Russian Orthodox theologian, Vladimir Lossky:

> God manifests Himself by His operations or energies. 'While we affirm,' says St. Basil, 'that we know our God in his energies, we scarcely promise that he may be approached in his very essence. For although his energies descend to us, his essence remains inaccessible.' This passage from the letter to Amphilocus. . . will have an importance of the first order for the doctrine of the vision of God. Byzantine theologians will often quote this authority in formuating [sic] the distinction between the inaccessible *ousia* and its natural processions, the *energeiai* or manifesting operations.[5]

---

[3]Soren Kierkegaard, *Philosophical Fragments,* trans. David Swenson and Howard Hong (Princeton: Princeton University Press, 1967), 46.

[4]Kierkegaard, 49.

[5]Vladimir Lossky, *The Vision of God,* trans. A. Moorhouse (London: The Faith Press and Clayton, Wisc: American Orthodox Press, 1963), 65; quoting Basil, Letter 234.

To speak in such a way carries language and thought to their farthest reach, beyond which lies the silence of non-discursive contemplation. For the present purpose, however, what is important is the distinction between what can be objectively analyzed and what cannot. Any statement that purports to designate or express an understanding of anything at all, whether actual or merely possible, must refer to what can function at least in some aspect as the object of some intentional operation, since apart from such operations it is not possible for a human inquirer to intend anything.

It is on this point that Lonergan's analysis of intentional operations is useful. There are, of course, many ways in which intending can take place, but one of the great values of Lonergan's analysis of cognitional process is that it demonstrates the reducibility of all forms of intention to the basic types described above or to combinations of the same. This makes it possible to sort out what could otherwise be a confusing plethora of meanings and to determine the conditions under which an actual intention can take place. The latter point is of considerable importance for the philosopher or the historian of thought, since it is possible that some statements, including some that may have become uncritically sacrosanct either to religious or to secular common sense, may upon analysis be discovered incapable of expressing any actual intention.

With these methodological reflections in mind it should now be possible to consider how intentionality analysis can be used to clarify the meaning of theological propositions. As was mentioned earlier the example here chosen for analysis will be the Trinitarian theology that developed in the fourth and fifth centuries among the Greek Fathers. This will be treated as a development that culminated in the Christological definition of the Council of Chalcedon in 451 AD. It is appropriate to consider this a distinct unit in Christian intellectual history, since after Chalcedon there were no further enduring new conceptions of trinitarianism on the part of the Greeks. The distinctly Latin development under the influence of Augustine of Hippo and of Marius Victorinus before him followed a different line of reasoning (that of analogy of the three "Persons" to the components of a human mind) and had its major influence after Chalcedon and then almost exclusively in the West.

An important benefit of an approach by way of intentionality analysis to the development of the doctrine of the Trinity, therefore, is that it can do much to clarify the difference between the Western and Eastern conceptions of the doctrine. It is a commonplace in the history of this issue that the Greek Fathers took their point of departure from our knowledge of the three concrete hypostases and went on to affirm their unity of essence *(ousia)* whereas the Latin line of thought took its point of departure from belief in the absolute unity of God and then inquired as to what there could be said to be three of within that unity. To phrase this in terms of the principles of intentionality analysis, the Greek discussion began with reference to what are known as three distinct objects of intention, whereas the Latin began with consideration of the unity of the subject who is God. Intentionality analysis can fit readily into the Greek line of thinking, since it can address itself to the question of what kinds of intentional objects *prosopa, hypostases, physeis,* and *ousiai* could be interpreted to be. The Latin approach, on the other hand, since it proceeds by analogy and inquires not into objects in the proper sense but into the self-relatedness of a subject, would seem to require a quite different method of analysis.

Much of the fourth and fifth century Greek discussion of the developing doctrine of the Trinity was a gradual process of distinguishing the meanings of the terms just mentioned, especially *ousia, physis,* and *hypothesis,* to the point that they could eventually function with the precision they do in the Chalcedonian definition. Just how gradual a process this was can be seen from the fact that although the Cappadocians developed a clear conception of the distinctions by the middle of the fourth century, numerous important figures, such as Athanasius and Jerome, continued to equate their meanings right up to the time of Chalcedon.[6] At that council, however, it was the generally agreed distinctions between *ousia, physis,* and *hypostasis* that made it possible to state an exact conception of their relations in the person of the incarnate Son. It will be helpful to consider the process by which these terms gradually took on the meanings they were to have.

During the course of its development the concept of *ousia* in theology took on several quite different meanings.[7] The initial ambiguity had to do with whether *ousia* referred to some kind of ethereal "matter" or "stuff" (which could at least in principle, therefore, be an object of sensory experience or of imagination), or to an intelligible form or generic definition (an object of intellection), or to the innermost, deeply

---

[6] Bernard Lonergan, *De Deo Trino: Pars Analytica* (Rome: Gregorian University Press, 1961), 206.

[7] George L. Prestige, *God in Patristic Thought* (London: SPCK, 1952), 190-192.

hidden core of subjectivity. In the last meaning, *ousia* would signify the divinity considered as an "existential object," in the sense in which this term was defined above.

There are examples in Patristic usage of all three meanings, but on the whole the divine *ousia* was identified primarily with that which is expressed not in a definition but in the divine "I AM," i.e., in a statement expressing the existential presence of the divine subject. The fundamental tendency in Greek Patristic usage, therefore, was toward the use of the term *ousia* neither in the empirical nor in the generic sense but in the existential. Such figures as, for example, Hippolytus, Athanasius, and Epiphanius explicitly rejected the generic sense in favor of the existential when applying the term to God.[8]

By the fourth century no theologian considered the divine *ousia* to be composed of any kind of matter. There was less agreement, however, regarding the question of whether it could be properly and not just analogously the object of an act of intellection. The writings of Basil of Caesarea can serve as an example of the ambiguity of discussions regarding this point. On the one hand, Basil could say that "the distinction between ousia and hypostasis is the same as that between the general and the particular; as for instance, between the animal and the particular man."[9] This would clearly place God in a genus and thereby make his *ousia* an object of intellection. On the other hand Basil also stated explicitly, as cited above in the passage from Lossky, that the divine *ousia* cannot be an object of human understanding because we know God from his operations, not from intellection of his essence (*ousia*). The operations attest the presence of a subject as their source. We can know *that* he is, in other words, but except that he is identified as the subject of operations, we do not know *what* he is. In the same place Basil also objected against those who insisted on a statement of the intelligible form of the divine *ousia*: "if I confess I am ignorant of the essence, they turn on me again and say, So you worship you know not what. I answer that the word to know has many meanings."[10]

---

[8] Prestige, 160, 167. This tendency continued also in the Latin tradition, as is exemplified in Aquinas' denial that God is composed of matter and form or that God is in any genus. (See *Summa Theologica*, I, q. 3, a. 2 and a. 5.)

[9] Letter 236, 6; quoted in J. Stevenson, *Creeds, Councils, and Controversies: Documents Illustrative of the History of the Church AD 337-461* (London: SPCK, 1973), 15.

[10] Letter 234; quoted in Stevenson, 116.

Basil did not specify what those meanings might be, but his words suggest the relevance of an analysis in terms of cognitional operations and their objects. It is one thing to know through experience some datum of sense or consciousness. It is another to know the intelligible as a formal possibility. And it is something else quite different to believe in the existential presence of the divine "I Am," which cannot be expressed in any definition and does not answer to the question "what?" but rather to the question "who?".

That *ousia* in the fully developed orthodox Trinitarian theology of the fourth century referred to the existential core of subjectivity rather than to categorical contents is clear from the way fourth century theologians conceived of the relation between *ousia* and *hypostasis*, which came to be used to refer to a concretely objective presence of the subject who was the *ousia*. As Prestige described it in a discussion of the usage of Athanasius,

> [t]his term [*hypostasis*]...is commonly translated Person, but
> it does not mean an individual person in the ordinary sense.....
> Applied to God, it expresses the idea of a solid and self-
> supported presentation of the divine reality. All the quali-
> ties which modern speech associates with personality, how-
> ever, such as consciousness and will, are attributed in Greek
> theology to the complementary term of the definition; they
> belong to the divine substance [*ousia*], the single being of
> God, and to the several "Persons" only by virtue of their
> embodiment and presentation of that unique being.[11]

Such "embodiment and presentation" of essential subjectivity is precisely the function of what was defined above as the "existential object."

The term *prosopon* is closely related to *hypostasis*, but it was also sufficiently distinct in meaning to have been preserved in the Chalcedonian definition as a separate term. According to Prestige, "strictly speaking, *prosopon* was a non-metaphysical term for 'individual,' hypostasis a more or less metaphysical term for 'independent object'."[12] The emphasis of *prosopon* (which could be translated by "face" as well as by "person") was an objective presence as apprehended, i.e., as an

---

[11] George L. Prestige, *Fathers and Heretics* (London: SPCK, 1948), 92.
[12] Prestige, *God in Patristic Thought*, 179.

object of experience or understanding. The emphasis of *hypostasis* was on the same concrete phenomenon as able to stand up to verification, i.e., as objectively real.

From the point of view of intentionality analysis, the relations between *prosopon, hypostasis,* and *ousia* in the Greek doctrine of the Trinity presupposed by the Council of Chalcedon, can be logically interpreted as involving a successive series of steps in the penetration to the existential core of an instance of concrete, objective presence of the subject who is God. This can be formulated as follows:

Prosopon would refer to the empirical perceptibility (in the case of the incarnate Son) and the intelligibility (in the cases of each of the hypostases) of the divine presence as manifested in particular operations. In terms of the theoretical framework assumed in this paper, the *prosopon* could be said to constitute the subsidiary or implicit "theoretical" object of the level three operation by which the concrete presence of the divine subject is known; i.e., it helps to define the focus of the operation of judgment. For the Greek Fathers, the operations of the Persons distinguished them and rendered them individually identifiable. It was a commonplace that the characteristic operation of the Father was to be the eternal source of all that is, that of the Son was to be revelation (i.e., presentation or manifestation), and that of the Spirit was to be sanctification.

Hypostasis would refer to the concreteness or objective actuality of such an identifiable and distinguishable presence. It constitutes the "real" object of the operation of judgment: "objective" in that it can be inquired into and known by way of intentional operation: "real" in that it is judged to be actual and not just conceivable or imaginary.

Ousia would refer to the inner core of subjecthood, the "I Am," wholly present in each hypostasis as the transcendent subject immanent in each. It constitutes the "existential" object that is affirmed when one judges that this real object (the *hypostasis*) is the presence of the one subject who is true God. As that which cannot be defined but only named as God, the *ousia* is unanalyzable into elements and therefore transcends intellection absolutely (since intellection involves discerning relations among elements). Here is found the inherently unspecifiable actuality of God, which is approachable only through apophasis, the way of negation.

Despite his somewhat different terminology, this analysis accords exactly with Prestige's comment that "when the doctrine of the Trinity finally came to be formulated as one *ousia* in three *hypostases*, it implied that God, regarded from the point of view of internal analysis, is one object [i.e., one subject or existential object]; but that regarded from the point of view of external presentation, He is three objects [i.e., real objects]; His unity being safeguarded by the doctrine that these three objects of presentation are not merely precisely similar, as the semi-Arians were early willing to admit, but, in a true sense, identically one."[13] Prestige phrased it in his own graphic analogy:

> ...if Christianity is true, the same stuff or substance of deity in the concrete has three distinct presentations–not just three mutually defective aspects presented from separate points of view, in the sense that the Matterhorn has a northern face and an eastern face and an Italian face, but three complete presentations of the whole and identical object, namely God, which are nevertheless objectively distinct from one another.[14]

To make the same point in the language of intentionality analysis, the Greek Fathers believed that God could be discovered as an objective presence along three lines of inquiry terminating in three distinct objects of understanding and judgment, each of which manifests the presence of a single subject who is present as a whole in each of the three. As Prestige phrased it, for the Greek Fathers, "as seen and thought, He is three; as seeing and thinking, He is one."[15] Or to stated it in my terms: as "real object" God is three; as "existential object" God is one.[16]

---

[13] *God in Patristic Thought*, 169.

[14] *God in Patristic Thought*, 168.

[15] *God in Patristic Thought*, 301.

[16] The idea that God is a single subject who is nevertheless three real objects could perhaps sound implicitly Sabellian, but Basil himself argued against Sabellianism in a way that can help to clarify the central issue. Basil's argument correlates closely with the terms of intentionality analysis as defined and applied in this paper. His objection was that "....merely to enumerate the differences of Persons (*prosopa*) is insufficient; we must confess each Person (*prosopon*) to have an existence in real *hypostasis*. Now Sabellius did not even deprecate the formation of the persons without *hypostasis*, saying as he did that the same God, being one in matter (*to hypokeimeno*) was metamorphosed as the need of the moment required, and spoken of now as Father, now as Son and now as Holy Ghost." (Letter 210, 5; quoted in Stevenson, *Creeds, Councils, and Controversies*, 112) Basil argued, in other words, that neglecting the question of the actuality of the *hypostasis* as real

The basic issue of the identity of *ousia* in the three objective *hy-postases* can be stated more explicitly in terms of a distinction between transcendent and immanent subjectivity. On the one hand, God, the one divine subject, considered as trinitarian Person or *hypostasis*, is immanent in the hypostatic operations and is in this sense intelligible as theoretical object by way of the characteristics he manifests in the operations. On the other hand, God, as the single identical subject of all the operations, is transcendent in relation to the operations that distinguish the *hypostases*. In the context of such an analysis, there-fore, God must be interpreted as one subject who is objectively present in his entirety in the intelligible and affirmable reality of three distinct objective presentations.

This consideration of the history of usage in the fourth century makes clear what the Council of Chalcedon was affirming in its en-dorsement of the trinitarian teaching that came to it from the Councils of Nicea and Constantinople, and it establishes the meanings of the terms *homoousion*, *ousia*, and *hypostasis*, in the Chalcedonian defini-tion. *Ousia* developed in the Greek theological milieu into a technical term referring to the existential reality of the one divine subject man-ifest in each of three concrete presentations (the *hypostases*). Among these, the Son was also phenomenally distinct (as *prosopon*) as well as distinctly knowable (as *hypostasis*) through a judgment of his ob-jective historical reality. The term *homoousion*, which Nicea had left undefined, took on in this context of usage the clear meaning of a refer-ence to the single identity of the one transcendent subject in the three *hypostases*. There was one God, in other words, who was concretely present as a whole in three presentations, each of which could be indi-vidually considered, inquired into, conceived of, and judged to be a real object (*hypostasis*) that was the actual presence of a single existential object (the concretely present *ousia*). The Father could be understood as the source beyond the world of presence of both the Son and the

objects of the operation of critical judgment, Sabellius reduced the objectivity of the Persons to something merely phenomenal. He treated them, that is, as objects only of experience and understanding, but not of judgment. For further discussion of Sabellianism, see Prestige, *God in Patristic Thought*, 160-162. Cf. Prestige, *Fa-thers and Heretics*, explaining the thought of St. Athanasius: "The entire difference between the Persons is one not of content but of manner. Nothing whatever exists to differentiate between the Father, the Son, and the Spirit except the difference of aspect with which each presents the whole reality of God. God exists Fatherwise, Sonwise, and Spiritwise..." (93)

Spirit in the world. The Son was knowable as the God-man in whom
the one divine subject (*ousia*) became incarnate as the performer of
human operations. And the Holy Spirit was the immanent, dynamic
presence of the same divine subject within God-man which he, operating as man, could reflect upon, inquire about, experience in immediacy,
and judge to be the presence of God within him. The title "Christ"
("anointed") as attributed to Jesus was a reference to the fact of the
abiding presence of the Holy Spirit as the principle of his inner life and
actions and was so understood in Patristic thought. The status of each
of the trinitarian hypostases as affirmed reality lay in the fact that each
could be known objectively by way of distinct lines of inquiry.

The focus of the Chalcedonian definition is not the doctrine of the
Trinity (which it presupposes), but its major corollary, the Incarnation.
The principal contribution of Chalcedon to the theology of the Incarnation lay in the clear distinction it made between *physis* and *hypostasis*.
Its use of the term *hypostasis* carried forward that developed in the
Trinitarian controversies of the preceding century. The only difference
lay in the emphasis placed on the fact that the *hypostasis* was the presence of a subject. For the earlier discussion what was emphasized was
that each *hypostasis* was an *objective* presentation of the divine subject;
for Chalcedon the emphasis lay on the fact that the second *hypostasis*
was an objective presentation of the divine *subject*. Chalcedon was concerned with the way in which one subject could be interpreted as the
point at which two natures became linked. The Chalcedonian explanation of the Incarnation was in essence that one and the same subject,
objectively knowable as the second *hypostasis*, could and did perform
operations according to the operative capacities of both the divine and
the human natures. The Chalcedonian definition does not, however, express the point in exactly this language. It will be necessary therefore
to consider the possibilities of meaning implicit in the definition itself,
especially with regard to the meaning of the term *physis* or "nature."

Physis can be interpreted in two ways, one essentialistic and the
other what might be called dynamic. In the essentialistic use of the
term, the "nature" of a thing is equivalent to its intelligible form or
"essence." In this use of "nature" it must be considered as the focal
object only of a level two operation.

A dynamic conception of *physis* or nature, on the other hand, would
be quite different. In this use of the term, the *physis* or "nature" of a
thing would be that which determines its operative capacity. If *physis*

is interpreted in the latter way in connection with the Chalcedonian definition, then its reference to the human *physis* refers to the capacity for specifically human operations, i.e., operations determined by the limiting conditions imposed on operations by the characteristics of a human organism. Since for Chalcedon the doctrine of the Incarnation has to do not with a static object of contemplation, but with concrete human operations on the part of God become man, it is clear that the term *physis* here must be interpreted in the dynamic sense, i.e., as referring to that which determines operative capacity.

Evidence for this interpretation can be found in the historical context as well. Part of this is the Tome of Leo, addressed to the council, which speaks of Christ as involving two "forms" (i.e., natures) in such a way that "each 'form' does the acts which belong to it, in communion with the other; the Word, that is, performing what belongs to the Word, and the flesh carrying out what belongs to the flesh ....".[17] This statement involves some ambiguity, since in the case of the human nature ("the flesh") it could on the face of it be interpreted as though it meant the nature were the subject of the operations, but it seems clear that what Leo actually intended was the idea that there is one divine Person ("the Word") who as subject performed operations by way of the human nature as well as by way of the divine nature. Leo stated this more clearly in a subsequent letter (after the Council) explaining the meaning of the Tome and trying to win support for the Chalcedonian definition: "...the actions were of one Person all the time...but we perceive from the character of the acts what belongs to either form."[18]

An additional part of the historical context is the use of the term *physis* among the Cappadocians, for whom, according to Prestige, the term was descriptive and bore on function, as compared with *ousia*, which was more metaphysical and bore on reality.[19] In the sixth century an essentialistic conception of *physis* did become prominent along with a similarly essentialistic conception of *ousia*, with which it came to be treated as virtually synonymous, but that was a later development.[20] At Chalcedon it is clear both that *physis* had to do with operative ca-

---

[17] Henry R. Percival, ed. *Nicene and Post-Nicene Fathers 14: The Seven Ecumenical Councils of the Undivided Church: Their Canons and Dogmatic Decrees* (Grand Rapids, Mich: Eerdmans, 1979), 256.

[18] Stevenson, *Creeds, Councils and Controversies*, 344.

[19] Prestige, *God in Patristic Thought*, 234.

[20] *God in Patristic Thought*, 273-275.

pacity and that it was distinct from *ousia*.

What, however, can be meant specifically by the concept of the divine *physis*, if *physis* is interpreted as the determinant of operative capacity? In the case of the human *physis* of Christ, what is referred to is the capacity to perform human operations. God operating as man in Jesus was able, this would imply, to operate under conditions of limitation, to perform cognitive operations, asking questions and seeking answers, moving from ignorance to knowledge by rational operations, and also to suffer pain as well as experience pleasure, emotional satisfaction, distress, and so on. It was such a capacity in Jesus that the Chalcedonian definition affirmed by the phrase "truly man, of a reasonable soul and body." To operate according to the capacity determined by the divine *physis*, on the other hand, would be to operate without such limitations. The term "divine nature," therefore, must refer to the absence of limiting conditions.

At this point it may be useful to clarify the ambiguity of the term "divine" in the Chalcedonian context. Like any other term that may be used to refer to the object of an act of judgment, it may be intended to refer either to the object as intelligible or to the object as actual. In the first case the term will designate a conceptual category; in the second it will designate the existential object, i.e., the actual subject. In the terminology of the Chalcedonian theology as explicated in the present analysis, when the term is used to refer to the divine nature, "divine" implies categorization: there is a category labeled "natures," with such subcategories as "divine," "human," "animal," etc. When used to refer to the existential object, on the other hand, the term "divine" refers to the subject of the operations manifested in the *hypostases*. Since this subject is interpreted not only as immanent in particular operations but also as transcendent in relation to both categories of operation, there is a single, identical subject who is the agent of each. This means that it is one and the same divine subject (i.e., God) who is the source of human operations and of operations that are divine in the categorial sense (i.e., operations according to the capacity of the divine nature).

The possible ambiguity of the term "divine" in the discussion of the Chalcedonian definition lies in the possibility of trying to apply it without the distinction between these two meanings to the operations of the God-man and to the subject who was incarnate as the God-man. What could be logically intended by speaking of the human intentional operations of the God-man as "divine" is not that they are operations of the divine nature, for this would imply that they lacked those limitations that make human intentionality possible. This is what the definition excludes when it speaks of "the distinction of natures" as "being by no means taken away by the union, but rather the property of each nature being preserved..." What it could logically mean, however, is precisely what is implied by the continuation of the statement just quoted: "...and concurring in one *prosopon* and one *hypostasis*, not parted or divided into two *prosopa*..." "Divine," in other words, has one meaning in reference to the divine nature and another in reference to the subject of both divine and human operations. The first is categorial; the second what might be called "nominative," i.e., it names the subject as "God" and thereby indicates him without defining him. To use the categorial meaning with reference to the subject would be to confuse an object of intellection with an object of judgment or a theoretical object with an existential object.

It would also undermine the central point of the Chalcedonian theology, which is that God, the divine subject, could and actually did become a man in the proper, literal sense of the word. This is something God could not do if he were limited to operating only according to the capacity of the divine nature, i.e., to performing only unlimited operations. The Chalcedonian affirmation is that the same transcendent subject who performs divine (in the categorical sense) operations could and actually did perform genuinely human operations, i.e., operations in which he operated not "as God" (i.e., without limitations) but "as man" (i.e., in a manner involving all the limitations characteristic of human operations).

As noted earlier, Lonergan's position was that consciousness is the experiential self-presence of a subject in operations; it is the subject's immediate experience, that is, of performing the operations in question and intending what they intend.[21] Applied to the Chalcedonian theology, this would imply that operating as man the divine subject is humanly conscious. It could also imply that operating as God (i.e., in a way that is not subject to limiting conditions) the divine (in the nominative sense) subject is divinely (in the categorial sense) conscious. A subject is conscious in his operations (i.e., he operates consciously), and therefore he is conscious in a way determined by the character of the operation. Consciousness, in other words, belongs to the subject

---

[21] See *Method in Theology*, 8.

as a function of the subject's operations and therefore of the "nature" according to which they are performed. Interpreted in such terms, the doctrine of divine Incarnation means that the one God could and actually did in a humanly conscious manner perform human intentional operations: experiencing, wondering, inquiring, interpreting, verifying, deliberating, deciding, and acting in a genuinely human way with all the limitations that are essential to genuine human consciousness. This is clearly what was implied at Chalcedon in the affirmation that the same Jesus Christ who was "truly God" was also "truly man, of a reasonable soul and body" and "in all things like unto us, without sin." [22]

It was such an understanding of the doctrine of Incarnation that culminated the line of inquiry running from the Cappadocians to Chalcedon. It was to clarify this central mystery of the Christian faith that the doctrine of the Trinity was developed. The distinction between the divinity of the Father and that of the Spirit-filled Son was implicit in the early Christian belief that in some as yet undefined way God had become man in Jesus. The development of the Trinitarian doctrine with its distinctions between *prosopon, hypostasis, ousia,* and *physis* made it possible for the bishops assembled at Chalcedon to state with concrete understanding and precision of expression the belief that the one eternal subject Who is God did without change take on the limitations of human nature and live both objectively and subjectively as a concrete human person, a man among men. What they achieved in the way of understanding through that long effort of clarification is easily lost sight of, especially if the imagination seizes on their terms and uses them imprecisely and in a reifying way. One of the great benefits of the methodological clarity to which Lonergan has contributed so much in his study of human intentionality is the possibility it offers of preserving (or perhaps recovering) what the Fathers won through such labor and bequeathed to the faithful of both East and West.

---

[22] Philip Schaff, *The Creeds of Christendom with a History and Critical Notes,* 2 (New York: Harper and Brothers, 1877), 62

Chapter 9

Cognitional Theory and the Role of Experience: Whitehead and Lonergan Contrasted

John C. Robertson

There are arresting similarities (at least at a formal level) between the respective philosophical works of Alfred North Whitehead and Bernard F. Lonergan. First, both accept and adhere to some version of the "subjectivist principle" of post-Cartesian philosophy.[1] That is, both break with what we might call "extroverted" types of thinking which begin directly with the external world of nature. For various reasons Whitehead and Lonergan believe such thinking misleading, indeed naive, and impossible for philosophy in its critical and post-critical phases. Rather they take the self's or subject's knowledge of itself as the privileged ac-

---

[1] See Alfred North Whitehead, *Process and Reality: An Essay in Cosmology* (New York: The Macmillan Co., 1929), chap. VII (Hereafter: *P.R.*) and Bernard J.F. Lonergan, S.J., *The Subject* (Milwaukee: Marquette University Press, 1968), *passim*.

cess to reality. Philosophy then for both men is nothing less than a fully-reflective form of self-understanding. Second, both men contend, however, that in knowing ourselves we know more than ourselves, inasmuch as the self provides us not only with a starting point for reflection but also with a paradigmatic *sample* of reality. In Lonergan's words, there is an "isomorphism that obtains between the structure of knowing (which self-knowledge grasps) and the structure of the known," which allows us to see that the "affirmation of oneself as a knower" contains also "an affirmation of the general structure of any proportionate object knowledge."[2] To understand ourselves is to understand also "the invariant form for which the sciences provide the variable matter."[3] Similarly Whitehead's "categorial scheme" is an extrapolation of the experiential occasion which the human subject himself is. Thus, Whitehead and Lonergan, while beginning with a cognitional theory based on the subject's self-understanding decline to believe with most moderns that an acceptance of the "subjectivist principle" must lead to a non- or anti-metaphysical position but hold rather that metaphysics is permitted and even required in order to render that self-understanding fully intelligible. Nor do they retreat from philosophy's traditional theistic orientation, for they contend that God is required as "the chief exemplification" of the transcendental categories exemplified by proportionate being.[4] As vital as this last point is to the role of religion in contemporary culture, discussion of the two positions at that level must be preceded by detailed comparison of the prior and more basic issues. This task, therefore, is the one taken up in this essay.

In his contribution to the 1970 International Lonergan Congress, Schubert M. Ogden, a thinker most indebted to Whitehead's process philosophy, calls attention to these formal similarities. He writes, "that we have here two philosophical-theological approaches which are strik-

---

[2] Bernard Lonergan, S.J., *Insight: A Study of Human Understanding.* Second (students') edition, revised. (London: Longmans, Green and Co.; and New York: Philosophical Library, 1958), 399, 523. (Hereafter: *Insight*)

[3] *Insight*, 498. See also Whitehead, *Modes of Thought* (New York: Capricorn Books, 1938; reprint 1958), chaps. VII-IX.

[4] *P.R.*, 519-536 and *Insight*, 634-686. Both Whitehead and Lonergan argue that God is required to ground the transcendental categories. Whitehead is more explicit than Lonergan in saying that God also exemplifies the categories; see, however, Lonergan's comment in Philip McShane, ed. *Language, Truth, and Meaning: Papers from the International Lonergan Congress, 1970* (Notre Dame, Indiana: University of Notre Dame Press, 1972), 311.

ingly parallel in their respective principles...."[5] This parallel, Ogden feels, is important even if not widely noticed. Yet the main intention of his article is not simply to correct *this* oversight but to contend that the two approaches also "at point after point, from cognitional theory to the metaphysical conception of God, directly *challenge* each other's position."[6] He argues, accordingly, that the *differences* between Whitehead and Lonergan—which are remarkable considering their common methodological decisions—are *as important and even less noticed than their similarities*. His article is an effort to analyze and to initiate an assessment of these differences. The orientation of the article is fruitful, I think, and the argument is provocative. I therefore propose to initiate this comparison between Lonergan and Whitehead with Ogden's account of the differences. I will certainly not deny that there are significant differences, but at certain points I will challenge, as well as supplement, Ogden's account of what these differences are and what they amount to. In doing so I hope to be responsive to his plea that "thinkers sympathetic to the two approaches (should reflect on Whitehead's and Lonergan's) mutual challenge" so little recognized or studied.[7]

Ogden's article has to do with (1) "cognitional theory" and (2) "the derivation therefrom of (a) metaphysics of proportionate and transcendent being." Because of limitations of space, I will in this paper concentrate on only the first issue.

Let us examine Ogden's account of the differences between Whitehead's and Lonergan's respective cognitional theories and also his reasons for doubting the "soundness" of Lonergan's position. Ogden's question in dealing with this topic does not have to do with the soundness of beginning with the subject; nor does he question that Lonergan intends so to begin.[8] Rather his question is "whether it is from this principle that his philosophical categories are derived."[9] To anticipate, Ogden finds in Lonergan "a further confirmation of Whitehead's statement that 'the difficulties of all modern schools of modern philosophy lie in the fact that, having accepted the subjectivist principle, they

---

[5] Schubert M. Ogden, "Lonergan and the Subjectivist Principle," *The Journal of Religion*, (51, 3), 172. (Hereafter: *L.S.*); subsequently published in McShane, ed. *Language, Truth, and Meaning*, 218-235.

[6] *L.S.*, 172.

[7] *L.S.*, 172.

[8] *L.S.* 158f.

[9] *L.S.*, 159.

continue to use philosophical categories derived from another point of view'." [10]

To understand the meaning and grounds of Ogden's critique here it is requisite to dwell a bit on Whitehead's position insofar as Ogden is using it in this context. Whitehead likens Descartes, commonly acknowledged as the father of the subjectivist principle, to Columbus who did not understand the full meaning of his discovery. Descartes and his successors discovered the necessity of beginning with the subject but inadvertently allowed certain categories which were based on another orientation to slip into their account of "the subjective enjoyment of experience...," failing to see that these traditional categories (e.g. substance-quality) are derived from a viewpoint other than the subjectivist principle. The difficulty with these categories is not that they are wrong, "but [that] they deal with *abstractions* unsuitable for metaphysical use." [11]

There does not seem to be a univocal understanding of "abstraction" in philosophy, so it is appropriate to note that for Whitehead an "abstraction" is a focusing of an aspect of a thing that leaves out other important aspects of the thing that a fully adequate account of the thing would have to include. [12] So Whitehead writes that "(the) notions of the 'green leaf' and of the 'round ball' are... high abstractions...." [13] It is useful for certain purposes to speak this way he admits, but it is, he argues, a way of speaking that naturally leads us into "two misconceptions": it suggests that the nature of things consists (1) of "vacuous actualit(ies), void of subjective experience" (e.g. balls and leaves) and (2) "qualit(ies) inherent in substance(s)" (e.g. roundness and greenness). [14] There are, Whitehead tells us, to repeat, pragmatic justifications for such abstract talk, but such talk, he contends, "penetrates but a short way into the principles of metaphysics." [15] The "subjective enjoyment of experience," according to Whitehead, is *not* best described as a "vacuous actuality" accidentally qualified by abstract qualities; *to use substance-quality thinking for metaphysical purposes is*

---

[10] *P.R.*, 253. Quoted by Ogden, *L.S.*, 159.

[11] *P.R.*, 253. Ogden, *L.S.*, 159 (italics mine).

[12] *P. R.*, 253 f. See also Whitehead, *Science and the Modern World* (N.Y.: The Macmillan Co., 1925; published as a Mentor Book, 7th printing, 1956), chapter X.

[13] *P.R.*, 253.

[14] *P.R.*, 253.

[15] *P.R.*, 254.

to fail to derive one's metaphysics from the "subjectivist principle."[16]

Similarly Whitehead distinguishes between "causal efficacy" and "presentational immediacy".[17] These refer to two modes of perception, of which "causal efficacy" is the more primitive and fundamental. In its pure form it is not conscious, yet it is present in all forms of experience at an early stage. It is the basic mode of receiving the impact of the past and it transmits that impact in a vague, massive and inarticulate way. "Causal efficacy" refers to the power of animal experience that requires us to conform to a degree to the thatness and whatness of the world that is antecedent to ourselves.[18]

"Presentational immediacy," however, is experience become conscious, refined and focused. It is the perceptive mode "in which there is clear, distinct consciousness of the....world.... In this 'mode' the contemporary world is consciously prehended as a continuum of extensive relations."[19] We can perhaps imagine experience on Whitehead's account as a pyramid lying on its side. The base and bulk of the pyramid is describable by "causal efficacy" and consists of experience largely unconscious, thick in emotional power but vague and inarticulate; it is the mode of inheritance from the past. The apex is the experiential process coming to a focused and conscious outcome and describable as "presentational immediacy". In this last stage of the process the content of experience has become sharp, precise, clear, distinct, spatially located, but "isolated, cut-off, self-contained temporally."[20] It is an *abstraction* from the whole of the experiential event.

We need not here go further into the details of Whitehead's complex account of experience except to observe the following. The totality of human experience, according to Whitehead, is a process consisting of both causal efficacy and presentational immediacy (in their pure and mixed forms). Presentational immediacy is then not the totality of experience, although it is that stage of experience in which intellectual functioning is prominent. It is a focusing of certain elements of experience already present in causal efficacy; therefore, it can be said to presuppose the latter. "In particular, causal efficacy contains sense,

---

[16] So Ogden, *L. S., passim,* especially 163.

[17] E.g., *P.R.,* 184-186.

[18] E.g., *P. R.,* 184-186.

[19] *P.R.,* 95.

[20] Donald W. Sherburne, ed. *A Key to Whitehead's Process and Reality* (New York: The Macmillan Co., 1966), 236.

but in a vague, ill-defined, and hardly relevant way. Presentational immediacy seizes upon these vague emotional feelings and transforms them into sharp qualities that are then projected into the contemporary region of that percipient occasion (i.e. unit of experience)."[21]

The fallacy of most modern philosophy, according to Whitehead, is that it is excessively intellectualistic. That is, with its passion for clear and distinct ideas it takes presentational immediacy and neglects all else, "abstracting" from the totality of experience of which explicitly intellectual functioning is only a part—and a late, derivative part at that.[22] But Whitehead insists that "the order of dawning, *clearly and distinctly, in consciousness* is not the order of metaphysical priority."[23] By the "order of metaphysical priority" he means the whole of a unit characterized by becoming in which intellectual functioning is the outcome of a total event of more or less self-structured experience. To limit our analysis of self-understanding to the late phase of the process which can be called the stage of consciousness is to fail to achieve the goal of radical and comprehensive inquiry. Ogden has this in mind when he recalls Whitehead's "law, that the late derivative elements are more clearly illuminated by consciousness than the primitive elements" and that, for Whitehead, "the consequences of the neglect of this law....have been fatal to the proper analysis of an experient occasion. In fact, most of the difficulties of philosophy are produced by it. Experience has been explained in a thoroughly topsy-turvy fashion, the wrong end first."[24]

Whitehead's critique of modern philosophy is complex, often a bit cryptic; and of course he was not in a position to assess Lonergan's rendition of "the subjectivist principle." Ogden drawing on Whitehead, however, can and does tell us what his difficulties with Lonergan's cognitional theory are. Lonergan errs, according to Ogden, in starting "from understanding to understand experience instead of starting from experience to understand understanding."[25] Lonergan of course is very clear that understanding presupposes experience (and Ogden notes this fact). Ogden contends nevertheless that for Lonergan "our only experience is conscious experience (i.e. experience only as it is given in the late stages of the experiential process) which is precisely the tra-

---

[21] Sherburne, 237.

[22] *P. R.*, 179-197.

[23] *P.R.*, 246. Quoted by Ogden, *L.S.*, 161. (Italics mine).

[24] *P.R.*, 246; *L.S.*, 162.

[25] *L.S.*, 164.

ditional position that experience presupposes consciousness instead of what I take to be the correct position that consciousness presupposes experience."[26] "Lonergan's position," according to Ogden, "is not simply that there could be no *knowledge* of objects apart from intellectual functioning," but, that Lonergan rather holds "that there could not even be an experience of objects, as distinct from mere data, unless intellect had already constituted them by directly intending being itself."[27]

Now I do not contend that there are not differences between Whitehead's and Lonergan's respective cognitional theories. Nor do I think that it is easy (or unimportant) to discern exactly what these differences are, once one has gone beyond the obvious differences in language. *I do not think Ogden's account of Lonergan's position is altogether accurate nor his attempt to specify the differences altogether successful.*

Let me explain my own understanding of Lonergan's cognitional position, insofar as it bears on the question before us. Lonergan distinguishes between (1) the world of immediacy and (2) the world mediated by meaning.[28] The infant shares with all sentient creatures the world of immediacy. It is the world of experience and feeling, without significant intellectual functioning. As the child's mind (including powers of speech) develops he gradually makes a transition into the world mediated by meaning. This does not mean, of course, that he leaves the world of experience behind, but that world is taken up and appropriated in a different way. Moreover, through further development, i.e. "moral conversion," the child's world is mediated by meaning and regulated by values—again without leaving earlier experience behind.[29].

But one can ask about the status of early experience and its content. Prior to intellectual functioning what does experience grasp—mere data or structured objects? Lonergan's position seems to be that the term "object" acquires different meanings in the various contexts mentioned

---

[26] *L.S.*, 165 (Parenthesis mine).

[27] *L.S.*, 165 f. (Italics mine).

[28] Lonergan, *Method in Theology* (New York: Herder and Herder, 1972), 76-86. [Hereafter: *Method*] See also *Insight*, 245-253. Also the world of immediacy and the world mediated by meaning are implicit in the discussion of the "two realisms" in *Insight*, 414 and in the discussion of the real—see, e.g., *Insight*, 154-157, 160, 235, 251f; 384, 388, 389, 412-415, 424 f., 499 f., 505, 673, and 676.

[29] Lonergan concisely describes intellectual conversion, moral conversion, and religious conversion and their interrelation in *Method*, 238-240, 240, and 240-243, respectively.

above. And the criteria for objectivity is similarly "field dependent," to use Toulmin's phrase. Category mistakes and epistemological confusions will result if the criteria proper to one context or orientation are employed in another.[30] In Lonergan's language, the naive realist thinks he knows objects simply by "taking a good look."[31] The empiricist empties his world mediated by meaning of everything not known by "taking a good look."[32] The idealist claims that knowing is not looking but answering questions and hence his knowing is a knowing of an ideal world.[33] Lonergan, however, distinguishes different worlds and different horizons, different meanings of "object," and different criteria of objectivity.[34]

Now to address directly the question about mere data or structured experience, let us note Lonergan's account of objects. Once again one must attend to the different contexts in which objects appear and in terms of which they can be discussed. Lonergan speaks in various places of (1) "partial objects," (2) "partially constructed objects," (3) "fully constructed" and "partially known objects," and (4) "fully constructed" and "fully known objects."[35] "Partial objects" (1) are objects of single acts of experience (e.g., tasting bitter or feeling smooth).[36] "Partially constructed" objects (2) are the objects of some combination of single acts of experience, (e.g. tasting, hearing, etc.) but excludes judgment.[37] "Fully constructed" objects (3 and 4) are objects of a combination of acts which combination includes judgment. Such objects are imperfectly but really known by men (3) and perfectly known by the unrestricted act of intelligence which is God's(4).[38]

This, of course, has immediate relevance for a key point in Ogden's critique. Ogden writes that Lonergan's position is not simply that there could be no *knowledge* of objects apart from intellectual functioning; he

---

[30] *Method*, chap. 10, especially 263. See also F.E. Crowe, S.J., ed. *Collection: Papers by Bernard Lonergan, S.J.*, (N.Y.: Herder and Herder, 1967), chap. 14.

[31] *Insight*, 384.

[32] *Collection*, 231-233. See also *Insight*, 245-250.

[33] *Collection*, 233-235.

[34] *Collection*, 221-239, esp. 235 f. See also *Insight*, 245-250 and 267-270.

[35] The distinctions between types of objects is implicit in the discussion of "Isomorphism" in *Insight*; e.g., see Index. For more on his explicit account see *Method* 12, 141, 263, and 286.

[36] *Method.*, 12, 141, 263, and 286.

[37] *Method*, 12 and 186.

[38] *Method*, 12, 263, and 286. See also *Insight*, the discussion of God and complete intelligibility, chapter XIX, especially 639-642.

holds that there could not even be an *experience* of objects, as distinct from mere data, unless intellect had already constituted them by directly intending being itself. But once again, this is a familiar position of the philosophic tradition—in this case, the position which, construing experience as mere "sense data" or "impressions", wrongly looks to intellect for the objectivity that experience as we actually live it quite adequately provides for itself.[39] Ogden's understanding of Lonergan is correct in (only) some respects and it is wrong in others. According to Lonergan we can speak of objects in the context of the world mediated by meaning only by referring to the activity of intellect. But these are "fully constructed" objects; and what makes them *fully* rather than *partially* constructed is the intellect understanding and judging them. And it is quite true that intellectual functioning requires the intervention of the notion of being.[40] Lonergan's position on this is that nothing is *known* to be so apart from the asking and answering of questions. And (1) the notion of being is operative in the asking of questions; (2) the thinking of being is operative (heuristically) in thought moving toward judgment; (3) something is known of being in a correct judgment of possibility or fact; and (4) the idea of being is the content of an unrestricted act of understanding, i.e. omniscience, which is God's possession and not ours.

This account of intelligence may be Lonergan's major emphasis, but it is not the whole of his position, as Ogden's criticism seems to assume. For Lonergan's account allows that, while we can *not* have *knowledge* of objects without intellect's functioning (which seems analytically true, even if often overlooked), in the world of immediacy we *can and do experience* objects—i.e. partial objects—without intellect's activity. Such objects are partial in the sense that intellectual functioning is missing and such functioning will help complete the object. Intellect helps quantitatively, since what intellect grasps is more than mere experience. It helps qualitatively, since intellectual activity is other than mere experience as such.[41] Still partial objects, even if partial, are still something; they force us to take some account of their thatness and whatness whether we are infants, asleep, or stupid.[42] Moreover partial object "X" is *not* absolutely other than fully constituted object X; *is*

---

[39] *L.S.*, 165 f.

[40] *Collection*, 236.

[41] *Collection*, 236; *Insight*, 3-32.

[42] *Insight*, 381.

just partial not full. The full object completes but does not destroy the partial object—its ancestor. This is Lonergan's account of *aufheben* or sublation.[43]

Of course what I am explaining is a theory, i.e. Lonergan's theory of human experience and cognition. To formulate and propound a theory is to move in the world mediated by meaning, even though this theory is about the world of immediacy as well as the world mediated by meaning. That is, knowing is one thing and what one knows is another. In this case, we know because of our intellectual functioning; what we know is that intellectual functioning in the mode of judging (i.e., knowing) is itself a variable of sentient life, coming on the scene late, preceded as it is by experience of partial objects and understanding of partially constructed objects.

One might ask, however, at this point whether it might not be possible that intelligence, always coming on the scene late, *always* misunderstands and distorts what was on the scene before it appeared. It is obviously true that sometimes reason "murders to dissect." But then it is reason itself that discovers that it sometimes does this. What would it mean that reason or intellect *always* and *necessarily* distorts or misconceives experience? How would one ever *know* that this is so without knowing what it is that one necessarily and always makes a mistake about (which plainly is not allowed *ex hypothesi*)? What would it mean even to say it is even possible that this is so? What is the point of calling some state of affairs possible when it is not a state of affairs that could even in principle be known to be actual?

In *Process and Reality* Whitehead characterizes and criticizes Kant as follows:

> ...for Kant, apart from concepts there is nothing to know; since objects related in a knowable world are the product of conceptual functioning whereby categorial form is introduced into the sense datum, which otherwise is intuited in the form of a mere spatio-temporal flux of sensations.... Thus for Kant the process whereby there is experience is a process from subjectivity to apparent objectivity. The philosophy of organism [i.e. Whitehead's philosophy] inverts this analysis, and explains the process as proceeding from objectivity whereby the external world is a datum to the

---

[43]*Insight,* 252 and 421-423; see also *Method,* 241.

subjectivity, whereby there is one individual experience. Thus. . . in every act of experience there are objects for knowledge; but apart from the inclusion of intellectual functioning in that act of experience, there is no knowledge.[44]

Now if Whitehead's account of Kant (whether or not it accurately describes Kant) also applied to Lonergan, it would be accurate to agree with Ogden that for Lonergan "[it is] not simply that there could be no *knowledge* of objects apart from intellectual functioning" but also that "there could not even be an *experience* of objects as distinct from mere data, unless intellect had already constituted them by directly intending being itself. . ."[45] We could, in short, conclude that Lonergan neglects "the objectivity that experience as we actually live it quite adequately provides for itself."[46] It is not clear, however, that Whitehead's description of Kant adequately describes Lonergan. *Lonergan would cast Whitehead's transition from objectivity to subjectivity differently:—as a transition from the world of immediacy to the world mediated by meaning.* Moreover, as we have seen, the world of immediacy is not a world without its own proper objectivity. It is a world of "partial" objects. The transition from this world to the world mediated by meaning is a transition to a context in which subtler criteria for objectivity obtain. Those criteria give us an objectivity which is the fruit of authentic subjectivity, indeed, of a lifelong authentic subjectivity of being attentive, intelligent, reasonable, and responsible.[47]

Part of the difficulty of contrasting Whitehead and Lonergan is verbal; Lonergan tends to use the word "experience" more narrowly than Whitehead. He does not tend to use "experience" as we might use it to refer to a "man of experience."[48] Indeed he sometimes speaks, as Ogden notes, of experience as "presentations and representations."[49] Sometimes he equates "experience" and "sensation" and characterizes sensations as "the Humean world of mere impressions."[50] Nevertheless one should note his uneasiness about this when he writes that "(t)he notion of the pattern of experience may be approached by remarking

[44] *P.R.*, 236.
[45] *L.S.*, 166.
[46] *L.S.*, 166.
[47] E.g., see *Collection*, 227 and *Method*, 265 and 292.
[48] Philip McShane, ed. *Language, Truth, and Meaning*, 310.
[49] E.g., *Insight*, 383, 348, and 357. See Ogden, *L.S.*, 165.
[50] E.g., *Insight*, 324, 382, and 514. See Ogden, *L.S*, 165.

how abstract it is to speak of a sensation. No doubt, we are all familiar with acts of seeing, hearing, touching, tasting, smelling. Still such acts never occur in isolation both from one another and from all other events. On the contrary, they have a bodily basis; they are functionally related to bodily movements; and they occur in some dynamic context that somehow unifies a manifold of sensed contents and acts of sensing."[51]

Even so Lonergan tends to use "experience" more narrowly. He does not speak of both "sensuous" and "non-sensous" experience.[52] The latter is employed by Whitehead to refer to our inner nonsensuous awareness of our selves and others as parts of an encompassing whole and the former to refer to outer perceptions or sensations whereby we *discriminate* the activity of discreet beings external to ourselves. Perhaps we can equate the former with what has come to be called *existential self-understanding* and the latter with *ordinary sensations* upon which natural sciences are based. The point is that Whitehead refers to both as types of experience and Lonergan tends to employ "experience" more restrictively to refer to the latter, i.e. for him "experience" *usually* (but not always, as we shall see below) means sense experience. I personally find this unfortunate to a degree, in light of the option of a broader use of the word made available to us by the phenomenologists and the so-called "radical empiricists" (Bergson, James, Peirce, Dewey, and Whitehead).[53] Nevertheless the verbal difference is not so important. The *question* is whether Lonergan has some account of all the reality included under the Whiteheadian "experience."

The broad Whiteheadian account of experience is obviously an alternative to what has been called "classical empiricism," i.e., the empiricism of Locke, Hume, Mill, and Russell. Classical empiricism tried to explain cognition in terms of experience—taken to be clear, discrete, and atomic sensations—and psychological principles of association. The classical empiricist assumes that all concepts have an "original" in the disconnected stream of sensations. Kant, as is well-known, found this account inadequate and supplemented it by positing the a

---

[51] *Insight*, 181.

[52] See Whitehead, *Adventures of Ideas* (New York: The Macmillan Co., 1933; published as a Mentor Book, 1955, 6th printing 1964), 181-183. See also Whitehead, *M.T.*, 150 and 143-171.

[53] See John E. Smith, *Reason and God: Encounters of Philosophy and Religion* (New Haven and London: Yale University Press, 1961), chapter 9, and Ogden, *L.S.*, 166.

priori reason standing behind experience. Whitehead's critique of classical empiricism differs from Kant's (and was anticipated to a degree by Hegel) in that it is double-barreled. Not only does he posit transcendental reason; he also faults the classical empiricist's account of experience. Classical empiricism is not wrong because it is empirical; its failure is partially due to its not being empirical enough. That is, it fails to note all that experience as it is actually enjoyed and suffered contains. This is to return to an earlier point we have observed: for Whitehead clear, discrete, atomic senses are a late variable of experience. They are on what technical reason focuses in the contemporary world; they are the content of a specious present; and as such they are abstractions. To equate them with experience as such is to commit what Whitehead calls the "fallacy of misplaced concreteness."[54] Whitehead's less "abstract" account of experience finds in experience as such not only nouns and adjectives but also conjunctive relations of various grades of intimacy, relevance, and externality. Experience is not simply of disjointed and isolated terms but contains transitions and tendencies. The invariant feature of experience is a dynamic and teleologically oriented process; it contains a continuity found in the passage of one phase into another within the serial history of the same organism or self. It is in this context, furthermore, that Whitehead can say that we ought to try to understand intellect in terms of experience and not vice versa: i.e., we ought to see how intelligence functions in and for the total life experience of the dynamic organism that the self is.[55] Or, to return to our earlier formulation: at the base of all operations there is the existential self-understanding of a self in terms of which all special functions should be interpreted.

Now how does it stand with Lonergan? With regard to the use of the word "experience," if it is clear that Lonergan does not adopt the Humean—i.e., restrictive—use of the term; it is also clear that he does not adopt the Whiteheadian—i.e., inclusive—use either. Whereas the latter refers to intending, deciding, and intellectual activities of all sorts as aspects of experience, Lonergan's does not. He prefers to differentiate between them. The verbal issue is interesting. The more interesting issue, however, has to do with the matter itself. Does Lonergan acknowledge as real those things of which Whitehead speaks (as aspects of experience) and if so how does he interpret them (if not

---

[54] *P.R.*, 11.
[55] *M.T.*, 209 ff.

as aspects of experience)?

Here as elsewhere an exact parallel between Whitehead and Lonergan is probably not possible to find. Nevertheless the distance between them may be lessened if we attend to the following. First of all, Lonergan's account of intellectual functioning is an account of a dynamic process. This is the reason he finds the notion of philosophy as a matter of logic alone wanting. Logic functions always within a stable context or horizon of meaning. It presupposes a steady state. But besides such states there is the eros of the mind which continually moves to higher and higher viewpoints—or else aborts itself in obscurantism (or "one dimensionality").[56] Second, and of even more importance here, intellectual functioning is only a part—although a crucial part—of the dynamism of the total self; it is only one of "successive stages in the unfolding of a single thrust, the eros of the human spirit."[57] For in addition to "intellectual conversion" (entrance into the sphere of refined intellectuality) there are also moral and religious "conversions." In the sphere of morality one cares about values as opposed to mere pleasures.[58] One cares about what ought to be done in addition to what is; whereas, in the world of intelligence proper the transcendental notion is that of being and it is this that functions heuristically for reason, in the world of morality the transcendental notion is that of value and it is this that moves us toward the good.[59] Moreover—to be especially noted vis-à-vis the charge of Lonergan's excessive intellectualism—the "apprehension of values and disvalues is the task not of understanding but of intentional response."[60] Emotions are therefore a component, for "such response is all the fuller....the better a man one is....the more delicate one's feelings."[61] "Intermediate between judgments of fact and judgments of value lie apprehensions of value. Such apprehensions are given of feelings." Because of the prominence of feelings, psychic laden

---

[56] *Insight*, 13-32.

[57] *Method*, 105.

[58] *Method.*, 27-56.

[59] I am indebted to Walter E. Conn, "Bernard Lonergan on Value," *The Thomist*, Vol. XL, 2 (April 1976), 243-257. He observes that in *Insight*, Lonergan has not yet developed a *transcendental* notion of value but discussed value as the good of order; whereas in *The Subject*, ten years later, Lonergan first presents an explicit account of the notion of value as a transcendental category. For Lonergan's mature view, Conn refers us to *Method*. See especially, 247-251.

[60] *Method*, 24 f.

[61] *Method*, 37.

images and symbols are important as lures.[62]

Not only are there the intellectual and moral stages included among the "successful stages in the unfolding of.... the eros of the human spirit,"[63] there is also the possibility of "religious conversion."[64] The religious question can be seen to arise like Toulmin's "limiting question," a question that emerges not within our moral experience itself but at its limits.[65] For in addition to questions about what we ought to do there is the question as to the point of acting at all. Is it all ultimately worthwhile? Is the universe malevolent or indifferent or friendly to values and the effort it takes to attain them? The answer to this question for Lonergan is the experience of the love of God, of God's love flooding our hearts and of our becoming a being-in-love with God (and his creation).[66] This event is "...the gift of God's grace,...the reason of the heart that reason does not know.... It is the efficacious reality that brings men to God despite their lack of learning or their learned errors. It is the crown of human development, grace perfecting nature."[67]

So we have the experiential, intellectual, moral, and religious as "phases in the single thrust for self-transcendence."[68] Yet while they are "distinct... [they are] not all that disparate."[69] What is more, while the order just given is "natural", de facto in the sphere of actual history the order is reversed. It is the experience of grace that impels one to want the good and to know the real in order to do the good and to be open to ever expanding experience to know the real.[70]

In whichever order we take it, however, we have here an account of the exigence of the total self. Some might call it a comprehensive account of human *experience*, although Lonergan prefers to use

---

[62] *Method*, 66. Cf. the work of Robert Doran, S.J., e.g., *Conversion and Theological Foundations: Toward a Reorientation of the Human Sciences* (Chico, CA : Scholars Press, 1981).

[63] *Method*, 105.

[64] *Method*, 101-124, especially 101-103.

[65] Stephen Edelston Toulmin, *An Examination of The Place of Reason in Ethics* (Cambridge: Cambridge University Press, 1961), 202-211, especially 204 f.

[66] *Method*, 115-117, and *A Second Collection: Papers by Bernard J. F. Lonergan, S.J.*, eds. William F. Ryan, S.J. and Bernard J. Tyrrell, S.J. (Philadelphia: The Westminster Press, 1974), 129 f.

[67] *A Second Collection*, 129 f.

[68] *A Second Collection*, 132.

[69] *A Second Collection*, 130.

[70] *A Second Collection*, 133.

the term "experience" more narrowly. At any rate, it is clear that intellectual functioning is not the whole of that total exigence. It is, however, an essential part. For if the self unfolds vitalistically and dynamically, it is a part of man's distinctively human nature to want to know.[71] (When dogs are well-fed they sleep, whereas humans ask questions.) Moreover, while knowing is justifiable as an end-in-itself, it is also required to help the moral man determine which values are most desirable and how they can be actualized.[72] For while it is true that values are largely apprehended in feelings, critical thinking is also required, for "when knowledge is deficient, then fine feelings are apt to be expressed in...lovely proposals that don't work out and often do more harm than good."[73] And critical thinking is required to root out biases, illusions, and pretenses that ever threaten to deflect human development from its good.[74] One should note, however, how intellect works here. For whereas the transcendental or invariant norm of reasoning is being, there are also categorical or variant norms,[75] and the categorical norms that governs the critique of human development per se is that of "genuineness" or authentic self-fulfillment in community.[76]

Conclusion

We are now in a position (as well as required by practical limits) to move towards a conclusion. We began by noting an arresting and fairly obvious (though strangely, not often noticed) parallel between Whitehead and Lonergan.

Both (1) accept the turn toward the subject as the starting point, seeing the self as the privileged access to and chief sample of reality; (2) deny that this decision must lead to solipsism or even to anti-metaphysical or non-theistic philosophy; and (3) aim at developing an integral metaphysics—isomorphic with the subject's fully reflective self-understanding—as a broad outline and heuristic structure in terms of which all else can be fruitfully understood. We aimed at studying, however, possible significant differences between Whitehead and Lonergan, prompted in part by Ogden's account of the matter. We especially

---

[71] *Insight*, 350 f.
[72] *Method*, 66 f.
[73] *Method*, 38.
[74] *Insight*, 476-477.
[75] *Method*, 11.
[76] *Method*, 41.

took note of Ogden's claim that there are big and important differences arising out of Whitehead's commitment to understand understanding in light of experience and Lonergan's commitment to understand experience in light of understanding.

We noted Whitehead's more and Lonergan's less inclusivistic use of the term "experience." Whitehead, in contrast to the classical empiricists, means by experience more than atomistic *sensa*; "experience" for him refers to the living process that we are, which consists not only of (a) sensuous perception of external objects but also and more importantly of (b) non-sensuous perception of ourselves in process, which process is a concrete unification of real relations, etc. For Whitehead, to talk in terms of the subject-predicate scheme is to employ a model taken from the visual experience (sensuous perception) of external objects (the green leaf) and not—as the subjectivist principle requires—in terms of the concrete actuality *we ourselves actually are.*

Lonergan, however, perhaps less sensitive to the debate between classical and radical empiricists than Whitehead, tends to use "experience" more narrowly. Nevertheless, even though he sometimes speaks of experience in Humean terms (sensuous presentations and inner representations), he differs with Hume (and Kant) in allowing that this talk is abstract and that what we encounter are *bodies* with their own structure, etc. We have also noted that he speaks of experiencing such non-sensuous "things" as our own understanding, judging, deciding, and being-in-love. *We can conclude, therefore, that the key trait of the experiential for Lonergan is the given which is to be understood.* Moreover, the to-be-understood, according to the terms of his acceptance of the turn toward the subject, is not only the self's experience narrowly understood; it is the total, interrelated, dynamic process of what the self actually suffers, does, and is. All of the levels of the exigent self—its experiencing, understanding, judging, deciding, and being-in-love—constitute the complex though single reality which is taken to be isomorphic with (teleologically ordered) reality.

Therefore, if Lonergan can not be claimed for radical empiricism, still his account of experience is such that Whitehead's critique of the classical empiricists can not apply *mutatis mutandis* to it either. This is not to say, of course, that this observation alone settles the decisive issues. We will recall that the real point of Whitehead's critique was to attack those cognitional theories which, misled as they are by ordinary language and its subject/predicate structure, generate "two

misconceptions: [1] *one* is the concept of vacuous actuality, void of subjective experience; and [2] the *other* is the concept of quality inherent
in substance."[77] According to Whitehead, it is preoccupation with external objects of visual experience that leads to this cul de sac. *If we
attend to that reality which we are rather than those objects which we
see*, we will not discover a substance with accidental qualities but a concrete experient consisting of focused relationships with other concrete
actualities. In place of a vacuous and static substratum (Whitehead's
definition of substance) we will find a subject in the process of actual-
ization. Descartes was right in turning to the "I think," but he erred
in not noticing that each "I think" is a *phase in an ongoing experience*.
Besides, we never just think; we always think something, and what we
are thinking is *constitutive* of the reality we are.[78] Moreover the scheme
of subjects with accidental qualities leaves unexplained the connection
between things. Consequently "the relations between individual sub-
stances constitute metaphysical nuisances." [79] Qualities are too abstract. They are abstractions from real relationships between a subject
and its environment. They are actually not adjectives but adverbs de-
noting how a subject can and does experience. The substance/accident
scheme fails to cohere with concrete self-understanding and does not
adequately interpret nature (as modern relativity physics presents it).

Now let us turn again to Lonergan. Initially, it is quite significant
to note that he prefers *not* to use the concept of substance. While he
expressed sympathy with Aristotle's "substantial form" (which he understands differently from Whitehead), he recognizes that the meaning of the English "substance" "has been influenced profoundly by
Locke....[and with the Cartesian] confusion of 'body' and thing [has
led] to an identification of substance and extension and then to the
riposte that substance is underneath extension."[80] As an alternative
way of speaking of things, he chooses to speak of central/conjugate
rather than substance/accident. There is the central form which is the
"concrete and intelligible unity, identity, whole" of a thing.[81] It is what
answers to "this." It is not posited substratum or vacuous actuality; it
consists of the conjugate forms which are "defined implicitly by their

---

[77] *P. R.*, 253.

[78] *P. R.*, 239 ff.

[79] *P.R.*, 208.

[80] *Insight*, 436; see 436 f.

[81] *Insight*, 435.

relations."[82]

The chief paradigm and source of these terms, for Lonergan, is oneself—experienced, understood, and affirmed. One experiences oneself experiencing the manifold, understanding the manifold, judging the manifold; one understands this process as well; and one affirms what one understands. The result is knowing oneself as "a concrete and intelligible unity-identity-whole."[83] If I am a unity and whole, the many parts are not irrelevant to me (as "accidents" would suggest), for I can be a unity only if there is a manifold and I can be a whole only if there are parts.[84] Indeed I do experience, understand, and affirm myself experiencing, understanding, and knowing the manifold in manifold acts. The manifold is constitutive of myself as an experiential, intelligent, and rational being. But to conclude here would be to be guilty of an oversight. For if I can experience, understand, and affirm my manifold acts in successive moments and precisely as *my* acts then I myself am not just many but am one. I am identical with myself.[85] To use Lonergan's categories now: the "concrete and intelligible unity-identity-whole" that I am is my central potency as experienced, central form as understood, and central act as affirmed. Further, the many that enter into the self-constitution of myself are conjugates: conjugate potencies refer to what is experienced, conjugate forms refer to that which is understood, and conjugate acts refer to what is as affirmed.[86]

This self-appropriation then is used by Lonergan to interpret all other items that are given in our experience. The metaphysical categories illustrated by the "thing" that we are, Lonergan argues, are "isomorphic" with the universe of proportionate being and are applicable to *every* other "thing" included in that universe.[87]

This analysis suggests the final comparison. In their own respective

[82] *Insight*, 435. In addition, Lonergan speaks of central potency and central act and conjugate potency and conjugate act. Something is in potency when it is merely given, in form when understood, in act when affirmed.

[83] *Insight*, 319.

[84] *Collection*, 223 ff. and *Insight*, 324-328.

[85] *Insight*, 325 and 338 f.

[86] *Insight*, 434-436.

[87] See the discussion of "things," *Insight*, 245-270, and of the "Elements of Metaphysics," *Insight*, chap. XV. For "isomorphism," see *Insight*, e.g. 115, 444-446 and 449 f. There is even an intriguing sense in which Lonergan and Whitehead agree in seeing God not as an exception to the metaphysical categories invoked arbitrarily but as their—to use Whitehead's famous phrase—"chief exemplification." But this is a topic for another study.

ways both Whitehead and Lonergan adhere to the subjectivist principle not only formally and in a minimal sense but in the sense of taking
the self's integral experience (not external objects) as the model for
interpreting all else. In this the view that Lonergan continues to derive
metaphysical categories from visual experience of external objects is
challenged and overturned. While he does not speak of "non-sensuous
perception" directly, he does imply experiences of realities not known
by "taking a look." And his basic instance of the metaphysical categories is the self and its operations as experienced, understood, and
affirmed, not the bodies presented to extroverted consciousness.

He has not used the substance/accident scheme criticized by Whitehead. Lonergan does find the need for a surrogate for substance/accident,
however, which he finds in central potency-form-act/conjugate potency-
form-act. It does not seem, however, that the former is a vacuous actuality (but a dynamic unity) nor the latter abstract, adjectival qualities
(but *relata*).

If Whitehead has no surrogate for substance, then Lonergan would
challenge him precisely on the basis of an analysis of self-understanding.
That is, do we not need some such surrogate to answer the question as
to the object of self-analysis other than simply "this?" Moreover, do
we not inevitably affirm ourselves as perduring identities and not just
disconnected flux when we affirm that we know the many in successive acts of consciousness? If we can accept W.A. Christian's analysis
of Whitehead's position on substance, however, we can find Whitehead and Lonergan not so far apart on this issue.[88]   For Christian
argues that Whitehead differs on this score significantly from the radical empiricists, inasmuch as his critique of the substance tradition is
dialectical; Whitehead found the need to account for the principles
of (1) "individuality," (2) "self-existence," and (3) "permanence" dis-
closed in experience.[89]   Consequently, Christian argues that with his
doctrine of "actual occasions"—which is the generic term for things
per se understood as acts of becoming—Whitehead was developing a
"reformed doctrine of substance."[90]   In this account, which I see no
reason to reject, Lonergan and Whitehead both have surrogates for
the substance/accident scheme: Lonergan's "things" consisting of cen-

---

[88] William A. Christian, *An Interpretation of Whitehead's Metaphysics* (New
Haven: Yale University Press, 1959), 105-119.
[89] Christian, 111.
[90] Christian, 115-118.

tral and conjugate potencies, forms, and acts and Whitehead's "actual occasions" consisting of stages of "concrescence."[91]

Even so, an important difference remains. Lonergan's central form is the form of a *self* perduring a life-time (prescinding for now from the question of subjective immortality). Whitehead's actual occasion describes an event of a shorter duration, the self (ordinarily understood) or person consisting of a series of such events. Lonergan's surrogate is closer, therefore, to the traditional substance than Whitehead's. The relevant question then becomes one of deciding whether Lonergan's or Whitehead's best renders the concrete reality which we actually live and are. One could expect the Whiteheadian to ask whether perduring central form is adequate to our experience of change, lapses of consciousness, mutations of identity, etc., just as one could expect a Lonerganian to raise questions about the adequacy of describing our experience of abiding self-identity in terms of a *series* of actual occasions. Both positions, of course, have their subtleties and the debate on this issue would be complex, as well as interesting and important. Practical limits prevent our taking the matter further here however.

I submit, nevertheless, that it is at this level and on this question—the question of interpreting the dynamic self-identity which we are–that a contrast and mutual challenge between Whitehead and Lonergan can best be made. For beyond and beneath the differences of vocabulary and style the differences in the respective renditions of the subjectivist principle seem not so radical as the earlier study cited contends. This being so, we have a good basis for further investigation of two important viable options in contemporary reflection on the place and validity of religion in modern secular culture.

---

[91] For Lonergan on "things," see *Insight*, Chap. VIII. For an account of Whitehead on "the phases of concrescence," see Sherburne, ed. *op. cit.*, chap. III, especially figure on 40.

Chapter 10

Foundations: Lonergan and Peirce

Vincent G. Potter, S.J.

I have a rather modest and limited objective in this paper: to support Lonergan's contention that Catholic philosophical and theological thought must shift its emphasis from "first principles" to transcendental method. My objective is limited in the sense that it takes up only one of the five areas in which, according to Lonergan, a shift must occur if Catholic thought is to achieve the effective *aggiornamento* mandated by Vatican II.[1] It is modest because I intend to support Lonergan's point by showing that over a hundred years ago an American philosopher proposed and defended a similar move. That philosopher is Charles S. Peirce whose thought only recently has had significant impact on the intellectual communities on both sides of the Atlantic. That two thinkers, separated by a century, coming from very different educational, cultural and religious backgrounds, should come independently to similar conclusions must strengthen the claims of each.

In what follows I suppose that the reader is more familiar with Lon-

---

[1] "The Future of Thomism," in *A Second Collection : Papers by Bernard J. F. Lonergan, S. J.*, eds. William Ryan, S.J. and Bernard Tyrrell, S.J. (Philadelphia: The Westminster Press, 1974), 50-52.

ergan than Peirce. Hence I will begin with a rather brief statement of
the former's views concerning first principles and then give a somewhat
more developed presentation of the latter's. In the process I will point
out the close similarities in these positions along with their differences.

10.1   Lonergan on First Principles

The point urged by both Lonergan and Peirce is that human knowledge
is discursive, not intuitive. This also means that there is no immediate
knowledge of anything. If *all* human knowledge is discursive and mediated, both the question of "first principles" and of the "foundations"
of human knowledge need to be re-thought in a radical way.[2]

Let us begin with a brief sketch of Lonergan's thought on these matters. In a paper entitled "Insight Revisited," Lonergan remarked that
rather early in his career he came to think of human knowledge "as not
intuitive, but discursive with the decisive component in judgment."[3]
This was the result of his indirect contact with the thought of Joseph
Maréchal, for which he was prepared by his previous disenchantment
with the central role ascribed to universal concepts by his professors at
Heythrop. The upshot of this realization was an emphasis upon the *act*
of understanding rather than upon the resultant concept. For reasons
that will become apparent, I draw the readers attention to the prominent role that *judgment* plays in Lonergan's view of human knowing.[4]
He saw that neither the act of simple apprehension nor the act of forming a proposition is the basic act of human knowing. Indeed there is no
knowing at all until there is assertion based on sufficient evidence, that
is, on the grasp of the virtually unconditioned. I stress this point not
only because it has become a commonplace among neo-scholastics but
also because Peirce substituted *inference* for judgment as the basic act
of knowing. Just as Lonergan realized that concepts are formed within
the context of judgment (and not that judgments are constructed *out*
of concepts), so Peirce realized that judgments are formed within the
context of the inferential process to express that process and,in turn,

---

[2]See "Theology in its New Context," in *A Second Collection*, 63-64. On the
"discursive" character in human knowing for Lonergan, see "Insight Revisited," in
A Second Collection, 269.

[3]*A Second Collection*, 265.

[4]See *Insight: A Study of Human Understanding* (New York: Philosophical Library, 1958) passim, especially chapters IX and X.

concepts are formed to express judgments. To this point I will return.

By "discursive" I take Lonergan to mean "going through intermediate steps." Thus all inference is discursive. It is the opposite of "intuitive." A cognition would be intuitive if it were immediate, that is, not determined by any previous cognition. A judgment would be intuitive if it were not determined by any previous judgment. It would be a premise which was not itself a conclusion. Otherwise it is discursive.

If one takes Lonergan's claim seriously that *all* human cognition is discursive and that judgment is the base unit of such cognition, then there are no judgments such that they are self-evident and self-justifying. It follows then that there are no first principles in the traditional sense. If every *judgment* is determined by a previous judgment, then there is an infinite regress of judgments. Aristotle, among others, considered this to be absurd since, if it were so, there could be no *sound* syllogistic demonstration, because although the form could be shown to be valid, the premises could not be shown to be *true*. Hence Aristotle concluded that there *must* be premises which are not themselves conclusions and these are the first principles.

What is at stake is the *grounding* of human cognition. What, if anything, is the sure and solid foundation upon which human knowing is based? For much of the philosophical tradition that secure base consisted in first principles. For another part of the tradition the foundation was one of the elements into which the propositions asserted in judgment could be analyzed (e.g., sense data, or "clear and distinct ideas" or "primitives" of one sort or another – linguistic, sensible, conceptual). This latter version of "foundationalism" is based on the supposition that human cognition is built out of atomic elements. Once cognition is analyzed into those elements there is nothing more to it. Complex cognition is "nothing more" than combinations of the basic elements. Furthermore, whatever those elements are in any particular version of reductionism, they were supposed to represent (or perhaps even "to mirror") nature (the real, what there is). That such a supposition is an act of pure faith has been pointed out by critics of this form of foundationalism.[5] Unfortunately, these critics sometimes conclude that because this reductionist representationalism could not ground human knowledge there is no grounding of human knowledge at all.

---

[5] See R. Rorty, *Philosophy and the Mirror of Nature* (Princeton: Princeton University Press, 1979) for a devastating attack on classical foundationalism. Rorty's own position on foundations are not in my view as sound as his criticisms.

The appeal to "first principles" in the traditional style has at least the advantage of avoiding the atomic building blocks assumed by the reductionist. It recognizes that the mind grasps connections and that it is those connections which reveal data to be intelligible. The difficulty with it is that its rejection of reductionism is not radical enough. It fails to realize that the act of judging a proposition to be true is the result of the more complex operation of inference. Lonergan implies this in *Insight* in the chapter on "Reflective Understanding" where he presents as the paradigm for assessing evidence to be sufficient the fundamental form of inference, *modus ponens*.[6] Lonergan sheds considerable light on his position concerning "foundations" in an article entitled "Natural Knowledge of God."[7] There he distinguishes two senses of "principle." The first sense is that of a self-evidently true proposition which can serve as a first premise. He has in mind the traditional Principle of Identity, Principle of Sufficient Reason, Principle of Causality, etc. The second sense is that of an originating power which manifests itself in activity. In the case of human knowing the activity is asking and answering questions. The originating power (principle) of that activity is the intellect itself. As the source of human knowing, it is neither in need of nor capable of justification, validation or verification. It is itself in its activity the source of all justifications, validations and verifications of any particular claim to knowledge. In this sense the intellect itself is the "first principle" and grounding of human knowing. This insight is the insight into transcendental method. To know what we know and under what conditions, we must first understand how we know. We must understand our intelligence in act. Our attempts to articulate that activity will be inadequate and open to revision, but that revision is possible because of our understanding of or insight into the activity itself. Errors in formulation or in theoretical explanation will show themselves as counter-positions which ultimately invite their own reversal. To the extent that our formulation and explanation is correct, it will be a basic position which invites further development.[8]

Lonergan sees clearly that self-evident propositions (analytic propositions) will not do as "first principles" which can ground human knowing. The reason is that in themselves they are merely tautologies, that is, they are "true" only in virtue of their meanings or their syntactical

---

[6] *Insight*, Chapter XI.

[7] *A Second Collection*, 126-128.

[8] See *Insight*, Chapter XI for the arguments in more detail.

structure. In order for them to become formulations of the intellect in act their meanings have to be verified in particular existential cases. But this supposes the grasp of sufficient evidence, an act of reflective understanding, and hence an inference (the conditions and their fulfillment in the particular case). Hence, even when dealing with what Lonergan calls analytic principles the human mind is discursive and not intuitive.[9]

10.2 Peirce on First Principles

Let us turn to Peirce's treatment of the same material. In 1868 Peirce (just turning thirty years of age) published a series of three articles in the *Journal of Speculative Philosophy*.[10] The views there set out remained central to his thought throughout his long career. In those articles he made a sustained attack on what he took to be the spirit of Cartesianism which, according to him, consisted in a preoccupation with removing skeptical doubt by establishing human knowledge as immediate, intuitive and certain. Peirce attributed this penchant to the empiricists as well, although what they claimed to intuit were sensible, rather than "clear and distinct," ideas. In place of this Cartesianism, Peirce offered a theory according to which human knowledge is thoroughly mediated and discursive. In a preliminary draft Peirce makes the point that *what* we think is to be understood only in terms of the proper method for ascertaining *how* we think.[11] He begins, therefore, with an account of cognition, then of truth and reality, and finally of the grounding of inference.[12]

The first paper, "Questions Concerning Certain Faculties Claimed for Man," centers on the issue of whether or not we have any immediate or intuitive knowledge of ourselves, of our mental states, or of the external world. By intuition Peirce means cognition not determined by previous cognition. In the case of judgment this would be a proposition

---

[9] *Insight*, 304-309.

[10] In *Collected Papers of Charles Sanders Peirce*, Vol. V, eds. C. Hartshorne and P. Weiss, (Cambridge: Harvard University Press, 1960) 213-357 (para. nos.). Also in the new Peirce edition, *Writings of Charles S. Peirce: A Chronological Edition*, Vol. 2 (Bloomington: Indiana Unversity Press, 1984), 193-272.

[11] See C. F. Delaney, "The Journal of Speculative Philosophy Papers," in the new edition, *Writings of Charles S. Peirce*, xxxvi-xlii.

[12] Delaney, xxxvi-xlii.

which can be a premise but is not itself a conclusion—a first principle
in the traditional sense. His conclusion on this point is negative. All
knowledge is inferential and mediated through signs. By introspection
Peirce understands internal cognition of our internal states not determined by external cognition. He concludes that we have no such power.
All knowledge of our mental states is by inference from overt behavior
and not by an inward looking.

The second paper, "Some Consequences of Four Capacities," focuses
upon a theory of cognition in terms of inference and sign-mediation.
The argument proceeds on the assumption that language as the external manifestation of mental activity is to be taken as a model of that
activity's structure. Language is a system of signs. Peirce works out an
analysis of signs and how they function. Mental activity then is viewed
as "inner speech." What is more, the thought process manifested in
language is inferential. Inferences are expressed in (and so can be analyzed into) a series of propositions (asserted in judgments). Judgments
in turn are expressed through (and so can be analyzed into) concepts.
But the thought process which is expressed in propositions and general terms and is analyzed into judgments and concepts is continuous
and inferential. It is not the case that judgments are constructed out
of concepts and inferences out of judgments. To so think would be to
make a mistake comparable to thinking that because a line segment can
be analyzed into points it can also be constructed out of points. The
linguistic representation of inference (say, in the syllogism) is static and
discrete. The process itself is dynamic and continuous. Such representation is no doubt useful but it is inadequate. It would be an error to
attribute to the process what is an attribute of its representation. It is
this error that generates Zeno's paradoxes. Later in his career Peirce
made this point very clear in distinguishing between an argument and
an argumentation.[13] The former is the living inferential process; the
latter is its representation in premises and conclusion.

If the human thought process is inferential, still that process is
differentiated. Just as the color spectrum is continuous but differentiated so too the inferential process is continuous but differentiated.
It can be analyzed into three sorts of inference: abduction, deduction
and induction. Abduction forms hypotheses (perceptual judgment is a
limiting case), deduction draws their implications, and induction tests

---

[13] Peirce, "A Neglected Argument for the Reality of God," *Collected Papers*, 6,
456ff.

their truth. This process is continuous, and hence there is no first premise which is not itself a conclusion. What, then, according to Peirce, grounds this inferential process?

At the close of the second article Peirce introduces three notions necessary to handle this foundational question: the notion of truth, the notion of reality, and the notion of community. From one point of view truth is what is the case independently of what anyone happens to think. From another point of view truth is what is *destined* in the long run to be agreed upon by investigators. It is not the agreement which constitutes the truth but it is the truth which brings about in the long run the agreement. The persevering application of the inferential thought process will correct error and bring about a convergence on the truth. Reality is that which is represented in the long run agreement. Here and now it is the knowable. In the limit case of the long run it is what will be known. Here and now reality is what is *intended* in knowing. In the limit case, it is knowledge of everything about everything. For Peirce there is no reality which is absolutely incognizable. Such a supposition is self-defeating. Truth and Reality, then, are convertible terms. These notions as merely intended by human cognition at any given time suppose the notion of a community without definite limits and capable of an indefinite increase in knowledge. To cite the last two paragraphs of this article, Peirce says:

> Finally, as what anything really is, is what it may finally come to be known to be in the ideal state of complete information, so that reality depends on the ultimate decision of the community; so thought is what it is, only by virtue of addressing a future thought which is in its value as thought identical with it, though more developed. In this way, the existence of thought now, depends on what is to be hereafter; so that it has only a potential existence, dependent on the future thought of the community.
>
> The individual man, since his separate existence is manifested only by ignorance and error, so far as he is anything apart from his fellows, and from what he and they are to be, is only a negation.
>
> This is man,
> Proud man,

Most ignorant of what he's most assured,
His glassy essence.[14]

The third article, "Grounds of Validity of the Laws of Logic," sets
out to justify inference in all its forms. Peirce begins with a consideration of deductive or necessary inference. He shows that each type
of categorial syllogism is governed by the *dictum de omni* and refutes
various classical objections to syllogistic reasoning. With respect to
abductive and inductive (probable) inference Peirce disposes of any attempt to justify them by turning them into a form of deduction or by
appealing to the uniformity of nature. Since both abduction and induction are inferences from part to whole, they are essentially a form of
statistical inference the validity of which depends upon the fact that in
the long run any item selected is as likely as any other to be included in
the sample. Peirce maintains that this in turn follows from the very notion of reality which he previously developed. Suppose that men could
not learn from induction. The reason would be that as a general rule
when they had made an induction the order of things would change.
But then the real would depend on how much men should know of it.
But this general rule could be discovered by induction and so it must
be a law of a universe such that when the rule was discovered, it would
cease to operate. But this rule too could be discovered by induction
and so there would be nothing in such a universe which could not be
known by a sufficiently long process of inference. But this contradicts
the hypothesis that men cannot learn from induction. Finally Peirce
stresses

> that logic rigidly requires, before all else, that no determi-
> nate fact, nothing which can happen to a man's self, should
> be of more consequence to him than everything else. He who
> would not sacrifice his own soul to save the whole world, is
> illogical in all his inferences, collectively. So the social prin-
> ciple is rooted intrinsically in logic.[15]

To illustrate how a continuous process can begin in time and yet
have no "first" member of the series, Peirce asks his readers to suppose
an inverted triangle gradually dipped into water (5.263). Clearly there

---

[14] *Collected Papers*, 5.316-317.
[15] *Collected Papers*, 5.354.

is a beginning in time of its being submerged, but there is no assignable first place on the triangle where it first contacts the water. Once the triangle is immersed, the surface of the water traces a line on it at some distance, say length a, from the apex. Such a line can be marked wherever one pleases and still there will be an infinite number of other places between it and the apex where it could be marked: at 1/2a or at 1/4a or at 1/8a .... *Because* the series is continuous, there is no "first place" which must enter the water first. The apex itself is not that "first place" since it is the triangle's boundary and marks where the triangle is not yet in the water.

Peirce suggests that we think of the triangle as representing cognition and of the water as representing what is distinct from cognition. Thus when the apex itself is at the water's surface, there is as yet no cognition. Now let each line traced by the water on the immersed triangle represent a cognition and let those lines nearer the apex represent cognitions which determine cognitions represented by lines further up the triangle. It is then clear that while every cognition is determined by one prior to it, there is no first cognition which is not itself so determined.

Peirce contends, therefore, that one can conceive, without contradiction, of *every* cognition being determined by another, while the whole process had a beginning in time. The term "first cognition" or "first principle" cannot mean "a cognition not determined by another" or "a premise which is not itself a conclusion." Whatever is to ground, or be the foundation of, cognition must be other than the "first principles" as abstractly conceived by some of the tradition at least.

It is here, I think, that Lonergan has something to offer Peirce. It is the proposal that what grounds the process of cognition (continuous as it is) is intelligence *in act*. The "foundation" of knowing is not itself an *abstract* knowing, but rather a concrete seizing of intelligence in action by the intelligent knowing agent. "First principles" (Identity, Contradiction, etc.) as abstract formulae are mere tautologies which have no truth value for anything outside the world of lexigraphical meaning. They are what Lonergan calls "analytic propositions." They are *principles* only insofar as they are grasped as existentially instantiated and this is possible only in the concrete act of knowing. It is there that their evidence is grasped as sufficient, that is, they are recognized as here and now operating because what conditions their operation here and now is fulfilled. If the evidence is challenged, the response is to point

out a *performatory* (not merely a logical) contradiction. This means
that if the challenge were telling, it would bring all intelligent acts to a
stop and reduce everyone to silence. To put it another way, the very act
of challenging the evidence produces that same evidence again. Notice
that this response is itself an inference and is determined by another act
of cognition. These concrete principles grasped in the act of knowing
are the conditions of possibility of that act, not abstractly and tautolog-
ically enumerated, but grasped as fulfilled in the act of knowing itself.
Hence they are *a priori* but not outside the conscious appropriation of
the act of knowing. They are *transcendental*, not in the Kantian sense
of an object ever beyond the knowing experience, but in the sense of
the immanent structure of every act of knowing.

10.3   Conclusion

I would like to close my remarks by returning to the three ideas central
to Peirce's theory of knowing as continuous inference. They are to some
extent already implicit in Lonergan and so might profitably be exploited
in realizing the shift which must take place in Catholic thought to bring
about its effective updating. These three central ideas are: the notion
of truth, the notion of reality, and the notion of community.

Peirce adds to the traditional notion of truth (what is the case independently of what any finite knower may think) an heuristic notion of
truth as that upon which the community of inquirers will agree in the
long run. This emphasizes the search for truth rather than its possession (although it does not deny the latter). It introduces an historical
and existential dimension which characterizes what actually goes on
within the scientific community. Lonergan recognizes this implicitly
when he points out that the canons of scientific method leave open the
question of further relevant issues and thus makes scientific inquiry a
fallible and so indefinite quest.

Peirce's account of reality explicitly endorses the scholastic insight
into the coextensiveness of truth and reality. There is nothing which
cannot be known, for if there were, it would be inexplicable and so
would block the road to inquiry. This is operative in Lonergan's notion
of metaphysics as heuristic and of being as whatever is or can be known.
It is at the heart of both Lonergan's and Peirce's argument for God.

Finally, Peirce's account of truth and of reality requires the explicit recognition of the role of the community. This is not just any group of people but the community of inquirers. Nor is this community merely a *de facto* requirement for arriving at the truth about reality. It is a necessary condition for the enterprise even to begin. This need for a community of inquirers does not mean that there must be actually an endless community of researchers. I can only suggest that this notion of the essential role of community rejoins Lonergan's insistence on the need for a series of personal conversions in order that there be any members of such a community dedicated to searching for the truth. This includes that final and perhaps most important conversion, "falling in love". Peirce could have written the following:

> When he pronounces a project worthwhile, a man moves beyond consideration of all merely personal satisfactions and interests, tastes and preferences. He is acknowledging objective values and taking the first step towards authentic human existence.[16]

Much of what Peirce proposed may be of real help in the shifting of traditional scholastic thought in the way Lonergan suggests: from logic to method, from Aristotelian to modern science, from soul to subject, from human nature to human history, and from first principles to transcendental method. I would like this essay to be a small contribution to that project.

---

[16] "The Future of Christianity," *A Second Collection*, 152.

List of Contributors

- Robert Doran, S.J., Associate Professor in Systematic Theology and co-director of the Lonergan Research Institute at Regis College, Toronto, Ontario.

- Vernon Gregson, Associate Professor in Religious Studies at Loyola University, New Orleans, Louisiana.

- Frederick G. Lawrence, Associate Professor in Theology at Boston College, Chestnut Hill, Massachusetts.

- Thomas J. McPartland, Lecturer in History at Seattle University, Seattle, Washington.

- Philip McShane, Professor in Philosophy and Interdisciplinary Studies at Mount St. Vincent University, Halifax, Nova Scotia.

- Hugo Meynell, Professor in Religious Studies at the University of Calgary, Calgary, Alberta.

- Vincent G. Potter, S.J., Professor in Philosophy at Fordham University, Bronx, New York.

- Nancy Ring, Associate Professor in Religious Studies at LeMoyne College, Syracuse, New York.

- John C. Robertson, Professor in Religious Studies at McMaster University, Hamilton, Ontario.

- Eugene Webb, Professor in Comparative Religion, The Henry Jackson School of International Studies at the University of Washington, Seattle, Washington.

INDEX

Abstraction, 162-163, 176.

African Religion, study of, 77-80.

Anamnesis, and philosophic self-appropriation, 103-4.

Arendt, H. 42-43.

Aristotle, 91, 183; and pedagogy of *Insight*, 11, 20.

Athanasius, 150, 153.

Augustine, 106.

Barthes, R., v, 31-34.

Basil, St., 146, 149-150, 152.

Being, notion of, 167, 172.

Bias(es), 43, 50-53, 105, 107.

Biography, philosophical, 102.

Cappadocians, 155, 158.

Categories, Theological (See Theology).

Censorship, and psyche, 51-53.

Chalcedon, 147, 148, 151, 153-158.

Charity, 39, 53.

Christian, W.A., 178.

Christology, and evil, 129-139.

Church, model of, 56-57.

Classics, role in Philosohy, 90-91.

Cognitional Theory, 160, 161-162, 165, 175-176.

Collaboration,in functional specialties, 17; cosmopolitan, 46, 51; crosscultural; interdisciplinary, 44; intellectual, 110-112; methodical, iv; in University, 19.

Collingwood, R.G., 24-25.

Common Sense, 49, 50, 82.

Communications, (functio- nal specialty), 67, 68, 78; in Philosophy, 101.

Community, vi, 110; as work of art, 49; academic, 110; communal reality, 89-92; (See Dialectic of Community).

Concupiscence, 105-109.

Consciousness, 2, 145; cosmological, anthropological, 55; cultured, 19-20; data of, 14; differentiations of, 17, 39, 54, 67; extroverted, 30; false, 25; Historical, 95-99, 112; Self-consciousness, 16; Soteriological, 54.

Conversion, 48; in philosophy, 98; and education, 20; intellectual, moral, religious, 17, 20, 98, 172-174; process of, 117.

Cosmopolis, 28, 41-43, 49, 50, 110.

Critical Theory, 43.

Crowe, F., iv.

Culture, (cultural) v, vi, 11-